There Might Be a Drop of Rain Yet

Brendan Lynch

CURRACH
PRESS

To the women in my life:
peerless Margie, Marlene, Cesarina, Karen,
little Hannah – and the mother!

1

Eight in the morning. Work not the best, he was filleting Tuesday's shopping list. A ray of sunshine crept along the Harry Kernoff woodcuts. God, how he would love to hit the road again. He recalled that Filipino film. Coconut-strewn beaches, harbour restaurants on stilts, beautiful women.

He jumped. The shrill ring of the table telephone reverberated around the living room. Since the *Irish Press* folded, he no longer had such early calls. A commission? Fruit would be reinstated! He reached for the receiver.

'Sister Luke here from the nursing home...'

It could only be bad news. His mother.

'Siobhán suffered a stroke...five this morning. She's resting now. I think you should come down as soon as you can.'

The pictures lost their sparkle. His poor mother. Eighty-nine. It had to happen some time. But he could never visualise it nor had wanted to. The receiver weighed a ton. Ironic that she should falter now; they had had got on so well since her recent great revelation. It was only a week since one of their best outings, a visit to his father's Toomevara grave followed by a Shannon salad. 'The first ice-cream I've had for ages and I have to spill it.' She brushed a white splash from the summer dress which outshone the Dromineer buttercups. She pointed across the Monet haze to her Scarriff birthplace. 'How the water dances in the heat. A pity I didn't have more of these days when I was cycling the four miles to teach the children in Bodyke.' She recalled the fair days and her favourite poem:

> She stepped away from me and she moved through
> the fair,
> And fondly I watched her go here and go there.

To hell with Jeremiahs! How could someone so animated be in danger now? The long-planned Clare holiday would yet go ahead.

But he had always known that a time would come when there would no more outings, no more concern about his driving. Had his mother finally reached the tomorrow which had diminished her every day? Even on the sunniest one, she had often looked skywards. 'There might be a drop of rain yet!' Like an automaton he dialled the car-hire company. Passing the door mirror, he congratulated himself on yesterday's beard trim. Appearances meant a lot to his mother. His elongated face reminded him of Jimmy's name for him, Quixote. His friend had always mocked his do-good proclivities.

As he hurried along the leaf-dappled towpath, he remembered his first tremulous visit to the post-war city. The crowds at the military tattoo. The cries of the gallowglasses, the thunder of the cannon and the smoke drifting across the arena from the battle of Benburb.

And his equally excited father, his gaberdine bulging with tourist guides and timetables. 'How much to Ballsbridge?' He surveyed the sly-eyed horse-cabbies on Stephen's Green. His parents would not recognise modern Dublin, with Grafton Street's scantily attired Diceman and the Celtic Tiger fall-out of overcrowded streets and foreign accents. 'That wasn't there last week.' Jimmy gaped, as they passed yet another new apartment block.

Only yesterday, outside the bow-windowed Teatime Express, he had remembered his mother over Morris West's *The Devil's Advocate*. The book which years before had encouraged him to reject her religious and political orthodoxy. How she had blamed England for everything! 'Weren't they awful robbers, God between us and all harm, the way they did us out of those Lane pictures?' But there were reasons for her animosity. Six months earlier, she confided her big secret about the War of Independence. A revelation which she had kept from the family for over sixty years. 'Perhaps, now you'll understand why I can never forgive the English?'

He averted his eyes from the sold sign over Parsons Bookshop; nothing was sacred any more. As he entered Murrays, he reflected on his current condition. Ten years back from London already. The frustration of no longer having his own transport was nothing to the indignity of renting.

'Two more flights to your garret?' Jimmy had paused for breath in Pembroke Street. 'By Jasus, some progress. When you left Ireland, you were only on the first floor.'

He had no choice but to sacrifice his faithful camper as a deposit for his little house. He paid for the hire-car with the credit card which had sustained him on his return, newly divorced and cashless. His mother queried its advantages: 'Sure that's only borrowing. Didn't I tell you always there was no future in that?' Keeping out of debt had been a lifelong priority. He remembered the accounts with Maggie Kennedy's emporium of lamp wick and Lamb's jam, which she cleared each month from his Garda father's insufficiency. Sometimes there were surplus eggs which could be set against an account, if not already misappropriated to bolster his own teenage funds.

"What are you coming over here for?" she repeated on his return. 'Your home's in England now, why don't you go back there to your wife and family?'

His imprisonment for banning bombs had shocked her. She knew before he ever told her that the marriage had ended, though the pagan reality of divorce took longer to digest. He spared her the consequent strained relations with his daughters. For the benefit of her twenty nursing-home neighbours, she opened the phone box door each Sunday: 'Give my love to Divina and the children.' She grew accustomed to his presence. But no doubt he headed the prayer list on her three daily visits to the chapel, her refuge from the ever-increasing permutations of clerical and political disappointments.

Regular newspaper features finally convinced her that he was making a living. 'You know your own business best.' When he acquired his Portobello dream home, she insisted on a generous contribution. They had achieved a dependence and, now, his mother needed his support. Would her setback also prove to be his biggest crisis? 'Come down as soon as you can.' the normally unflappable Reverend Mother had insisted.

You've got it. A stirring swansong. How well Roy Orbison, Carver and Hopper had sung the Great American Lonesomeness. Strange, how sadness could be uplifting. But it wasn't sadness which possessed him now but worry. How would he find his mother?

Would she be able to speak? Foot to the floor, he overtook every car. 'Slow down, you're going much too quickly,' she would admonish, as soon as she spotted anything on the horizon. Each time he left the home, she doused his car with holy water.

The Laois hills skirted his route like a caravan of dromedaries. He breasted the silhouetted Rock of Dunamaise. His mother's Moore ancestors were chieftains here, before being ousted by Cromwell. 'Did you know that Tom Moore is a cousin of ours?' Standing by the massive masonry, she once recited:

> 'When proudly, my own Island Harp I unbound thee
> And gave all thy chords to light Freedom and Song.'

Ivy-clad Rackett Hall, their regular Roscrea eating place. He'd made good time. He braked for the bend between the round tower and the Romanesque gateway, and swerved into Parkmore's flower-bordered grounds. The engine silent, he heard the stream which had reminded his mother of their original riverside house. And the front garden in which she had read and often quoted:

> 'For men may come and men may go,
> But I go on forever!'

But he knew now that she would not go on forever. Would she at least be conscious? Would she be able to recognise him?

'You flew – as usual.' The Reverend Mother's blue-and-white uniform crackled as she rose from her desk. Her ready smile proclaimed the unwavering faith that would carry her through the Colosseum and out the other end. He liked Sr Luke. 'You're a rare Irish phenomenon, you practise religion,' he told her. She bustled down the corridor ahead of him. How uniforms attenuated physical characteristics; he was never sure whether she was thirty or forty. They entered the room which had become so familiar to him since his return. His mother's pink bedspread brightened the beige interior; white pillows propped up her grey head. The Reverend Mother announced her guest; his mother reached out a pale arm: 'Is that you, Brendan?'

'I heard about your bad turn. I'm here to remind you about the holiday.'

'I'll be all right. Thank you for coming.'

She could speak! But her eyes remained closed. Her almost bloodless features mirrored the hair which had earlier been dark and lustrous. He noted for the first time how fleshy her once thin face had become.

His mother drifted back to sleep. He took up station at her bedside. She looked more tired than ill; her habitually anxious expression was relaxed for a change. Her rosary beads were coiled around her right hand. The stroke had paralysed her left side; she frequently moved her right hand across to feel its inert companion.

The room seemed to have shrunk; it was no Vermeer interior. The books and papers which had made it homely had been removed; her collection of religious objects had been reinforced by a silver cross and two candlesticks. He remembered helping her dispose of his father's clothes, which he had taken to the convent for the town's poor. He came back to find her prostrate with terror and loneliness. 'What's there for me now but the grave? I can't live without him.'

It was then that he returned to Ireland. Disenchanted with Grand Prix motor race reporting, he had already mapped a long voyage east in his camper van. But his mother was ageing and alone; his wandering could wait. How the decade had flown. Would he still be capable of realising those travel dreams? 'Settle down like the rest of us; your teenage days are over,' Jimmy said scornfully in Nesbitts.

The nuns called every hour. Many residents also visited; Miss O'Meara shook his hand: 'Now, don't be worrying. A strong woman, she'll soon be all right with the help of God.'

'We'll be down the week after next.' Forgotten but not gone, their lonely limbo was a reminder of the various humbugs who had promised to visit his mother. Villager Jim Shanahan joked: 'Sure they're too busy making money and going to church.'

There was a knock at the door – the newsagent's girl. 'Oh! I didn't know about your mother. I'm very sorry. Where will I put the *Nenagh Guardian*?' His mother suddenly stirred. Was she going to speak? She vomited. 'You can dab her lips with a spoon of whiskey and water,' the nurse advised. As she drifted back to sleep, she resumed her unconscious praying. Every now and then, she touched her lips with the rosary beads.

'She'll go straight to heaven.' Sister Pauline paused by the bed. 'The Apparition', his mother had christened the quiet lieutenant, whose serenity, unbidden, alleviated the most intractable emergency.

'Not for a long time yet.' He brandished the spoon.

The Reverend Mother remembered: 'The room next door is free for a week. You're very welcome to stay there, if you don't mind being our youngest guest!'

A succession of sparrows danced across the window sill. But there were no accustomed titbits; their benefactor's breathing filled the room with increasing urgency. He lunched at Rackett Hall, beside the marshland which had once encircled the abbey of Mona Incha. Cemented by love in more reverential times, the Romanesque ruins stood high and dry on a rocky island pile, distorted by the pressure of the broad beeches which now sheltered champing cattle. How typical of Ireland's perverse charm that a place so remote could boast such a Poussinesque evocation of the triumph of art, nature and scholarship.

'A summer symphony! Will you listen to the creaking of the branches and the buzz of the insects.' His mother held his arm once. 'The sound the monks, Lord rest them, would have heard. Before Cromwell came and hanged them all.'

'Where is the other half today?'

'Lissadell's your natural home,' he had often meant to tell the willowy manageress.

It was just six days since his mother's belches had embarrassed him here, as he allayed her habitual concern about his financial situation. Worry had blighted her life. A calm day heralded a storm, sunshine a deluge. Recently, she had become uneasy about directions. 'Are you sure we're on the right road?' For a special treat, he once drove her up to the Devil's Bit, the landmark hill which overlooked their village. Whitethorn and early summer plants perfumed their car. But as branches brushed its sides and the way narrowed, she began to fidget. 'I don't think you know where you are at all. This is not the way. We should have stayed on the main road.'

A grassy ridge appeared in the centre of the roadway. 'Stop and turn around. I don't care about the view. I know we're lost. For God's sake, be a good boy, take me home immediately.'

> In the early morning rain,
> With a dollar in my hand.

The manageress's mention of her Kilimanjaro holiday reawakened his unfulfilled travelling and writing instincts. He recalled the prevaricating Francis Macomber. His London doctor had queried the contrasting studies of Bertrand Russell and Ernest Hemingway. 'Doers rather than talkers, each made a rare and sustained contribution,' he had explained.

What about his own contribution? 'Be careful you don't wind up with my epitaph.' The Bard of Kensington once wagged a finger. 'He lived a life of "doing soon" and died with nothing done!'

His life expectancy and opportunities had suddenly contracted; death was no longer something that happened to someone else. He had his fill of passive socialising and would dearly like to escape again. Even Jimmy had grown restless with modern Ireland.

'The cloud of humbug over this bloody country would put Hiroshima in the halfpenny place. The police broke up your Apartheid protest, but we led the stampede aboard the Mandela bandwagon. Thanks to our blind eye for paramilitaries, murder's a way of life, every other pub bought with laundered money. We slide through shit to the drycleaners, while developers launder millions in the Caymans. And none can say we are inconsistent. After campaigning against French letters, one of our bishops turns out to be a father!'

Fast-changing Ireland increasingly taxed his own sense of humour. 'Three hours waiting already, the Celtic Tiger sleeps at night.' A Mater casualty pensioner wiped her eye. 'Scumbag,' belched a millionaire editor in Nesbitts, not about the killers, but their afternoon RUC victim. Joycism was now a profitable business, Leeson Lounge poet Michael Hartnett tilted his head: 'Seven towns contend for Homer dead, through which the living poet begged his bread.'

Now, indeed, was time for him to be up and doing – to be

travelling or writing, if he wasn't to sink into the same quicksand of opportunism or extremism. His mother's illness was giving him a sharp lesson on impermanence. His mother? He left his salad. Three older nuns were keeping vigil. 'She's had a great rest.' Sister Pauline furled her rosary beads. 'It will do her the world of good.'

His mother looked fresh and well in her newly made bed. But he began to accept that they would not see Lahinch this weekend. When the nuns had tiptoed out, he brought his chair up to the head of the bed. He held her left hand: 'You're right to rest for your holiday.' He knew she couldn't feel him, but he didn't want to impede her good hand which regularly moved her beads. When he did touch her right hand, she lifted both it and the beads to her lips, mouthing prayers he could not hear. He let his hand go easily with hers; he was happy to think that she was aware of his presence.

He reflected for the first time on how much he owed his mother. It was she who had introduced him to the printed word and the treasury of art and ideas. Mary King of Parsons bookshop had chuckled at the irony: 'Your mother's learning and books paved the way for your development – and for your estrangement from her!'

'No encyclopaedia, no London,' he had often meant to joke. Now, he might never have the opportunity. The *Guardian* lay crisp and unread on the locker which housed her secret hoard of biscuits.

'Off with you for five minutes.' Nurses Ryan and O'Grady took an arm each.

His mother's stroke had left her incontinent; he waited outside while they changed her clothes. Despite a lifetime liberating himself from his Catholic brainwashing, he was uplifted by the tangible holiness he felt around him. The nurses, nuns, staff and residents cared. These were not the preachers of his youth. He recalled his various office jobs, all that intrigue for power and a few shillings. Nurse Ryan patted his arm: 'We'll be popping in regularly. When you go to bed one of us will stay the night; you'll have nothing to worry about.'

He remembered his father, fastening his clips and cap band and cycling into the night to guard a disputed farm: 'I am only doing my duty.' Strange that his father had been so capable in keeping order in their village, but it was his mother's voice which had been most heard at home.

'Didn't your father die just in time, before the corruption stories started to break?' Miss O'Meara cornered him in the corridor. Her dragonfly figured belied the home's liveliest resident.

'After his generation's hard work to build up the ould country, wouldn't the new religion of greed have broken his heart? All those politicians and businessmen working hand-in-hand and just laughing at the rest of us.'

His mother looked relaxed and strong, though she hadn't eaten all day. Her breathing was more laboured, however. Was she worse than he wanted to acknowledge? But his father had rallied after his stroke; she would also show them. The leather elbows of the doctor's tweed jacket brushed the bedspread, as he focused his stethoscope. 'Stroke victims do recover. Your father was twenty years younger, however, and his attack was not as severe. We must be realistic; your mother is quite ill.'

The evening Angelus rang, the crows congregated outside the window. As a child, he had marvelled at their evening homecoming to the Shelley's Cross beeches. The familiar cawing and gurgling stream reassured him that his mother could not have spent her final years in more agreeable surroundings.

The door opened at speed; it could only be Sister Luke. 'Your mother knows you're here; you need have no doubt about that. Come and speak to her.'

'This is Brendan. I've just had tea, are you hungry yet?'

Afraid to interrupt her rest by loudness, he wasn't surprised that she reacted with only a slight movement of her lips. The Reverend Mother bent over the bedspread. 'Siobhán! Sr Luke here. How are you now?' His mother's eyes remained closed but she replied in her strong Clare accent, 'I'm OK, Sister. Thank you.'

He wasn't to know it, but these were the last words she would ever speak. Throughout the evening, he reassured her: 'Don't worry, we'll get you back to Clare soon again.' What would he be doing now, if she hadn't fallen ill? *On a Saturday Night,* always a radiant Scott Fitzgerald somewhere. If he had money, Bruce Springsteen to get him in the mood before he headed for the Rajdoot or Botticelli restaurants. Otherwise Nesbitts, smoky Grogans or the civilised oasis of the Arts Club. But how lonely this room was, how isolated his mother had been from the world.

Miss O'Meara marshalled a final gaggle of visitors. 'A grand lady; we're all praying for her. She's looking better already.'

Though outside it was still bright with midsummer light, most residents had already retired to their rooms. The lounge television was switched off. The rattle of delph faded as the last table was set for breakfast. Wardrobe doors closed, the shuffling of feet ceased. Snores competed with his mother's breathing.

He remembered their Toomevara village bedtimes. He would have been packed off earlier, while his parents listened to the Irish Hospitals' Sweepstakes programme. He yawned as he recalled the compere's silky voice and the signature tune, 'When You Wish upon a Star'. How swiftly his mother's life had flown from those cosy wireless evenings to this Spartan setting. The new check nightdress was not her own; all that remained from their original home was her old May altar Virgin and battered statues of St Martin de Porres and St Jude. Her fingers occasionally turned the amber beads which had launched the evening rosary. In a continuous chant, her voice rose and fell as she held on to each prayer-extended breath. 'Like a racecourse bookie, God forgive me,' Jack Hackett once whispered. Now, she fought for her breath.

A clock chimed midnight. Nurse O'Grady held the door open: 'Twelve hours you've been there. You won't help your mother by killing yourself, it's bedtime.' He knew she spoke sense. Something to which he was not always amenable, his mother had frequently reminded him. 'Your own country and church weren't good enough for you. You had to flee abroad and waste your energy on so many strange ideas – and I think you still haven't got sense.'

'How is my mother really?'

The nurse took over his chair. 'She's holding her own. But tomorrow will be crucial.'

He was tired. It had been a long day. He fell into the unfamiliar bed, his mind teased by long-forgotten images of their little village and his mother's healthier days. 'When You Wish upon a Star', he tried to remember the words:

> When you wish upon a star,
> It makes no difference who you are,
> Anything your heart desires will come to you…

2

'So early in the morning! See who's at the door,' his mother shouted from upstairs, as she got her hat for half-eight Mass.

'Bad news, Mrs Lynch.' Dan Casey from the garage wiped his hands with an oily rag.

'You go into the dining room.' His mother prodded him. He left the door open.

'Poor Mrs Smyth's gone, she died at two this morning.'

'God between us and all harm. I knew she wasn't well. But to go so quickly, I can't believe it.'

Only a week ago, Mrs Smyth had given him sweets in her little house on the other side of the post office. How could she be dead?

''Twas the heart. Fr Kenny said she had a very peaceful end, Lord rest her. They're laying her out now.'

'Well, it's God's mercy she's suffering no more, and she's gone to a happier place. Fanny Troy and young Eileen were a great help to her. She couldn't have had better care. Thanks for telling us, Dan. May the Lord have mercy on her soul.'

His mother called him. 'Mrs Smyth's dead; you must say a prayer for her at Mass.'

Mrs Smyth was the first person he knew who had died. He could not believe he would never again get a sweet from her, nor see her leaning over the railings on her way to Darby Kinnane, the butcher. He would have big news for Colm, when his elder brother cycled home from Nenagh secondary school.

'Will you brush your clothes and, for God's sake, straighten up.' His mother's dark hair touched his face, as she tugged his jersey and sprinkled him with holy water. 'Walk properly, or you'll have a stoop like Maggie Kennedy.'

'Do as your mother says.' His father looked very straight as he checked his blue uniform. His face was bright and red. 'Always on the go, the healthiest man in the village,' Auntie Maggie said.

They crossed to Looby's corner and set off up the slope past the pump and the grassy square. His mother crossed herself opposite the ruined abbey where Tom and Jim Devaney, who had been killed by the Black and Tans, were buried. 'Are you sure you closed the door, Paki?'

Beyond Donovan's pub, Maggie Kennedy was shutting her door. The little shopkeeper always twisted him a generous *tóisín* of conversation lozenges for his penny. As she limped across to the chapel, he could see that she was bent all right. He straightened his back. They passed the lane that led to the river. Mollie Barney was already leaning over the half-door of her galvanised-roofed cottage. 'Good morning, Sergeant and Mrs Lynch. Another lovely summer's day, thank God!'

'There might be a drop of rain yet.' His mother pointed to the sky, before telling her about Mrs Smyth.

'Reidy and Keogh will surely be at the funeral. Another fight, Sergeant?' Mollie looked up at his father, as she took off her apron for Mass. The two farmers had boxed each other outside the hall six months before. Who would be saying Mass? If it was Father Kenny it would take half an hour. But, racing through the words, Father Cosgrave would do it in half that time. 'A new record!' Tommy the timeleeper displayed his watch one morning. 'Twelve minutes. Master McGrath couldn't match him.'

From Donoghue's thatched house, they crossed to the chapel which stood beside the school. It was a lonely place, surrounded by a stone wall and constantly whispering trees. 'They're crying for the dead,' his brother, Colm, had told him.

The wicket gate swung violently in the windy gusts. One day, it banged shut and cut off Tommy Howard's fingertips. Where would they dig Mrs Smyth's grave?

His parents sat close to the altar in the side aisle, where the Stations of the Cross started and where the Christmas crib was set up. To their right stretched the cream-painted chapel's long aisle and choir gallery. Under the nearest window was a statue of Mary and her bloodstained son, Jesus, who had just been taken down from the cross. In the opposite window, bearded St Patrick displayed the gold crosier with which he had banished the snakes from Ireland.

The varnished sacristy door opened and Father Cosgrave came

out. His head was at an angle, as if his glasses were too heavy for him. He envied the altar boys who accompanied the priest. He couldn't wait to be big, so that he could also wear the white surplice and black soutane. 'And, then maybe, you'll become a priest,' his mother said to him hopefully. It would be wonderful to be a priest. To be so close to God, to be able to say Mass, maybe to go on the foreign missions and convert the poor pagans his mother always prayed for. To wear those glittering vestments and be saluted by all the people. But he wouldn't want to be killed like those priests in China and Russia.

'*Introibo ad altare Dei.*' Father Cosgrave turned the pages of the missal. Soon the congregation bowed their heads for the consecration and, unlike the crowded Sundays, they were quickly back from communion. The priest's green vestments twirled as he swung around. 'Mrs Smyth died this morning. Lord have mercy on her. She'll be brought to the chapel this evening. Remember her and the souls of all the faithful departed in your prayers.'

'Poor Mrs Smyth. She's a hard life with only that little plot to keep the three of them.' His mother once showed him her plot on a walk to Ollatrim. As he knelt on the bare wood, he envied the O'Mearas in their cushioned pews in the opposite gallery. They owned the post office, a pub, grocery and many village dwellings, including Mrs Smyth's and his parents' riverside house.

'Porridge time!' First to rise, his father cooked the oats every morning. He also emptied the chamber pots and filled the bedroom ewers with water from the backdoor tar barrel.

'Cock-a-doodle-doo!' He liked their riverside house, whose kitchen overlooked the busy hens in the backyard. The dining room with its pictures of the penal Mass, Pope Pius XII and famous explorers, and the mahogany table under which he could play; the carpeted sitting room with its bookcases and bouncy three-piece suite, and the four upstairs bedrooms with all their hiding space.

His mother taught him a poem about a house which he always liked to think was theirs. She was very proud when he recited it for visitors.

> I remember, I remember,
> The house where I was born,

The little window where the sun
Came peeping in at morn.

It was written by a man with a strange name, Hood. His mother
said that he was a nice man but that the rest of the English had
done terrible things to Ireland.

Their house was beside the bridge, right in the centre of their
village of three streets and eleven shops, six of which were pubs.
And the hall which fronted the abbey and the square, where the
travelling shows parked their colourful caravans. He enjoyed sitting
on their front garden seat. Flowers danced inside the white railings,
the river sounded like music as it flowed out from under the bridge.
He watched the farmers going to the creamery, while he awaited the
distant hum of the green bus that went all the way from Limerick
to Dublin.

'Here's Billy Delaney with the cows for milking!' Even on wet
days, he could see everything from their glass porch. Postman Jim
O'Rourke chatted to villagers on his round, farmers went into Matt
O'Meara next door for foodstuffs. Big Jim 'Boss' O'Meara on the
other side of the bridge came out to check the weather. Lonely
asses and carts with milk churns waited outside Harty's and French
Shea's pubs.

'When they fly low, it's a sign of rain. When they play high in
the sky, the sun will shine.' His father and he watched the fork-
tailed swallows building their upside-down nests under Looby's
eaves. Their chirps filled the air each evening, as they dived and
played between the houses. Birds which had flown all the way from
Africa!

After breakfast, his father read the death notices in the *Irish
Press*: 'Poor MacTomáis has gone.'

'God rest him.' His mother put down her teacup. 'Sure the poor
man was riddled with bullets, a miracle he lasted so long at all. Sad
to see the Independence veterans dying out so quickly.'

His father brushed his navy hat and shone his uniform buttons
and whistle. He would like to be as tall as his father, who was five
foot ten, just taller than his mother. His father put the hat on his
own smaller head. They all laughed as the peak covered his eyes, so
that he could see only his father's shiny black leggings and boots.

'*Slán leat.*' His father walked over the bridge and down to the barracks which stood on the Nenagh end of the village. He didn't want to be a Garda himself when he grew up. He heard his mother telling Auntie Maggie: 'God help us but you can't have friends if you're in the Force.'

Johnny Sullivan said bad things about his father, after being prosecuted for ill-treating a donkey. Mrs McCarthy made more trouble. 'Sergeant, come immediately. My fur coat's gone, my best coat from Switzers in Dublin. I'm sure Nellie Hegarty took it.'

'Far from fur coats that one was reared.' His mother put down her duster. His mother's grey tweed was many years old.

His father found the coat in the maid's house and returned it to the farmer's wife. 'Nellie was tempted in the cold. I've given her a good telling-off.'

Mrs McCarthy shouted in front of passing villagers: 'I don't care if she's poor. She's a thief. I'll write to Dublin if you don't prosecute her.'

'Nellie and her family are hard-working people, I'm sure she will never do anything like this again,' his father told the judge. She got off with a small fine and her name was in the paper. The McCarthys, who sat close to them in church, never spoke to his father or mother again.

On the village's only typewriter, his father tapped out letters and explained government documents to neighbours who could not read or write. He drew maps of accident and assault scenes. 'Whatever you do, you must do it well, no matter how small. You respect people for how they work, not for what they do.' He blotted the fountain pen ink.

District Justice Coffey complimented him: 'Congratulations, Sergeant, your sketch detail is worth a thousand words.'

His father also had a collection of chisels, planes and saws and a black iron last, on which he heeled and soled all the family's shoes. Neighbour Din Ryan admired the new chest of drawers. 'But how did you manage that bookcase?'

'Very simple. I measured the glass, cut it with the diamond and stuck it in with putty.'

'You should have been a carpenter, Sergeant. A lot less aggravation and a lot more money!'

'You can sit on the seat – but don't leave the garden.' His mother put on her apron before starting the baking.

Dick Casey's waistcoat hurling medals flashed under his grey hat. The change jingled in his trousers pocket as he waved from his garage across the road. 'I'll give you a halfpenny if you'll come over for it.'

If only Colm was here. Dick twirled the ends of his yellow moustache as he walked up and down beside the red petrol pump. 'Keep away from the porch,' his mother laughed once, when he imitated the garage owner by curling the moustache he made out of a long sweet paper.

One Sunday morning, Dick ran out and took the bicycle from under a man cycling to Mass. 'You can travel in style again when you catch up with the payments.'

On the Sundays of the big hurling and football matches, Dick invited locals into his house to hear the wireless. He propped the window open with a Peggy's Leg jar, so that those outside could also hear Micheál O'Hehir's commentary. 'He's forty yards out. He's sidestepped Christy Ring. He's steadying the ball. It's an impossible angle. But it's over the bar, Tony Reddin, another point for Tipperary!'

"Come on Hough and Shanahan,' the locals shouted for Toomevara's own county players.

His mother liked Dick as he also supported Dev, the man who had freed Ireland from the English. Dick sold his father the three-speed Raleigh which, according to the big metal advertisement, could outpace the fastest jungle lion. 'You can be in two places at the one time now, Sergeant.' Din Ryan marvelled at the Sturmey-Archer gears.

The brass bell rang as Pat Tierney came out of his shop opposite their house. Pat looked small without his hat. 'How's Benny Lynch this morning?' he punched the air like the famous boxer.

Every Christmas, the children gathered around Tierney's window to see the new toys. Pat sold drapery and also habits for the dead. Mrs Tierney was taller and dressed very well. Each summer, she hung a striped cloth to protect their hall door from the sun. His mother shook her duster. 'That one has more airs and graces than Maureen O'Hara.'

Mick Ryan Dalkey slowly crossed the road from Looby's corner. After looking down at the river, he adjusted the binding twine which held his trousers and pulled himself up on the bridge. He took out a broken clay pipe from one pocket of his oily jacket and a plug of tobacco from the other. With a penknife which looked too small for his hands, he peeled off the brown flakes and rolled them for a long time. He filled the pipe, struck a match against the bridge and soon there was smoke all around him. He settled the pipe's cap, a bottletop with holes in it, as he watched the O'Mearas and the farmers go to and fro and occasionally pushed back his cap to scratch his head. Many of them laughed at Mick but he only smiled back and puffed away. 'Dalkey's a bit cracked,' Colm had explained.

Suddenly, Mick put his hand to his ear. 'The buzz's coming,' he called into the garden.

He heard the bus changing gear, before its green bonnet came around McLoughney's corner and it stopped outside Boss O'Meara's. The conductor whistled 'MacNamara's Band' as he ran down the steps and into the shop, Dubliners had much livelier airs than his mother's favourite, 'Three Lovely Lassies from Bannion'.

To be a bus conductor would be great! To see all the places his mother had shown him on the map: Limerick, Roscrea and Kildare, where St Brigid had hung her cloak on a sunbeam. He envied the passengers inside the big glass windows. Tonight they would be far away in Dublin. He wished he was the driver, sitting high beside the engine. As the bus moved off, he and Dalkey waved to the driver, who beeped his horn and nearly frightened Mick into the river. Standing at the railings, he watched the bus accelerate up Church Street, past Delaney's and Guard Coleman's and off towards Moneygall on its long journey.

The midday Angelus bell rang. Mick Dalkey got down from the bridge and headed across the road for home. His mother knocked on the porch glass. 'Dinner! Come in and wash your hands.' His father returned and they all sat down to eat their bacon, cabbage and potatoes. His mother filled their glasses with milk from the jug: 'Do you think Din Reidy and Jimmy Keogh will be at the funeral?'

'They were both friends of Mrs Smyths; we can't stop people from going to funerals,' his father laughed.

His mother waved her fork. 'If they've drink, there will be violence, make no mistake.'

After lunch, he helped his mother put the dishes in the basin for washing. She poured in the hot water. 'Mrs Smyth was fond of you. If you're a good boy you can go to the wake when your brother comes home from school.' He felt afraid to go, but he wanted to see what a dead person looked like. Funerals were sad. After Mass, everyone shook hands with the relatives. The women all wore black dresses and scarves, the men black ties and black diamonds stitched on their jacket shoulders. 'Forty ponies and traps – that man was very rich,' his brother said after one funeral. Not so many people had followed Paddy Dwyer's poor sister, Maggie, to the chapel. Mrs Smyth would hardly have a big crowd.

Doctor Murphy passed their porch. The doctor had a big stomach and he walked the street every day with a long tube around the collar of his grey suit. 'That's for listening to patients' hearts,' his mother said as she watered the geraniums. He wondered if the doctor had heard Mrs Smyth's heart.

'Because of the funeral, I'll do the Stations of the Cross early. Then we'll go to Looby's before your brother comes back from school.'

He liked visiting the two small sisters. Though they were both widows and dressed in black, Auntie Hannah's and Auntie Maggie's stories made even his strict mother laugh.

The chapel's heavy door closed behind them. It was nice to sit in the coloured light from St Patrick's statue instead of having to kneel. The air was so still and the village sounds so distant, he felt he was in a different world. His mother genuflected and prayed before each of the fourteen stations. She and his father visited here three times each day.

His mother pushed Looby's door open. 'God bless the house. Anyone at home?'

Auntie Hannah, the thinner sister, seated him at the table by the riverside window. Auntie Maggie brought him a jug of buttermilk and their deck of playing cards to build houses with. The three women sat around the cream Aga cooker, under the hanging flitches of bacon.

Auntie Hannah steadied the teapot. 'Isn't that terrible about

Mrs Smyth? A good Christian and a dacent neighbour.'

'It's hard to see the oul' shtock going.' His mother held out her cup. She suddenly raised her voice: 'Did you see what that rip was wearing at Mass again this morning, no respect or modesty at all?'

Auntie Maggie winked at her sister. 'The new teacher, Miss Carey, and her bright clothes?'

'They get all those pagan fashions from England; those English papers should be banned.' His mother banged her cup on the saucer.

'She's a bit theatrical all right, Mrs Lynch.' Auntie Maggie shook her head. 'And, speaking of the stage, what did you think of *Mungo's Mansion?* It finished in the hall last night.'

'You can't bate an Irish play. And they couldn't have had anyone better than Pat Tierney as King Mungo.'

Auntie Hannah refilled their cups. 'I thought Paddy Carroll and Liam Walsh were great.'

'But I never laughed so much as I did at Mungo's son, Billy Delaney. Sure they were all as good as anything you'd see above in the Abbey. With your lovely Clare accent, Mrs Lynch, you could also be a great asset to the players!'

Auntie Maggie stood up, held her head in the air and imitated the wife of a rich shopkeeper. She pretended to plaster powder and paint on her face to copy the Last Rose, the schoolteacher, Mrs Hackett. His mother shocked him by laughing when Auntie Maggie described a shopkeeper: 'That boshtun! Sure I knew him, God forgive me, when he didn't have an arse in his trousers.'

His mother brought him to the post office to send her monthly postal order to the insurance company. He put her halfpenny in the Missions box and watched the African boy's head nod up and down. 'Dublin in the morning.' Matt O'Meara's watch chain jingled. He looked very important with his neat moustache and dark striped suit, as he banged the rubber stamp with the name of *Tuaim Uí Mheadhra.*

'Maybe one day we'll all go to Dublin on holiday.' His mother opened the gate. She was always in good form after a visit to Looby's. It would be great if she was like this all the time.

The latch lifted on the back gate. He raced out to the yard and took his brother's schoolbag. 'The wind was in my face today.' Colm undid the clips on his grey patched trousers and freewheeled down to the shed, his face as red as his hair.

He liked his brother, who was not much taller than him despite being six years older. He was not a bully, like other big children. They also had a sister, Patricia. But she lived with their grandparents in Scarriff since going there years earlier when their mother was sick.

'Mrs Smyth is dead!' He put the schoolbag on a chair. 'Dan Casey said that 'twas the heart that killed her. She's laid out now and our mother said that you can take me to the wake. There might be a fight as well! Mollie Barney says Din Reidy and Jimmy Keogh will be at the funeral.'

After Colm had his dinner, they went to see Mrs Smyth. Fanny Troy opened the door: 'You're very good to come, boys. I've some lemonade for you after you've said your prayers.' They knelt down beside the black iron bed and for a while he was afraid to look at Mrs Smyth. She was dressed in one of Tierney's brown habits, just like the mission priests who visited their village. Her eyes were closed. She held her rosary beads tightly. He thought she was only asleep but she lay there very stiff and white-faced. She didn't breathe at all. That was what it was like to be dead, not to breathe any more.

The Gunner and Paddy Dwyer did not seem so sad, as they drank bottles of stout beside the fireplace. 'Now, put that in your pipe and smoke it, Dan,' Paddy laughed, as he finished telling a joke.

When they went home, their mother pulled down the blinds in the front rooms. 'Call me when your homework's finished and I'll check it.' She closed the dining-room door on his brother. Afraid that he was late to see the crows, he ran across the yard and into the back garden. 'Green fingers,' Auntie Maggie called his father, after inspecting the cabbage, carrots and parsnip, and the drills of Golden Wonder potatoes which stretched down to the end hedge. Hundreds of crows circled noisily over the neighbouring fields. They gathered together in one giant flock before flying off to their nests at Shelley's Cross.

At six o'clock, Ger Devaney rang the chapel bell. From under the sitting-room blind, he watched his neighbours carry Mrs Smyth's dark coffin along the street. Fanny Troy and Eileen were crying. His father chatted to Doctor Murphy and Dick Casey. Guard Coleman and Guard O'Gara walked together. Guard Howard was probably on duty. The shopkeeper Tim Delaney looked very large beside Jim Shanahan, Din Reidy and little George Powell, who never missed a funeral. Retired postman Ned Kinirons and the baker Joe O'Dea talked with the two Tommy Ryans, Barney and the Timekeeper. Darby Kinnane looked at the red-faced Gunner and Paddy Dwyer, who didn't seem to be able to walk too well. The teacher, Mrs Regan, laughed at Auntie Maggie, who must have told her a joke. Jimmy Keogh walked at the back with Gordon Birch, the saddler. He was well away from Din Reidy. A pity; there would hardly be any fight. The street was empty. Poor Mrs Smyth was gone. A few minutes later, Gordon Birch turned the corner, his hand on his hat. 'He's a Protestant and can't go into the chapel,' Colm explained.

His mother cut the bread for their tea when his father returned. 'Only a funeral would make you miss the news.' His father listened to the six o'clock news every evening on the wireless. Villagers often leaned over the railings: 'What's the latest, Sergeant?'

They were in the middle of their tea when there was a loud banging on the front door. It was Boss O'Meara: 'Sergeant, quickly, the Civil War again.' From the porch, he could hear the shouts of Din Reidy and Jimmy Keogh on the other side of the bridge. Their jackets were on the ground. 'God blast that little blackguard, Mulcahy. He murdered the seventy-seven.' Din waved his fists, as he tried to pull up the sleeves of his grey shirt.

'At least he was Irish, unlike that foreigner who killed Collins.'

'Collins did England's dirty work, you bloody Blueshirt.' Din reached up and tried to hit Jimmy. But he missed and tripped over Spriggs Donoghue, who was watching with other O'Meara's drinkers.

'He was Ireland's greatest man. Unlike that half-blind Spanish troublemaker.'

Din tried to throw Jimmy to the ground. 'Don't you say anything like that about Dev. I'll break your bloody neck.'

More drinkers moved down the street from Harty's and French Shea's pubs. Jimmy prodded the smaller man. 'He started the Civil War. He killed Collins and Ireland's best men.'

Din's cap flew off as he swung another punch. 'Your crowd

signed the Treaty; you're to blame for everything. I'll bloody well kill you.'

Jimmy dodged. 'Where were you in 1916 anyhow?'

'I did my bit. I wasn't sitting on the fence like your lot, waiting to see how the wind would blow.'

'By Jasus, I'll kill *you*.' Jimmy took a swipe at Din, who ducked. 'If I hadn't a drink on me I'd make mincemeat of you.'

Spriggs retreated a safe distance. 'Hit someone your own size.'

'You and all belonging to you were useless articles, all wind and piss.' Din jumped up and down trying to land a punch.

'I'll show you who's useless, I'll swing for you, you little renegade.' Jimmy grabbed Din with both hands

'Now, that's enough of that!' His father ran in between the two men. 'The Civil War's over. No one else in going to be killed in Toomevara this or any other evening. You should be ashamed for carrying on like this after a funeral.'

'Sorry, Sergeant.' Din wiped his forehead. 'But if that fella says anything derogatory about Dev ever again, he'll be going home with his head in a sling.'

'But nothing! If you two can't conduct yourselves, stay away from each other for a while. You've both drunk too much. If I see either of you near a pub for the rest of this week, I'll arrest you.'

Din pushed his shirt back inside his trousers and picked up his jacket. He walked his bike towards the Mines' Cross. He turned back and, when he noticed his father wasn't looking, he waved his fist at Jimmy, who was driving his pony and trap into the Pallas road.

'Spriggs was the only casualty,' laughed the Timekeeper. The shoemaker examined his bruised foot and they all went back inside the pubs.

He opened the gate for his father. He thought he was a great man to come between the two fighters. His father put his cap on the table. 'Don't leave that there while we're eating.' His mother removed it to the dresser.

His father stood with his back to the fire. 'That's the Civil War until the next anniversary!'

'Disgraceful to hear Dev being insulted like that; the drink again.' His mother cleared the table.

Auntie Maggie called to the door. 'Did you ever see the bate of it, Mrs Lynch? Sure neither of them buckos, or anyone belonging to them, ever went within a mile of a gun or the fight for independence.'

'By the way, Mrs Regan was well oiled at the funeral. She'll have be more careful, I think.'

'It's a hard life being a widow.' His mother shook her head. 'But I hope she doesn't get into any trouble.'

When Auntie Maggie had left he asked: 'What's wrong with Mrs Regan?'

'You're a very bold boy to be listening. There's nothing the matter with Mrs Regan. She's a very good teacher, as you'll soon find out.'

They all knelt down on the dining-room's brown linoleum for the rosary. There must be something very strong in that drink to make little Din Reidy so brave. His parents and brother recited the five decades between them, he said the *Amens*. His mother prayed to her favourite, Saint Jude, and for all the pagans in Africa and China. She asked God's blessing for the emigrants, for the faithful departed and especially to guide Mrs Smyth's soul to heaven.

'Will you play a game of rings?' But Colm had to do his homework. He never saw much of his brother, as he left for school each morning at half eight and wasn't home until half four. After dinner, he had so much study that they seldom played together.

Sometimes, his father told him stories about his Donegal home and of the great Ulster chieftains, the O'Neills and Red Hugh O'Donnell, who escaped from Dublin Castle on Christmas Eve, 1592. And of Brian O'Linn, the world's most cheerful man. 'When Brian drank poitín and fell into the river, he said: "Never mind, we'll go home by water."'

His mother studied a book by the fireside, while he tried to read the *Irish Press*. He could already understand some of the big words. He wanted to be able to read and write. His mother had told him: 'Reading is like a key. You turn it and you will learn about everything in life.' The paper didn't always bring good news. Once, his mother cried as she read of the sinking of one of the last big sailing ships. He looked at the *Irish Press* every night in order to delay his bedtime. If his mother was in good humour, she would say:

'Is it trying to dust me again you are?' But she was too clever. 'Nine o'clock, bedtime!' She lit the candle and took him up the shadowy stairs. When he had finished his prayers, she tucked in the blankets. She left the candle on the mantelpiece and the door open, as he was afraid of the dark. He studied the ceiling cracks, which made shapes like the countries in Colm's atlas.

The cups and saucers rattled downstairs, as his parents sat down and listened to the Hospitals' Sweepstakes wireless programme. If they had visitors, he might be allowed to stay up and hear the programme himself. He could hum its tune, 'When You Wish upon a Star'. His father had taught him a poem about stars:

> Twinkle, twinkle little star
> How I wonder what you are!

What trouble could Mrs Regan get into? Colm said she was a very nice lady. He thought of Mrs Smyth, locked up and all alone in the empty chapel. To-morrow night she would be under the ground. O'Meara's dog barked and another dog answered down the Pallas road. How was it that you could hear things so clearly in the night? He shivered and hugged his navy blanket closer.

3

'How the time flies!' Autumn leaves swirled around his mother and Auntie Maggie on the way home from Mass. But to him a year was a lifetime, particularly when he started going to school.

'With the teacher's help, you'll soon be able to read all the *Irish Press* – and then you'll know as much as us,' his mother encouraged him. She and his father were very clever; would he ever learn as much as them?

The class of twenty boys and girls sat on forms under the ceiling mushrooms. The Last Rose looked very strange with her pale face and red-painted cheeks. A fellow-infant told the teacher that he had said a bad word. He cried as she sprinkled him with holy water and hit him on the head with *cipíns*, the fire kindling sticks. She flung back her red scarf: 'Kneel down in front of the Virgin Mary and pray for forgiveness.'

The Last Rose handed the rough lino squares to the dunces. 'This is good enough for you; you'll never learn anything.' She gave her favourites the slates, from which it was easier to wipe off the chalk. She put the pupils whose parents had provided the most turf nearest to the fire. Mickey Butler, who walked barefoot from Grenanstown, shivered on the outside.

'Ring-a-ring a rosies, pocket full of posies. Atishoo, atishoo, All fall down.' As they played outside, he could hear the cries of the upstairs boys who were being beaten by the shiny-suited master, Mr Larkin. Noel Searson told him a riddle. 'Which is quicker, telephone, telegram or tell a woman?'

Noel held his nose as they ran past the lavatory. 'Only the bluebottles could stand that stink.' The lead pencils and plasticine smelled nicer but he did not like school. He looked at the three stone steps which led down to the street. The empty churn danced, as Johnny Hayes jogged home from the creamery on his donkey and cart.

Why were larger ladies always happy? He hoped nothing would

happen to his First-Class teacher Mrs Regan. She started every morning: 'Now, students, the fireside first. A warm body makes a warm brain.'

Mrs Regan taught him how to use his N-pen without making inkblots. She praised him in front of the class for being able to point out London on the wall map, which showed such faraway places as Prussia and St Petersburg. After school, she often parked her ass and cart outside O'Meara's pub next to their house. His mother called him in from the porch. 'She's shopping.' He crept into the pub one day. It was dark and his teacher was nowhere to be seen. Suddenly, he heard her reciting 'My Dark Rosaleen' in the snug. After a long time, she came out. The harness jingled as she mounted the cart. She sat down with a very straight back and adjusted her tartan skirt. 'Grenanstown!' She flicked the reins. The little grey ass shook his head and set off for their home.

'I've seen her coming from school. Once clear of the village, she lies down and falls fast asleep. If the PP catches her drunk, she'll lose her job,' Colm told him.

Mrs Shanahan overheard them: 'If she has a Baby Power for her health, it's the poor woman's own business. She's a very lonely oul' station, God help her.'

His mother hated the drink. He couldn't understand this; most of the men seemed happy when they left the pub. And they were generous. Dick Hassett often gave him a penny on his way home from French Sheas. 'But don't tell the Sergeant,' he said with a wink.

'Did you see Tommy Smith falling in the street again, after spending all day and all night in O'Mearas?' His mother held the door open when his father returned one day. 'No wonder their children are in rags and his wife has to beg for everything. It's a disgrace.'

The parish priest gave a sermon on the evils of drinking. His father raided the after-hours pubs but didn't catch anyone. His mother flung down her book: 'Little wonder, half the guards are drinking there themselves. You're too soft. You shouldn't let them off so easy; they'll have no respect for you.'

'We are trying to save family budgets, not reduce them by fines!'

Despite her dislike of the drinking, his mother made porter

cakes at Christmas for Paddy Dwyer and the Gunner who both lived alone. The dining room filled with a musty smell when they called. Colm made a face. 'They don't wash every day.'

Mrs Regan knocked on the door. 'Mrs Lynch, Christmas will never be the same again. The PP's been made a canon. He's going to celebrate with a midnight Mass!'

'The chapel will be overflowing.' His mother invited her in for a cup of tea.

'By the way, how's Colm? I see him cycling off to the Nenagh Brothers every morning. He's a very refined boy, I wouldn't be surprised if he joined up himself. Have the Brothers spoken to him yet?'

'He's a better chance of a vocation than this fellow. They're coming down from the Dublin novitiate to tell him about the order but keep that you to yourself.'

Was Colm going to go away with the Brothers? Even though they were seldom together, he would miss him. But neither his mother nor brother would tell him any more about what was happening.

'Adeste Fideles'. The chapel was repainted a brighter cream for the midnight Mass. It was packed long before twelve with everyone in their best clothes. The largest candles he had ever seen lit up the sanctuary. The harmonium played and incense perfumed the aisles. His mother bent over to his father: 'Did you ever hear the choir sing so well?'

'Oh, my God!' His mother looked up from her prayerbook. Huge flames leaped from a vase of reeds beside the biggest candle. In a flash, John Joe McCormack leaped over the altar rails with a jug of water from the font. Before those in the back realised what was happening, he had quenched the fire. He had never seen so many at Communion. Even Canon O'Rahilly seemed surprised and he gave his shortest-ever sermon. 'As Christians all over the world gather to remember the birth of the infant Jesus, there can be few celebrations to match what you have shown this special night. You have great faith. I am very proud of you. May God bless you all and grant you a happy and peaceful Christmas.'

His mother nudged his father, who looked so different in his brown suit. 'I think he's crying, Paki.' He wondered if the canon was sad, going home alone while everyone else had their families.

The congregation gathered around the crib which the sacristan Ger Devaney had built. 'Happy Christmas!' they greeted each other, as they walked home past the candlelit windows. He had never been up so late, nor seen the sky so full of stars. There was nowhere else in the world that night as beautiful as his own little village. Tim Delaney shook hands with his parents. 'More power to John Joe, the place could have gone up in flames.'

'Can we go to the crib after tea?' The chapel was so mysterious at night; the only light came from the sanctuary lamp and the manger lantern. As they knelt over the sweet-smelling straw, the lantern's shaky shadows made the animals come alive. Its heat was their breathing which warmed the infant Jesus and his poorly-clad parents, Mary and Joseph. The clatter of his mother's collection-box penny echoed around the emptiness. A mouse rustled the straw. He moved closer to his mother.

'A leg each, so there'll be no fighting. Who's for crackling?' As well as Santa Claus, the holiday brought iced cake and roast goose, which they ate in the dining room. A red cloth covered the mahogany table, paper decorations hung from the ceiling, holly brightened the base of the paraffin lamp. Brian O'Higgins Christmas cards illuminated the mantelpiece and a bag of turf stood in the hallway, so that his father would not have to go out in the cold. He seldom got the toys or the train sets he had seen in Tierneys. His mother insisted: 'We're not buying anything that's made in England.'

'Owing to the big war, Santa now has to make many of his own toys,' his father read from the *Irish Press*.

On Christmas morning, he woke to find a little yellow wheelbarrow which was inscribed: '*Do Bhreandán ó Santa Claus.*' The paint had run on the opposite side, where Santa had first started to write. 'It's very hard to paint at the cold North Pole at night.' His father examined the barrow.

'Pick whatever book you like, the bigger the better.' Tierney's doorbell rang as the Gunner dragged him into the shop with some of his wren-day money. He chose a picture book on all the jungle animals. The Gunner was cracked since he was shellshocked in the Great War. On St Stephen's Day, he became a wild animal himself.

He dressed in a black mask and red cloak, and leaped through the streets waving a long staff. Most of the children joined the Gunner's parade, and he took more money than all the other wrenboys put together. But the children ran away from him afterwards, as he staggered from pub to pub. 'You can't bate the Christmas, better than armistice day in Wipers.' Dan dragged Ould Mate, the other war pensioner, around the village until the wren-money was gone. He felt sorry for the two men. Many villagers looked down on them because they had been in the British army.

One morning, it was strangely quiet. Colm shouted into his room: 'Look out the window; it's like a Christmas card.' He opened the curtain. Toomevara and all the countryside as far as Keeper mountain was entirely covered by snow! The roads, every roof, windowsill, garden and field. Even Casey's oily petrol pump wore a dazzling coat. Everything was so clean and still. The only sound came from the river flowing by the snow-wrapped flowerbeds and the postman, who made funny crunching noises as he walked. Lumps of ice floated in the water which his father brought in from the frozen tar barrel. 'I had to use the hatchet!' They put out bread for the birds. Neighbours cut pathways to their homes through drifts as high as himself. The snow stayed for two months. Mrs Regan's ass slipped on the ice outside their house. It took Mrs Regan longer to get up than the ass. His mother ran out when she heard the commotion. 'Come in now and have a cup of tea.'

His teacher nearly tripped over the chair. 'Many's the fall between cup and mouth, as Tommy Barney says.' He was shocked to see that she was drunk.

His mother poured the tea. 'We've never seen a winter like it, thank God. Sure 'tis amazing that any poor animal can stand up at all.'

Unkindly called Humpty Dumpty by some children, Tommy Barney was the best carpenter in the village. His wife, Mollie, kept track of village life over the accumulating shavings, while he sawed and planed and recited the adventures of the rapparee, Brennan on the Moor:

But what he'd taken from the rich, like Dick Turpin
and brown Bess
He always did divide it with the widow in distress.

Tommy carved him a top which he played in the light from Tierney's window. If the road was icy he was sometimes able to slide with Colm and the bigger children. Most frosty nights, his parents brought them for a walk to Shelley's Cross. As they came out of the dip, he could see Knockane castle against the sky, which danced with twinkling stars.

'When you're bigger, you'll learn all about the stars.' Colm pointed. 'That's the plough, and there's the evening star that keeps the moon company.'

He risked the danger of the ice-covered potholes to study the moon. Snug and warm in the green jersey and gloves knitted by his mother, he wondered if there really was a man there, as his parents had suggested. His father pointed his navy glove upwards. 'The *Titanic* would have been saved had the moon shone that night.' The distant flashing of the *Aurora Borealis* made him wonder about the Lapps and the Eskimos, who lived up at the North Pole in igloos made of snow. A falling star flashed across the sky. 'God bless the poor soul on its way.' His mother crossed herself.

Two important visitors called, Christian Brothers from Dublin. His mother sent him to Kelly's to buy a sponge cake. 'What are they doing here?' He expectantly unwrapped the cake.

'They've come to see Colm. They often visit homes to see if there's a vocation in the family. But you're not to tell anyone.'

Was Colm going to join the Brothers? That would be almost like having a priest in the family. Maybe he would get his bike; he would love to be able to cycle.

The new year progressed; the trees turned green. 'You can do the bottom bar.' His father paused while repainting the white front railings. He loved the spring smells. The fresh paint, the Brasso and polish as Moll Ryan helped his mother change the furniture around. And the new flowers from the Dublin seed catalogues. Two beds of wallflowers, marigolds and pansies surrounded the porch, a third ran along the river wall. Lupins, roses and sweet pea brightened the sheltered corners. When they had visitors, his mother provided tea and scones on the seat under the sitting-room window. Din Ryan puffed his pipe beside the gate. 'An oashus, Mrs Lynch, the liveliest spot in the village.'

Mrs Quinn stopped on her way back from Kelly's bakery. 'Mrs Regan was found snoozing near the crossroads yesterday. The ass found a nice piece of grass and forgot all about Grenanstown!'

When she had gone, his mother shook her head at Moll Ryan: 'That's the trouble with the drink. It lowers you to the level of ignoramuses like her. If she doesn't give it up, she'll be in trouble, I'm afraid.'

'Himself will be no ignoramus,' Moll laughed, as he tried to read the *Irish Press* on the seat. But reading was hard work. '*Ration* – what does that mean?' He interrupted his mother again. 'But why is it spelled with a 't' when it sounds like 's'?'

He was allowed to go with Noel Searson along the Pallas road riverbank. They crossed the stile and Noel whistled 'Blaze Away', the old march tune made popular again by Josef Locke, as they stepped along the avenue of high trees in Robinson's beech walk. Spiders' webs glistened in the hedgerows, as they picked buttercups and cowslips in the marshland opposite the little bridge. 'Solid silver.' Noel scooped up the flaky stones which sparkled in the bottom of sandy pools. His older friend showed him the birds nests and told him the names of all the trees. While he picked haws, Noel tried to tickle a trout from under a river rock. 'I've got to be careful of the crayfish. One took the fingers off a man beyont in Latteragh last week.'

'Mary, Mother of Mankind, we are honoured to celebrate your feast again.' Each year, his mother set up a May altar on a small table in a corner of the dining room. She placed the Virgin Mary's blue-and-white statue and two silver candlesticks on the lace cloth. Vases of fresh flowers flanked the Virgin; taller jars of lupins and lilac from their back garden stood behind. Sometimes, he risked the briars to bring wildflowers from the Pallas road. As he knelt on his scratched knees for the rosary, he knew that the Virgin was happy with him for his sacrifice. There was nothing as beautiful as the lilac's perfume. It also forecast the summer holiday freedom of long evenings, lettuce and salad cream.

His father wasn't the only painter in Toomevara. They woke

one morning to find an election slogan whitewashed on the bridge. With his thumbs in his breast pockets, his father addressed the likely artists: 'The Prime Boys were out last night. We must make sure they don't decorate anyone's wall.' The village was divided into two lots of people, the Fianna Fáil supporters who read the *Irish Press* and whose leader Dev had freed Ireland and the usually richer Fine Gael supporters who took the *Irish Independent*. 'God between us and all harm but you can always recognise a Cosgrave sliveen,' his mother told Mrs Gleeson. 'They look so mean and guilty. And no wonder, after doing Churchill's dirty work.'

He never visited any of the Fine Gael children's homes during elections. Some of them made him cry when he was giving out leaflets for the Fianna Fáil presidential candidate: 'Sean T. O'Kelly with the big fat belly.'

Sometimes, there were fights and his father would patrol the streets at closing time. The Timekeeper called to check the time on the wireless. 'You're great, Sergeant, the way you can handle them all without a gun like in the old days. But I don't know why they're arguing. Didn't I see the two candidates go into Donovan's pub together after meeting on the square yesterday!'

The candidates put posters on the school tree after Sunday Mass and gave speeches from the wall. 'Hear, hear!' their supporters cheered. 'Keep down the price of the pint,' shouted little Con Flaherty. When they had finished, Con jumped up on the wall. He waved his arms and imitated the candidates: 'I come before you, to stand behind you, to tell you something I know nothing about. The opposition promises change, but I'm the only one here who'll give you real change.' The children dived to the ground, as he showered them with new pennies which flashed and spun in the morning sun.

The republican Éamon de Valera was his mother's hero. She always cheered up when his name was mentioned. 'He gets more votes in my county than any other candidate in the country!'

'Up Dev!' she clapped and shouted when he spoke on the wireless at the end of the war. She ran over to Dick Casey: 'He's the only one who could ever stand up to that Churchill.' When the *Irish Press* published the speech, she cut out the photograph of Dev at the microphone. His mother reminded Dick of how Dev had visited her Scarriff home during the 1919 election. 'And as long as I live, I'll never forget the day we all cycled to Ennis to hear him speak after his release from prison. He stood up and when there was finally silence, he began: "As I was saying before I was interrupted…"'

'Well, you never heard anything like it, Dick. Sure they didn't stop cheering for ten minutes. There wasn't a man or a woman there that day who wouldn't have died for the Chief.'

His mother brought him out to Shelley's Cross to greet her favourite on his way back to Dublin. They both saluted as the two big cars approached. Inside the second car, he thought he saw a dark-clad man wave back. 'God bless you, Dev!' his mother exclaimed. She still saluted after the cars had passed them. 'Dev's gone.' He turned around but she continued to wave long after the car sped down Maher's hill and he was shocked to see that she had tears in her eyes. He knew then that the Chief was more important to her than anything else in the world.

'Dev's a great man all right,' he agreed, as they walked slowly back, past the Protestant church and Williams's bicycle shop.

While Colm did his homework, his parents often took him curdeeking to Gleesons' house near Ollatrim Cross. Mrs Gleeson was a sister of Wedger Meagher, the captain of the famous Toomevara Greyhound hurlers. 'Toome's greatest day, when they played the All-Ireland at Croke Park! Stephen Hackett may be rickety on the bike now, but you should have seen him that day. No one could catch him; that's why they were christened the greyhounds.'

Mrs Gleeson was also a Fianna Fáil supporter. As she sliced a steaming apple tart, she recalled the 1932 election when Dev's party had beaten Cosgrave's Fine Gael, known then as Cumann na nGaedheal. 'They come in a gale all right, Mrs Lynch and beJasus – may the Lord forgive me – they went out in a bigger one.' His mother remembered the War of Independence, as she held out her plate. 'Wouldn't it make you proud, Mrs Gleeson, to recall Wedger and the boys? With only hurley sticks and a few rifles, they stood up to the machine-guns and armoured cars of the Tans. And the flying columns! Sure, the English never knew where they were going to come from next. Wasn't it great that a few of our own were able to run rings around Lloyd George and the rest of Maxwell's gangsters. We'll never see the likes of Wedger and his comrades again.'

His parents also visited the Hacketts on the Nenagh road. His mother held out her teacup to the former teacher: 'Wasn't it an awful shame we had to resign when we married? The reading helps but all the books in the world can't compensate for the lack of work.'

'Work? Sure, aren't we slaving from morning to night? It's a man's world, Mrs Lynch. But I do envy Mrs Regan sometimes; she got back to the teaching when poor Tom died. The bit of money must be a big help with her shopping!'

Jack Hackett was the creamery manager. He had all the latest farming gossip and an opinion on everything. 'You'd put George Bernard Shaw in the halfpenny place,' his mother laughed, as they discussed Baron Hanley. The Baron was a Limerick man who had risen from rags to riches in America. The *Irish Press* announced his annual return in a big green, white and orange coloured car. A shamrock was painted on each door; Irish and American flags flew on the car wings. As he slowed through Toomevara, the Baron saluted everyone with his white-gloved hand. But Jack was unimpressed. He moved his hat back on his head. 'Sure, what can a millionaire do only have one dinner and wear one suit and sleep in one bed, like the rest of us? Baron my backside!'

'What's that terrible noise?' His mother and he looked up at the sky as they left for Mass one morning. Just like the photographs: an aeroplane! The green aeroplane roared right over them and across the fields towards Gurtagarry. His mother grabbed his arm and pulled him all the way to the chapel. 'Jesus, Mary and Joseph! we'll all be killed.'

'Did you see this morning's paper?' They met Auntie Maggie on the way home. 'Six planes went out and ten came back. You could never bate the English for the lies.'

Many nights, the windows rattled to the roar of motorcycle patrols and the rasping of military lorry tyres. A German plane crashed at Dromineer. Colm cycled out to see it. 'The cockpit glass was so thick a sledgehammer couldn't break it. The pilot burned his secret documents before the guards arrived.'

'Allies Advance.' He could now read big writing.

'Hitler will be beaten,' he informed classmate, Chris Shanahan. He looked forward every day to the *Irish Press* maps, which arrowed the war's latest advances and retreats. It was as exciting as draughts and Ludo. Each night, the maps joined the press cuttings which his father filed away on the kitchen door hook.

'Forty paces to MacBirney's from O'Connell Bridge.' The *Irish Press* also featured Captain Mac's children's column and funny picture advertisements for Mac's Smile razorblades and O'Dearest mattresses. His favourite cartoon appeared each weekend: 'Today is Saturday. Don't forget your Lemon's Pure Sweets!'

'"Roddy McCorley". You can't beat Billy for the whistling.' Colm watched as Tim Delaney's son herded the cows up the sunny street.

Summer brought the most exciting sounds. The thump of Perry's Ale barrels and the clinking of Dwans' lemonade bottles outside the pubs. The horses' clip-clop and the rolling of carriage wheels, as Miss Trench of Loughisle estate went to shop in Nenagh. The whirring of the Dubliners' laden sportscycles, as they headed for faraway Kerry. The rattle on the slate footpath of his cycle wheel bowlie. The whine of the saws from Boland's mill, the evening cries of the canon's rainbow-coloured peacocks.

'I passed the caravans coming home.' Colm heralded his favourite melody, the clang of sledge-hammers against the metal pegs which anchored the travelling show tents. The village also rang with the tapping of the Tinker Quinns, as they repaired and soldered saucepans, frying pans and kettles, while their horses grazed on the Pallas road verges. And their rich Clare accents as, in return for a bucket of potatoes, they told his mother the latest Scarriff gossip: 'Magician Biddy Earley's secret bottle will soon be found; there's a *meitheal* of men searching Lough Graney night and day.'

The sun melted the main road tar the day that Ireland's greatest sports commentator called on Big Jim O'Meara. The publican showed Micheál O'Hehir all his tricks, including one he himself longed to learn, how to turn a penny into a florin. Jim asked the commentator to choose a card. He flung the deck up at the bar ceiling where one card remained stuck.

'Would that be yours, Michael?'

Shortly afterwards, the Heaneys arrived with their latest wire puzzles. 'Better than any book, these'll keep you going all winter!'

The Emergency brought rare night-time adventure, when his

brother and himself joined the villagers in the harvesting. Tilly lamps swayed on the horsedrawn reaper and binder they followed in the fields above Boland's mill. Din Ryan cocked his ear: 'You can hear the whirrin' of the threshin' from the four provinces.'

Teams of villagers cut the sheaves and filled the bags with flowing wheat. Men dodged the threshing machine belts and used words he had never heard at home. Frankie Smith ducked. 'That fuckin' belt nearly took me head off.'

Dick Hassett pushed him back on the straw. 'You'd be the first man to die for Ireland this war.'

'It's like the Aurora Borealis.' His brother said, as they watched the beams of huge battery lamps flash across the countryside. The government paid villagers to catch rabbits. But the dealer, Johnny Meagher, didn't make his expected fortune. Jim Shanahan leaned over the railings. 'Mrs Lynch, the prime boys are removing the rabbits through the back door, and presenting them at the front for another payment!'

Many villagers joined the Local Defence Forces. Some even became film stars. Despite getting lost on manoeuvres, a Toomevara platoon was picked for crowd scenes in the battle of Agincourt, the highlight of the film *Henry V.* 'Evening, General. What news from the front?' Din Ryan saluted Paddy Dwyer, who looked very important in his new uniform. Many people made fun of Paddy, who could neither read nor write. When manoeuvres ended, Colm, John and Tony Donovan and the bigger children staged their own wars on the Shelley's Cross sandhills. With *camáin* and wooden swords, they marched home singing:

> Will you come to Abyssinia, will you come?
> Will you bring your bread and butter and your gun?

His parents helped to start Red Cross and Local Defence Force branches. His father loaded his carrier with manuals, bandages and splints, and cycled out to give first aid lectures in Ballymackey and Gurtagarry. Dick Casey put the carbide in his father's lamp. 'You're a real patriot, Sergeant. A few more like you and this would be a great country.' Two bags of flour arrived from his father's sister, Aunt Bridget, who lived in New York. When it had all been used and some given to poorer neighbours, the Moneygall tailor Chris Quinlan converted the bags into trouser linings for Colm and himself. Chris surveyed the lining slogans. 'The only boys in Toomevara with "Gold Medal" pants.'

It was to be the last short trousers his brother would wear in Toomevara. The Christian Brothers called again. They spoke to his parents and Colm for a long time in the sitting room. His mother came out: 'Colm's joining the Brothers.'

'Toome's first Christian Brother!' Mrs Tierney congratulated her.

He played for the final time with Colm, when they experimented with the port wine his mother kept for visitors. He didn't like the taste. 'It's like the Mass wine. I'll have another drop.' His knowledgeable brother put the bottle to his mouth.

'Be careful. You'll be singing like Mrs Regan, and then our mother will find out.'

They topped up the bottle with water. A few days later, they studied Father O'Brien as he took a glass in the sitting room. 'A very nice port, Mrs Lynch,' he said. But his brother and he noticed the face the priest made on his first sip.

A week later, two Brothers came to collect Colm. He was sorry to see him go; now he had no one at home to scheme with. 'Mind my bike,' Colm said, as he climbed on to the bus with the green painted wooden suitcase their father had made. It was strange to be drawing up only three chairs for the rosary. There was a pause when Colm's decade came up, before their mother started: 'Hail Mary, full of grace.' She cried as she concluded: 'But thank God for his vocation.'

His mother suffered one of her illnesses shortly afterwards. 'You've been overdoing it again, Mrs Lynch,' newly-arrived Dr McCann told her. She stayed in bed for a week. Every day, his father prepared her a beaten-up egg. The doctor added to her store of medicines in the dining-room dresser: Milk of Magnesia, Syrup of Figs, Vino's cough medicine, Parrish's Food, Beecham's Powders, Kruschen Salts and Andrews Liver Salts. His father could never explain her maladies to him. 'It's her nerves, God bless the poor woman,' he overheard Mollie Barney telling a neighbour.

He crashed many times, as he tried to master his brother's

bicycle. 'You look like the Elastoplast advertisement.' Din Ryan said, looking in the door of Sis McDonald's pharmacy. But within a short time, he was able to go for spins with his father down the Pallas road. He made his first big trip to Doll's shop in Clash, where he chewed Cleeves slab toffee beside the fireside tea chest while the adults chatted. Mrs Cullen filled a bag of tea. 'Regan was late again for school last week. A terrible example for a teacher to be giving. She's gone too far, we're going to see the PP.'

One Saturday afternoon, Jack Hackett banged on their door. 'Sergeant, come quickly! Jim Larkin's lying on the Nenagh road, covered in blood and surrounded by a swarm of flies.'

His father cycled off and found the headmaster unconscious near Phil the Sailor's cottage. His bicycle's front fork had broken. He had to be taken to Nenagh hospital. Auntie Maggie called. 'If it was Mrs Regan, I could understand. Poor Jim, sure he never took a drink in his life.'

But the headmaster's accident shocked his fellow-teacher. Auntie Maggie met them on the way from Mass a week later. 'A miracle. Poor Mrs Regan was so frightened by Jim Larkin's crash that she's taken the pledge!' From then on, his teacher always went straight home from school. His mother stood in the porch one evening: 'You'd miss the oul' ass.'

His father brought out Colm's cycle after one Sunday Mass: 'You can ride to the big match today!' His parents loaded their bikes with the rug, scones, mugs and a flask of tea. 'Greyhound' Stephen Hackett and ballad singer Billy Walsh set off with them to Moneygall, where Toomevara was playing the local team.

'Wait for me!' His shorter legs had to pedal much faster to keep up with the adults on the four-miles trip. Stephen picked him up when he swerved into the ditch at Loughisle. By the time they reached the hurling field, they were all singing Billy's new song:

Hay and oats for the Moneygall goats,
Eggs and rashers for the Toomevara dashers.

The big bus at last! They all went to Dublin to see Colm. For mile after mile, they drove along the tarred roads through villages and towns. He heard new accents at each stop. The names on his school map came to life. 'There's St Bridget's tower,' his mother pointed in Kildare. They approached the city. He had never seen so many houses in his life, nor so many people, motor cars and delivery lorries. He counted six bridges, each wider than the preceding one, before the bus stopped. His mother explained: 'A traffic jam. We can't go until the guard waves the other cars through.'

Noisy buses called trams sparked and screeched their way across the city on rails. '*Herald* a'*Mail*,' barefoot newschildren shouted from the street corners. His mother showed him a house with six storeys and the Dáil, from which Dev ruled Ireland. And the river Liffey and O'Connell Bridge, from which they counted out the forty paces to McBirney's. Outside Trinity College, he pulled his mother's arm: 'Look. Look. A black man!'

Colm's life was very different now. 'There's over a hundred of us here. We don't have our own rooms; we all sleep in dormitories. The Brothers are strict. I'd rather be back in Toomevara. Are you minding my bike?'

Colm wasn't allowed out. His father looked back as they left. 'You'd think they'd let him free for a few hours.' But he soon forgot his brother, when they went to the Ballsbridge Military Tattoo. The drums rattled and the cannon roared, as the army acted the battles of Benburb and Clontibret. How he cheered, as the Irish soldiers charged and their guns flashed through the smoke and the English ran away.

The holidays made summer race. A whole year had flown and he was back to school again. Mrs Regan told him: 'My class is only to prepare children for all they will learn in the big grades upstairs. The more you study, the better a job you will get when you are big – and the more questions you will be able to answer on *Question Time*!' He missed the bright evenings. But autumn brought the compensations of hazelnuts, Halloween barmbrack, snap-apple and the exciting wireless quiz. As he stripped the slim trees in Loughisle Wood, he dreamed of finding the rapparee Galloping Hogan's buried treasure. But he was as unsuccessful as he was at Blean, where he had sought the outline of a crock of gold in the tree-rimmed fairy rath.

His father surprised him: 'Would you like to go to Kilkenny?' But it was a sad trip, as his father brought orphan Tom to the children's home. He was allowed to keep the six-year old boy company until he was led away crying by dark-habited nuns. The dashboard instruments of Dan Casey's Ford Prefect shed a warm glow as they headed across the dark roads to the comfort of real home. 'Why couldn't Tom stay in the village with his aunt?'

His mother wrapped the rug around him. 'The nuns will look after him very well.'

Their wireless was rationed, as the dry batteries were expensive and the wet ones had to be regularly charged at Boland's mill. *Question Time* was their favourite programme, after the news and the weekend plays. Each Sunday night, he raced home from Devotions and warmed up the set in time for Joe Linnane's introduction. Mrs Regan called one night to hear the programme. He was very proud that he could answer some of the two-mark and even four-mark questions. He was learning all right. 'He'll soon be reading books,' the teacher cheered his mother. His mother asked him to whistle the signature tune for their visitor. They laughed when he insisted it was the *Question Time* music and not what they called 'Perpetuum Mobile'.

'How's Colm getting on?' his teacher enquired.

'He's doing well; he loves it there.' He was surprised, Colm had said no such thing.

'Would you like a refreshment, Mrs Regan?'

'Nothing stronger than lemonade, thank you, Mrs Lynch.' She taepped her Pioneer pin.

4

'There's not much happening in Toomevara.' His mother gathered the dead geranium leaves from the porch shelf. 'When you're older, I will give you extra study. Education will take you to some better place.'

'But soon we're going to your home in Scarriff!'

'The sooner, the better. We'll be able to relax for a change. With your father being the sergeant, it's no fun here.'

He was as happy as his mother to be going to Clare. More freedom, more friends – and fishing in the perch-filled Graney. He sat on a special saddle on his father's bike and the three of them set out to cycle the thirty miles. Moll Ryan waved them off. 'Safe journey. I'll look after the hens.'

A Nenagh tea stop fuelled them for the long ride past the hurler Rody Nealon's house to Portroe hill. They all looked through the trees for their first glimpse of the Shannon. 'Lough Derg!' he shouted, as he spotted the silvery water through the trees. They stopped at the Lookout. His mother took off her cream summer cardigan and pulled three bottles of Club Orange from her front basket. 'Nothing could ever beat that view. Mountshannon and Holy Island, as if I never left them.' She handed the bottles to his father for opening. 'Isn't it great that you'll be out of that uniform for a fortnight?' They sat on a fallen bough. His father pointed to the hills above the road. 'Galloping Hogan led Sarsfield through there to attack the besiegers of Limerick:

> And yet one blow for freedom –
> One daring midnight ride,
> And William may be humbled yet,
> For all his power and pride.

His parents cycled abreast and talked about locals they had known. He had a great view from the crossbar, as they freewheeled around the green-shaded bends and Big House entrances towards Ballina. 'God bless the work,' his father greeted the council men. Birds sang and watched from telephone wires. His mother inhaled in appreciation. 'Smell that woodbine. Wouldn't it do your heart good.' When they reached the bridge over the Shannon, they dismounted and leaned the bicycles against the parapet. His parents blessed themselves and they all prayed at the memorial where the Black and Tans had shot Alfie Rogers from Scarriff and three comrades: 'God bless you, who gave your young lives for us. We will never forget you, may the Lord have mercy on your souls.'

His mother blessed herself. 'Why are you crying?' he asked, as they picked up the bikes and walked into Killaloe.

'You go ahead now and be a good boy.'

'Ah, I see you were at the bridge again, Siobhán.' Mrs Daly welcomed them to her riverside house. 'Paddy says we must try and put the past behind us, though I know that's especially hard for you. But it's great you're both looking – and your timing's as good as ever. Sit down there now while I take out the rhubarb tart.'

'I heard Colm went off with the Brothers. I hate to see them going off so young. How's he getting on?'

'Most of the boys there are around fourteen.' His mother pulled her chair up to the table. 'We have a letter once a month. He's still missing home; there's not much rhubarb tart there! But, please God, he'll get used to it in time.'

Mrs Daly's tea and the local news set them up for the final lap. Through the sunshine and tree shadows, they pedalled past Gleesons of Tinerana and the house of the failed priest. 'Paradise,' his mother said, looking across Lough Derg to their Lookout picnic spot, as they walked up the long Ogonnoloe hill. From Raheen hospital, they soared down into Tuamgraney. 'Music for Pythagoras,' his mother cried, as they heard the clanging of the blacksmith's anvil.

Big Tom waved a glowing tongs from his forge's open door. 'Siobhán and Patrick, you're like the swallows, you always return.'

His mother dismounted from her bicycle. 'You don't know how nice it is to be home.'

While his parents and Tom chatted, he raced up the hill to his grandparents. Two steps above the footpath, they kept an open house where the kettle always boiled on the hob. Under prints of *Napoleon's Retreat* and *The Battle of Cremona*, visitors took snuff and played cards until the early hours. 'Hould your diamond till the last!' The chair creaked under his grandmother's weight as she outwitted her Forty-Five companions yet again.

'They dragged them out and destroyed their homes.' Joe Minogue shuffled the pack and recalled the Bodyke evictions. 'And only thirty year since they raided this house too. By God, the Tans met their match in you, Mrs Moore. Dropping Jim Daly's revolver into the stirabout was the best ever!'

'Where else would I put it? Who was going to stick his arm into a bubbling pot?'

His grandmother managed the finances and cooked for three lodgers. When she wanted a pee, she stood over the backdoor drain and lifted up her ankle-length black dress, even on the coldest nights. He was not surprised that she had been unafraid of the Tans.

She rebuked his mother once: 'We put all our money into giving you a good education – and then you went off and got married.'

'When I cycled home from teaching all day I had to clean up the house and cook. Don't you remember how I had to hand up my wages? I'd to beg for a shilling to go to the odd dance.'

Known as 'Dada Moore', his grandfather looked very silvery with his white hair, light-grey cap and suit. He only beat him once, for walking Emmet Henchy across the parapet of the Graney bridge. 'Your brother never did anything like that.' Every morning at six, Dada Moore started the big engine in Sparlings Bakery. 'Squirt that oil in there when I turn the wheel. Then, we'll make some bread.' After a snort and a backfire, the machine started. The flywheel revolved, the belts slapped, the valve pushrods slurped up and down, the bakery came alive with the smell of oil and the miracle of motion. After stoking the furnace, his grandfather showed him how to mix the flour, yeast and milk. The dough stuck to his fingers as he filled the rectangular tin which his grandfather thrust into the oven on a long wooden paddle. An hour later he upended the steaming brown loaf: 'Now, show that to your mother.'

Dada Moore was a Labour party supporter. 'Fianna Fayal and Foine Gale only fill their own nests like the bosses. They're all hiding behind the sacrifices of real men like James Connolly. Only a Labour government will put this country on its feet.'

'With that moustache of yours, you're a dead-ringer for Uncle Joe Stalin,' Ned Moloney joked.

'What was my mother like when she was small?' he asked his grandfather.

'She worked hard at home and at school. She was a good scholar, I wasn't surprised that she became a teacher.'

'She's a bit cross sometimes.'

'Did your mother never speak to you about the Troubles?' His grandfather looked up from cleaning the dough mixer.

'She told me about the Scarriff men who were killed and showed me their grave above in the churchyard.'

'That's all? The Troubles brought big problems and changed many people's lives. Your mother might tell you more about it some day. She got a big shock when those men died; they went to school with her. But I'll tell her she must be nicer to you in the future!'

Was that why his mother was so often sad – because her schoolfriends had been murdered? And why she spent so much time in church and worried about everything? All the other parents he knew were so cheerful compared to her. But in Clare she was always more carefree: 'Off you go then with Emmet, but be sure and be back for your tea.'

Every night, she visited old friends, even sometimes walking as far as Moynoe and Tuamgraney. 'You don't know how nice it is to be among your own,' she told Mrs Boyce. 'People aren't so friendly in Tipperary; there we'll always be blow-ins.'Twould be great if we could move back but with Patrick in the Force, we can't do that.'

Scarriff was a lively place. Every Saturday morning Mrs Phelan undid the twine which released the latest *Beano* and *Dandy* adventures. Mikey McMahon, who spoke through his nose, sold him the bamboo cane and line with which he caught his first perch in the swirling Graney. 'Go for the red ones,' Emmet Henchy directed from the wall, as they raided Miss O'Brien's orchard.

Dick Grimes, oil tanker driver, cradled his teacup on the top doorstep. 'You can't bate the fair day for excitement.'

'You mean for the rivers of shite and piss.' Paddy Moloney rubbed his eyes against the caustic smell which hung over the town. Crowds thronged the streets from early morning; all the shops were shuttered against the heaving cattle. The market house was surrounded by stalls. Hawkers sold twine, penknives and bottles of cure-all medicine: 'Good bye to lumbago and the rheumatics.'

'Five pounds for that animal? Five pounds of good meal would hardly bring her back to life.'

An accomplice bent down. 'You'd read the *Clare Champion* through the poor beasht's ribs.'

The buyer and seller spat on their hands to cement the deal. 'By God, you've an Ennis Show winner there.' The seller counted the notes. 'The only show's the one I've made of myself. I need a pint to recover.' The buyer tethered the cow to a telegraph pole and they all went into O'Brien's bar.

His grandmother made breakfast and lunch for the hungry farmers and drovers. Auctioneer Jim Rogers hit the hanging flypaper with his upraised fork. 'More power to you, Mrs Moore, that bacon and cabbage would melt in your mouth.'

Cigarette and pipe smoke wafted up the stairs with the whiskey fumes. Joe Minogue looked up from *Moore's Almanac*. 'An eclipse of the moon in September.'

Nellie Riordan told drovers their fortunes from the tea leaves. Jim Rogers mimicked: 'This is your line of fate. And this is your line of sorrow. If you don't shite today, you'll surely shite tomorrow.'

Red-faced Paddy Moloney folded his short legs and threw himself into the Cobbler's dance. Jim Rogers outshouted the street ballad singers with 'The Stone outside Dan Murphy's Door' and everyone joined him in the ballad of the West Clare Railway:

Are ye right there Michael, are ye right?
Do you think that we'll be there before the night?

In the evening, his grandmother allowed him to play Roy Rogers and John Philip Sousa on the big gramaphone with its twin needle boxes. He wound the handle, while the lodger Mick Gallagher stood beside the louvred cabinet and sang 'The Old House' with Count John McCormack. But his biggest adventure was in the nearby cinema. Liam Treacy preceded him up the narrow stairway. 'Bring that drum of film; we'll splice it in the projection room.' He rubbed shoulders with Hollywood as he arranged the display stills of Ann Blyth, Rita Hayworth and Alan Ladd. MGM's roaring lion and Columbia's torch-bearing Liberty Lady became his new icons. As the projectors clicked into life the flickering images excited wild cheers from far below. The music swelled, a cattle rustler aimed, the audience shouted: 'He's behind you, Gabby!'

For weeks after he returned home, he would stretch on his bedroom window sill. His eyes trying to pierce the Graves of the Leinstermen peak, behind which lay the scene of his happiest childhood experiences. His mother was always cross after the holidays. His father poured her tea one evening: 'If we win the Sweep we'll go back and live in Clare!'

His mother frowned over her son's monthly letter. 'Colm's finding it hard again.'

'He was always a bit slow to mix.' His father looked up from the *Irish Press*. 'No matter how you look at it, it's a strange life they have up there. But give him a bit more time and he'll be all right.'

He was sorry that his brother couldn't paddle in the river beside their house, catching bricíns and building dams. 'Be careful of the broken glass. I'm not sure if I should let you play there at all,' his mother warned. Sipping wagtails shook their tails, sparrows and occasional robins danced from rock to moss-covered rock. The river connected him to the great outside; he wondered about its faraway sea home. The flowing water muffled the village sounds; it was a magical peaceful world. But he ran up the steps in tears one day when he stumbled over a bag of newly drowned kittens. His mother would only allow him to stay out for short periods. 'Ten Minutes,' the village children called him. Workers let them mix cement when the new cottages were being built. In the evenings, they swung like acrobats from the crossbeams. Someone reported them to the sergeant, who discovered that one of the trespassers was his own son. Thereafter, Chum Shanahan was his sole companion. They made aeroplanes with spinning sycamore leaves and dug trenches in the garden. With discarded council pipes as guns, the trenches became outposts which they defended like the Gunner.

'Halt! Who goes there?' they mimicked the soldiers they had seen on manoeuvres.

'We'll go halves on anything you find.' The hall caretaker, Paddy Fitzgerald, let them search thorough sunbeams and stale cigarette smoke for coins lost during the previous night's whist drive. He left Chum in Looby's barn, thinking he would soon tire of being 'kidnapped' and find his own way home. But his friend fell asleep in the warm hay. Hours later, Mrs Shanahan knocked on the door. 'Have you seen Chum? We've searched the whole village, we can't find him anywhere.'

'You're a terrible child, frightening all our neighbours. No more outdoors for you.' His mother sent him to bed early. Luckily he had discovered books. 'Reading is like a key.' His mother had been right. The wireless and the *Irish Press* had introduced him to the big world outside Toomevara but it was the books which really unlocked all the wonders of life. The county council's fortnightly library introduced him to Biggles and Patricia Lynch, with whose roguish tinkers he soon roamed Ireland's hills and valleys. After reading Arthur Ransome, his river dams became lagoons which led to adventures on distant shores. He discovered real-life adventurers among the dull-covered adult books with their pencilled curses against the English and the communists. Round-the-world sailor Joshua Slocum, pioneering flyers Alcock and Brown, Amelia Earhart and Captain Fitzmaurice, the Irishman who made the first flight from Europe to America.

Auntie Maggie struggled up from the wooden council box. 'I don't know why you come here at all, Mrs Lynch. Sure you have a bigger library at home – and bookcases with windows.'

He was proud of his parents' book collection. With the curtains drawn and the lamp on full wick, there was nowhere as cosy as the dining room for reading. His legs reddened and covers warped, while his mother turned the pages of Annie M. P. Smithson on the opposite side of the fire. A downdraft filled the room with smoke. His mother pushed back her chair and quoted Padraic Colum:

> My eyelids red and heavy are
> With bending o'er the smouldering peat!

He often read a hidden book in bed. With his mind full of fantasies of distant lands, he fell asleep to Toomevara's familiar night noises. The croaking of the Robinson's pool frogs, the howling of faraway dogs, the cries of lone drunks staggering home, the squeaking of a bicycle receding towards Ballymackey, the swish of O'Meara's wind charger. And if the wind was right, the wavering whistle of a goods train rattling through the night near distant Cloughjordan.

Wouldn't it have been great if the railway went through their village, with a signal that rose and fell with each arrival? Then, it wouldn't be as backward as his mother had said. How Mick Dalkey, the Gunner and all the old people would enjoy sitting on benches under ivied telegraph poles with rows of white insulators like resting birds! Watching the great smoking engine and those passengers who had travelled all across Ireland from Kerry, Cork and Limerick.

His favourite books were the seven big volumes of Cassell's *Book of Knowledge* with their blue covers and gilt spines. Contrary to what his mother had told him, he discovered that there were many good English people. The lifeboat rescuer Grace Darling, pioneering nurse, Florence Nightingale, Wilberforce who had abolished slavery and writer Samuel Johnson, who had often helped poor Oliver Goldsmith.

While the cornerboys smoked by Boss O'Meara's gable wall, the flick of a page transported him to exotic lands where people picked oranges from outside their windows or travelled the streets of Venice in gondolas. Photographs showed the Taj Mahal and beautiful buildings in Italy, dykes and windmills in Holland, children tobogganing in snowy Switzerland. And sad images too, blind soldiers holding each other's shoulders as they shuffled home from the Great War. They would never see Florence or even their families again.

'Study those and learn something about your country's history.' His mother opened the glass bookcase. On the shelf under the Oxford Dictionary and A. J. Cronin's novels, were copies of the *Capuchin* and *Wolfe Tone* annuals and her favourite books on the fight for independence. Dan Breen boasted of killing fellow-Irishmen who were escorting gelignite along a country road. 'But weren't Constables Patrick O'Connell and James MacDonnell only doing their duty as my father does?' His question startled his mother. Photographs showed the bodies of ambushed Auxiliaries littering a country road and policemen burned to death in their barracks. In Clare, republicans buried a magistrate on a strand where the tide drowned him. Surely this was as cruel and cowardly as anything the Black and Tans had done?

He interrupted his mother again. 'The gunmen killed war victims recovering in Dublin hospitals, poor men like the Gunner. Tom Barry shot the 75-year old singing beggar Tom Sullivan, then used his body as an ambush decoy. How could it be murder for the British to shoot Irish people, but heroic for us to kill the British?'

His mother lowered her Ethel Mannin book: 'I'll let you off this time, but never again say anything like that about the brave men who freed our country. Never!'

'But don't the Commandments say: "Thou shall not kill"?'

She shook the book at him. 'Now, that's enough, don't upset me any more. There are many things that you are too young to understand.'

For the first time, he thought his mother was wrong. A terrible event reinforced his new sentiments. His parents rejoiced when unarmed Gandhi liberated India from the British Empire. But they were shocked by the six o'clock news announcement: 'Mahatma Ghandi was assassinated today by Hindu extremists.'

Dan Casey called over to discuss the news. Jack Hackett and the teacher, Tom MacDonald, arrived soon afterwards. His mother made tea and they all sat down around the dining-room table. 'It's a tragedy, after all his sacrifices for others. He was a real Christian.' His father straightened his chair.

"Gandhi proved, like Christ, that the only way to justice is through peaceful means,' Tom MacDonald agreed.

'Violence degrades man and breeds more violence. We've seen that in Ireland. It took Europe a thousand years to restore civilisation after the northern invasions. Look at England, whose parliament has become a model for so many countries. No more civil war, they settle their affairs peacefully in the House of Commons. That's progress, that's civilisation.'

"All very well to talk about the long view, Tom.' His mother refilled their cups. 'But some thieves only yield to force. It's

Christian to turn the other cheek, but we've also a responsibility to protect our homes from the invader. Despite all their promises, the English only gave us our freedom after brave men and women were prepared to die for it. Men from my own town were shot like dogs by the Tans, without even the comfort of a priest's last visit.'

"Well, Mrs Lynch,' interrupted Jack Hackett. 'I saw those thugs in action too. Didn't they murder my friends Tom and Jim Devaney who are lying over there in the square? But we're living in different times now and the lure of the gun is, I think, a bigger menace than those blackguards. Everywhere I look, the gun brings misery and destruction. I'm worried now that those bloody brainless killers – excuse my language – who murdered Gandhi may have opened the door to even greater bloodshed. And he after freeing them and India without a single shot! The more I think of it, the more damage the gun caused here too, killing all our best men bar one. I've sometimes wondered if we'd listened to Redmond, there might be a lot more people alive today – and a lot less bitterness.'

It was the first time he had heard patriots being criticised in their house, or his mother being swayed by an argument. 'Maybe there's something in what you say, Jack. Poor Gandhi, India's Parnell.'

Though he was Protestant, his mother remembered Parnell every Ivy Day. She polished his portrait medal and arranged it with flowers and ivy on the dining-room mantelpiece: 'Charles Stewart, Ireland's uncrowned king'.

> He fought the might of England
> And saved the Irish poor.

His mother and he went to Cis MacDonald for Andrews Liver Salts. Cis stepped down from the stool: 'Have you read Maura Laverty's latest? *Never No More*. I'll lend it to you when I'm finished.'

His mother searched in her purse. 'Without the reading, I'd be lost. Only the books kept me going when I had to stop the teaching. 'Twould be great to be back in the school again, doing something useful.'

Din Ryan didn't think much of the reading. 'Them oul' books will only mix you up.' He puffed his bull's-head pipe on a chair outside his new council house. His mother called their illiterate neighbour 'the Oracle' because of his regular pronouncements. A rich farmer boasted of the time he saved with his new tractor. Din removed the pipe from his mouth: 'And what did you do with all the time you spared?' When asked to account for the bad summer, Din pointed up through his own Rich-Cut clouds. 'Bums, bums. It's all dem atum bums. Mark my words, they're not natural.'

He laughed at Din but, perhaps, he was getting proud with all his book knowledge? The mission Passionists, who terrified the villagers every two years, included pride with the other deadly sins which would consign one to hell for eternity. Under the chapel wall, Roscrea traders sold shiny medals and pictures on their stalls. 'One shilling only for the scapulars, half a crown for the brand new missals.' But inside, the air was heavy with fear and guilt. The cross swung violently on the missionary's black cassock as he waved his arms and shouted about the terrible fate awaiting those who died without repentance. 'Even a bad thought can condemn one to an eternity of hellfire and brimstone, an eternity of unbelievable torment and suffering! Eternity, *Eternity*! Do you know how long that is? Imagine trying to count the drops of rain – or the grains of sand in the sea! It's not for a year, nor a decade, nor a lifetime. But for an *infinity*! An experience and duration that is beyond the understanding of mortal man.'

The men and scarved women knelt on opposite sides of the aisles. Only odd sighs and the sound of a shifting foot disturbed the silence. No one lazed on one knee or dared to cough, not even Biddy Walsh, who always interrupted the canon's sermons. The Passionists scared him. But he could never believe that God would condemn even the most roguish villager to such torture. 'Surely, religion shouldn't be frightening people?' he asked fellow-altarboy John Coleman, as they followed a funeral. But for his mother, religion was everything. She told Tom MacDonald: 'Wasn't it only the church which gave us strength and self-respect in the face of oppression? And keeping the faith is surely one of Ireland's greatest achievements?'

'Do you want to ring the Angelus bell?' Ger Devaney handed him the chain which hung from the abbey's ivied wall. He felt part of history and heaven as he announced the evening prayer to his village from the lofty belfry. He had often tried to visualise heaven's elusive glory. Particularly when the hymns soared with the thurible's incense and brilliant reflections flashed from the golden monstrance:

Tantum ergo sacramentum
Veneremur cernui.

He had often wondered how souls ascended to heaven until, as he was cycling home from Clash one afternoon, a sunburst sent great rays of light down to the ground all around him. In that marvellous moment, he realised that souls sped up those ladder-like rays, to a world which he could also one day experience if he remained good and pure. As he floated homewards, he thought of Paddy Dwyer, one of the first to reach the site of the Blessed Virgin's appearance at Curraheen. Paddy's regular attendance convinced pilgrims that he also had been touched by the Divine Presence. With donations received for touching their rosaries, he acquired a gold wristwatch. But when Mrs Tierney requested a hand on her expensive beads, Paddy consulted his timepiece: 'Sorry, mam, no blessings after six.'

God punished him for his bad apparition thoughts, when he almost missed being confirmed. He was assisting Dr Rogers when, after the last pupil had been touched on the shoulder, the bishop rose and returned to the altar. Other altarboys laughed as he tugged at the bishop's vestments: 'Will you get your crosier again, please; you forgot to confirm me!'

With donations from neighbours, including the Barneys who were not so rich, he and his classmates paid Paddy Boland twelve and sixpence to drive them to Roscrea monastery. He felt big and proud as he sat in the front seat of the black V-8 Pilot and adjusted the legs of his first long trousers. But getting big brought its own problems. His mother insisted that he spend more time studying. 'We've got your future to think of; we must prepare you for secondary school.'

She set him special courses in history and Irish, and berated him when he answered a question incorrectly or complained of tiredness. 'You'll never be any good. Mark my words, you'll become a corner-boy, watching everyone and doing nothing, like most of the people here.' He knew his mother was unhappy in Tipperary. But why could a person who prayed also be so angry? Was it because she did not mix as much as the other villagers? He once overheard his father: 'You can have too much of those books, Siobhán. You should go out more often.'

His parents were invited to the wedding party of farmer Johnny Reynolds. He was looking forward to their going out, Moll Ryan would let him stay up late. They went to change their clothes. Soon, his mother appeared in a bright dress which smelled of mothballs. She stood by the landing mirror, trying on her hats. 'Will Molly Smith be there – and that Mrs McCarthy? You know I can't stand them.' She finally stuck a pin in the chosen hat: 'Paki, I'm not used to this going out. I don't know if I should go at all.' They returned to the bedroom. After a long time, his father came out alone wearing his uniform. 'Your mother's not well, we won't be going.' He fastened his cycle clips and went to tell Moll Ryan. He thought of his mother in Scarriff, stepping out every night of their holiday. 'Life's short; better to look on the bright side,' Auntie Maggie often joked but his mother didn't heed her. She was always worrying, about his father's work and about Colm, and particularly about money, as each month she had to buy food on credit until his father was paid. Was this why she was so religious and so often ill?

One night, his father cycled home from Brownstown with bloodied hands and torn uniform. 'The lamp was going down, I didn't see the pothole in the dark.'

Since then, his mother fretted constantly when his father was out searching for an escaped prisoner or minding a disputed farm. 'All those farmers think of is making sure their neighbour doesn't have one yard more than themselves. They'd never die on Killaloe or any other bridge. Why can't you let some of the others go for a change?'

'I am the sergeant. It's my responsibility.'

On bad nights, he was allowed to stay up and keep his mother company. As the rainy gusts increased, she cried: 'God protect us, but every tree in the parish must be down.' The wind tugged at the doors and windows; the paraffin lamp flickered constantly. He had visions of his father's caped figure lying under an upturned beech.

His cap blown over the ditch despite its leather band, the wheels of his mangled bicycle spinning in the moonlight. His mother knelt under the Sacred-Heart lamp: 'Dear Jesus, bring your servant Patrick home safely. Listen to our prayer, we beseech you.' She paced the porch until the light of his father's bicycle emerged from the dark. The rain flowed off his cape; the dying carbide flickered. Red-faced, tired and hungry, he bent down to undo his bicycle clips. 'They got away again!'

His mother also feared his own fascination for the yellow and red swingboats which arrived each year with the travelling shows. But he was thrilled by the scary excitement of propelling himself higher than Treacys and the nearby houses. He became an equal to the swallows when the creaking boat stopped in mid-air, before plunging down and up again the other dizzy side.

> There's a yellow rose in Texas,
> That I am going to see.

His big show hero was Bert Patterson, whose banjo and sheriff's star danced with the floodlit moths as he brought the Wild West to Toomevara. Bert held his hand up: 'Hopalong Cassidy told me in Gulch City to be sure and give his regards to everyone in Toomevara.' The audience cheered and stamped the wooden floor.

Another show introduced moving pictures to the village. A confetti of black and white spots announced the first shaky title and brought new heroes to Toomevara: Charlie Chaplin, Buster Keaton, Laurel and Hardy. 'Did you ever see the bate of it?' Paddy Armstrong's eyes opened wide, as the white screen was transformed into a frantic chase, whose speed the piano player tried to match on his badly-tuned keyboard. Generator breakdowns added to the drama. Rain plopped through the tattered canvas, as a gunfight reached a blazing finale in sun-soaked Arizona. Each night's performance concluded with a tantalising episode of the *Last of the Mohicans* serial.

He cried when the shows left and the square reverted to the goats and grass again. As the caravans disappeared into the dust, he dreamed of following them one day, to where there was drama and diversion, unlike the sameness of his quiet and gossipy village. His mother looked out the yard window after hearing again from Colm. 'I don't think he tells us everything in the letters. Maybe, he was too young to be going off after all, the poor craythur. I don't think he's happy there.'

His father put down the paper. 'There's only one way to find out and that's to speak to him ourselves. As soon as I get leave, we'll go up and see him. And have a little holiday for ourselves as well!'

A second trip to Dublin: that was something to look forward to. Another unexpected distraction followed, an airmail letter from war-flour benefactor, Aunt Bridget, in New York: 'I'm flying home in a fortnight.' His mother cleared a front bedroom. His father painted the galvanised lavatory a bright green; he hammered in a new nail for the smartly scissored *Irish Press* paper.

Aunt Sarah and her husband Michael arrived on their way to collect Bridget. Their new black Austin smelled of fresh leather. 'We'll first see where that plane crashed last week,' Michael said, and turned off the tarred road. Kerosene fumes rose from the estuary scrub, as Michael lifted him up on the Constellation's long silver wing. He could see all the instruments inside the cockpit glass. A plane that had crossed the mighty Atlantic – like *The Spirit of St Louis!*

'I hope you like candy.' Bridget handed him the biggest bar of chocolate he had ever seen. She was a dress designer and her two-piece navy costume put his mother's cotton dress to shame as they posed for a garden photograph. The visitors left in the shiny Austin. As his mother put away the china set, she sobbed, 'God help us, Patrick, but you'll never have a motor car. You'll walk those streets forever and get neither gratitude nor reward.'

Toomevara enjoyed its own brush with the modern world. A crowd gathered on the bridge to welcome the first tanker of fuel going to newly opened Rineanna airport. The red leviathan's headlamps lit up Church Street, as it slowed to a crawl in response to his father's waving flashlight. None of them had seen a monster like it. Pat Tierney turned to Ned O'Donoghue. 'With that shape, it could race Henry Segrave's *Golden Arrow*.' The villagers cheered as the tanker moved off. The driver added to the excitement with a siren blast which set all the village dogs barking. As the lights faded into the darkness of the Nenagh road, he realised that his village would only ever be a place of transit. Even the locals often quoted the tramp's remark: 'I passed through every village in Ireland, but I ran through Toomevara!'

The following evening, his mother discovered him drawing a picture of the oil-tanker, when he was supposed to be studying. She slapped him. 'Do you want to end up a council labourer, leaning forever on a shovel on the Clonolea road? Don't you think I have enough concern already with Colm? For God's sake, study your books. Then, you at least can leave this dead place and do something with your life.'

5

'Brendan is a most attentive server.' The visiting Father Robinson walked to the square with them one morning after Mass. 'He has the makings of a fine priest.' He liked Father Robinson, who was so dignified and always spoke so softly. His mother grasped her missal in both hands: 'Colm is with the Christian Brothers, of course. But this wild man will have to study a bit harder before we can make anything of him.'

He was flattered by the interest of the travelled Dominican. Neither of his parents' families had a priest. He felt now that his mother was pinning her hopes on him. He had seen letters addressed to her from the St Joseph's Society, which helped families educate their sons for the priesthood. 'If you do well at your studies, we could get you into St Flannan's College,' his mother said, opening the gate. 'We'll ask Tom MacDonald to give you some coaching.'

After reading about Cardinal Stepinac's trial, she told him, 'Always remain true to your faith. Despite torture and persecution, the church stood by us. Even the Penal Laws couldn't crush the priests, whom the British hunted like animals across the bogs. Never forget the sacrifices of Blessed Oliver Plunkett and Father Murphy of '98.'

But a *Sunday Press* feature angered him when it defended the republican burning of the homes of Horace Plunkett and George Moore. 'Plunkett organised food committees for starving Dubliners after the Easter Rising. He and Parnell and O'Connell did much more than the gunmen. Isn't patriotism supposed to be about love, not killing and destruction?'

His mother flung down her paper. 'You don't know what you're talking about. You're becoming another little shoneen.'

She hit him so hard that she overturned his rosary armchair. 'Brave men and women of the independence movement died for you, you ungrateful cur. If it wasn't for them, British soldiers would be marching up and down our village.'

He cried on the floor. For his confusion and shock, as much as for the pain. How could someone be so unfair and cruel? How could his mother condone thuggery? Like so many neighbours was her religion all just talk? He wondered if Tom MacDonald had been right after all. 'His politics are very strange,' his mother had ridiculed the teacher's opinions. But, one of the medal-less few not to embrace the victorious gunmen, was his teacher the real civilised and courageous Christian of their village?

Father Robinson sent them a postcard of his monastery in Switzerland. 'Fribourg's a beautiful place, a town of bells. Every night, we can hear the peals of St Nicholas's Cathedral. They've been ringing since the thirteenth century. You can write to me if you ever want to know more about our order.' It would be great to be in a foreign country! Switzerland looked wonderful; the monastery was surely something special. But did he really want to be a priest? He admired the monks in Roscrea but they weren't allowed to talk. He shivered when he thought of his brother locked away in that Christian Brothers place. Were his parents also going to board him?

His mother continued his extra studies. 'If you don't work properly, we won't take you to Dublin when we go to see Colm.'

'My eyes are hurting.'

'Well, that's an excuse you won't have for much longer.' She turned up the wick. 'Toomevara's about to join the twentieth century; we're soon going to have the electricity!'

Some villagers already produced weak light for their own use. Bolands had a turbine, Jack Donovan a petrol-powered generator and young Jim O'Meara had built a windcharger. But only a Sacred Heart light brightened the hallway of his own house. The kitchen boasted a hanging lamp whose wick was turned up when they had supper. A grander globed lantern illuminated the dining room. Candles led the way to bed; a flashlight lit the dash past the ashes pit to the outside lavatory.

That Friday's *Nenagh Guardian* forecast the end of the paraffin era. 'Light at the touch of a switch. Electricity is coming to north Tipperary. Not only will every house have the new light but each village will also be lit by streetlamps.' Despite not being able to read the *Guardian*, Din Ryan prophesied: 'Soon you'll be able to boil water without a fire!' A few neighbours refused to have anything to do with the electricity. The Timekeeper stopped his father: 'You'll be paying for it all your life, Sergeant. And the government will know everything we're doing.'

'Electric? A good pair of hands was good enough for all before me.' Bill O'Rourke sent sparks flying from his anvil. The blacksmith often let him blow the bellows, before bending red-hot iron bars into horseshoes and wheel-bands. The water hissed and steamed as Bill drenched the glowing bands to contract them to the size of the wooden wheels. 'The axles will go first!' Excitement mounted as the line of poles advanced like soldiers towards their village. 'We're putting up the electric.' Children ran cotton thread between the bushes. John Joe McCormack concealed wires under their floorboards and behind the walls. 'You needn't worry. No mouse will get through that cable, Mrs Lynch.'

The night after the last wires were connected, a big crowd gathered in the dark around the hall. They all stopped talking when the retired teacher and *Nenagh Guardian* correspondent, Ned O'Donoghue, stood up to speak. 'As we stand in the shadow of the old abbey we can be justly proud of Toomevara's great past. But the world is continually progressing and we must move with it. Of all the changes happening for the good, electricity is one of the greatest. It will make our work easier, our nights brighter, our leisure time more rewarding. Tonight, we banish the darkness from Toomevara. Tonight, our village joins the great outside world lit by electricity.'

'Hear, Hear!' shouted his audience. The canon pulled the switch which immediately lit up the village street and most of its houses. Night-time was suddenly transformed into daytime. The cheering grew even louder. No one had seen anything like it. 'It sure bates Times Square,' remarked returned-Yank Tom McMahon as he shaded his eyes. Ned, the canon and all the locals did a tour of the village. 'We'll see the sergeant coming now,' laughed late-night drinker, Dick Hassett. The streetlamps banished the dark shadows and the sprint from one pool of shop light to another. They stripped Donoghue's haunted house of its terror and extended the night-time spinning-top territory. Pat Clancy jostled Matt O'Gara: 'We can play all night, now!'

Din Ryan predicted even greater miracles. 'The world will shortly come to Toomevara. The electric wireless will bring New York as close as Borrisoleigh.'

A new Pilot radio replaced their unreliable battery wireless and its keening valves. There would be no more battery-charging delays, no more rationing of dramas and concerts. His father turned the switch: 'You're a happy woman now, Siobhán. Sean O'Casey plays and *Ballad Maker's Saturday Night* at the touch of a button.'

When his parents were out, he listened to the Westminster chimes and Big Ben – live from London! On the illuminated dial, he summoned foreign stations from Hilversum to Hamburg, and short-wave signals which he imagined came from the *Flying Enterprise*. Chris Shanahan listened with him. 'Isn't Captain Carlsen a great man, to stay with his sinking ship for a whole week?'

But his mother wouldn't allow him to listen to the pop music station, Radio Luxembourg 208. 'Jungle wailings. Listen to real singers like Delia Murphy or Josef Locke.'

'You said that last year about "Bingo Bango Bongo, I Don't Want to Leave the Congo" but I often heard you humming it since.'

He envied Chris Shanahan, who taught him 'Five Minutes More', which had been banned on Radio Éireann. One evening, he gave his friend a lift home from Harty's Pallas road farm. 'What do you think of Jo Stafford?' Chris settled himself on the crossbar, after the bump of Robinson's Bridge.

'He's not the worst.' He resumed pedalling, not realising that the hit-parade leader was a she.

His parents invited Father Kelly for tea when he returned from his parish in Manchester. 'A bit busier than Toome all right! My parishioners are mainly Irish. Between weddings and births, and socials and dances to keep the lads off the drink, we're on the go from morning 'til night. We could do with some help – maybe your son will join us when he's bigger?'

'He spends too much time playing and listening to the wireless. But, I suppose, miracles are possible.'

His mother wondered how Father Kelly managed, surrounded by Protestants. But he had found the village's few Protestants more interesting than many of his own religion. 'What in the name of God's that noisy contraption?' His mother put down their bucket at the fountain, as Harry Bentley sped towards them in a strange machine. The running boards were planks, an engine hopped up and down in the front of what seemed a bed on wheels. Harry steered from one side of the street to the other before stopping for water. 'It's my new car,' he shouted.

'What are you going to call it?'

'A Bentley, of course!'

'They were together again last night,' the saddler Gordon Birch joked through the Sweet Afton smoke which curled around his jaunty hat.

'Who?'

'The two cheeks of my arse!' He smacked his wax-hardened apron.

He spent hours in Gordon's workshop, paying for his keep by waxing thread and teasing horsehair. The saddler sang 'Silver Threads among the Gold' while he transformed sheets of leather into bridles, stirrups and saddles. Even on the darkest day, he always had a twinkle in his eye. Dan Casey called over, 'It's cold this morning.'

'Put your shirt around it.' Gordon waved his half-moon knife.

They played draughts in the evening while Mrs Birch knitted by the fire. 'I'll give you a tune on the jew's harp, while you try to get out of that.' The saddler left him double-cornered again.

Travelling Heaney's wire puzzles were no problem for Gordon: within minutes the intertwined pieces would be lying separately on the table oilcloth. He cut out the *Guardian's* mention of his Nenagh Show awards for shallots and flower bulbs. 'The Birches are dacent hard-working people who could teach a lot of us how to live better. For Protestants, they're a grand family.' His mother surprised him. But one pre-election day, Gordon and he argued over Dev's butter price increase. He shouted to the saddler: 'You don't care about the poor people of Ireland. All you want is the bloody Protestant English back again.'

He knew instantly that what he had said was neither right nor fair. He also realised by the glint in Gordon's eye that it was time to be off. He sprinted like Zatopek across the yard and ducked just as the saddler's favourite mallet overtook him and shattered against the wall. He lost another favourite when Con Flaherty was taken off to the Clonmel asylum. 'Like the other candidates, I'll be back for the next election.' Con bowed his head as his father helped him into the car. An alcoholic farmer was confined by relatives. One of the best customers of his own pub, Mick French Shea leaned against the door, his hat askew: 'Mrs Lynch, they're afraid he'll drink the inheritance; it's a disgrace. 'Tis as bad as sending the ould ones to the county home. How long can any of them survive, so far away from their friends and their pets and haunts? And I believe half of them sleep on the floor. Are we Christians at all?'

His mother prepared a county home sandwich for Billy Hayes, who brought his LDF jacket with him to Thurles. Though the war was over, Billy marched into the barracks each week, stood to attention and saluted his father: 'Loughisle Wood inspected, Sergeant. Nothing seen or heard.'

One rainy morning, she put a steaming brown cake and some apples into the oatmeal sack which contained Paddy Dwyer's few clothes. 'Good luck to you, Mrs Lynch, and all belonging to you. Maybe you'll come and see me some time?' Paddy wiped his eye, as the smoke rose from the last threepenny Woodbine he would enjoy in Toomevara.

He thought his mother was wrong to be always so strict but she at least showed some consideration for the poor people. No one else appeared concerned. Were his neighbours only talking about Christianity? Though his mother worried about Colm, she was as proud of him as if he had been a priest. On the way home from Mass one morning, she showed Mollie Barney a photo of Colm in his black soutane. 'He's finished the novitiate. He's training now for the teaching in O'Connell's Schools.'

'A lovely photo, Mrs Lynch. We're all looking forward to his ordination.'

'This progress is a funny oul' business.' Din Ryan surveyed the quivering swollen rabbits at Shelley's Cross. 'Them great scientists can invent myxomatosis but they can't find a cure for it.'

There was something wrong about adults putting their expertise into exterminating small animals. Dick Hassett showed him how the rabbits had damaged his crops but were grown-ups so great, after all, if their only defence was to kill? 'Sissy!' his classmates chanted. He wondered what Din Ryan had felt as the villagers ridiculed his atom-bomb theories. Maybe the Oracle was right?

He was twelve years old and as he read his Cassell's books, he sometimes wondered what it would have been like to have been born in a different country. 'Sure if we were born in Africa, we'd be pagans too – and as black as the ace of spades.' Din Ryan searched for his penknife. 'And if your parents were born in the North, maybe they would be unionists!'

His mother a unionist; he was shocked. But after thinking about it, he had to agree with Din. So why was everyone fighting then, when they were really all the same? And why was England blamed for everything, when so many villagers had to go there to feed their families? 'Now, we can't be holding the queen responsible for the weather,' Jack Hackett chided his mother one night. His father disliked people going to England but he always helped with their travel documents. 'What's it like in Birmingham?' he asked Paddy O'Brien, who came home wearing a suit.

'Well, actually, Sergeant, the traffic's so great that at first I thought it was a big funeral! But every second week, there's a real funeral when someone is killed on the buildings. When work is finished there's nowhere to go but to the pub for a bit of company. Actually, it can be a lonely enough oul' place.'

'Actually, I'm from Brownstown bog,' his mother mocked, as she made the tea.

One night, at Shelley's Cross, they met Tim O'Riordan and his wife who worked in London. Mrs O'Riordan wore slacks. 'Did you ever see anything so disgusting or unnatural?' asked his mother, looking back at them. 'Aping the English. No respectable person would dress like that. No Irishman or woman should go there or bring their vulgar ideas back here.'

Was his mother jealous of the emigrants because they were richer and had travelled more? Could she not see that it was English money which kept many families going? And if Dev was such a great man, why couldn't he help Irish people stay and work in their own country?

Their Dublin holiday opened his mind to even more ideas. He had always been proud of their framed map of the world, whose *Links in the Chain of Discovery* border featured portraits of such famous explorers as Scott, Amundsen and Shackleton. But in the

Dundrum house owned by university lecturers, there were more pictures and books than he had ever seen before. And writers with foreign names like Balzac, Tolstoy and Marx.

He was disturbed by a book which luckily his mother did not see, *Why I am Not a Christian* by a man called Bertrand Russell. The dustwrapper said that he had been imprisoned for helping pacifists during the Great War – but surely that was a Christian act? These authors spoke of another exciting world to be discovered one day, as did the colourful reproductions which did not impress his mother. 'Paki, will you look at these daubs. Matisse if you ple-iss! Sure the Bodyke children would have painted better.'

He was happy to think that there were people in the world like the lecturers, who might not laugh at himself or Din Ryan. He knew now that there was nothing wrong in having different opinions. He knew that he was right not to agree with anything that he thought unjust. He dreamt of one day having a house with books and pictures, where one could think nice things and be happy and free.

They took the bus to Marino to see Colm. They waited in a room full of religious pictures and statues, until a senior Brother brought him out. Though Colm looked much bigger in his new soutane, he was even quieter than he had been before. 'Are you happier here now?' his mother sat down beside him.

'I'm well used to it.'

'Can we go out and walk around the grounds?' his mother enquired.

The big Brother frowned. 'He must be back in fifteen minutes for lunch.'

His mother told him to wait on a seat while they walked with Colm. As they left the college afterwards, she fell behind his father and himself. When he looked around, she was crying.

Tom MacDonald admired their library one day. 'Ours would be a great country, with no corner boys and no crime, if we had more education.'

'From a Munster vale they brought her.' The schoolteacher and Bill O'Meara compiled *The Spirit of Tipperary* anthology of their county's writing, which included the work of Grenanstown poet, Richard Dalton Williams.

After lessons, Tom taught his pupils how to make fishing flies and grow shrubs and fruit plants. He told them of Toomevara's monastic past and showed them slides of foreign countries with a big brass projector. 'There is in every village a torch,' said his mother, quoting Victor Hugo.

The teacher coached him for the entrance examination to St Flannan's College, which was renowned for its high quota of priests. His mother was delighted when he won a scholarship. 'But it's only a day scholarship. How will you get the extra money for me to board?'

'The St Joseph's Young Priests Society will help us.'

Mollie Barney watched as his mother wrote his name in indelible ink on the lining of all his clothes. 'Brendan will be on the foreign missions yet. Or maybe even a bishop, like Dr Rogers, another Flannan's man!'

He didn't want to leave home but neither did he want to cycle the round trip of fourteen miles to Nenagh in the cold winters. College might be a great break from his strict mother. He became excited about travelling all the way to Ennis.

The head prefect showed him where to sit in the study room. 'Newspapers are not allowed!' How could he know what was happening to Professor Picard and his bathyscape, Doctor Mossadeq in Persia or even Doctor Noël Browne nearer home? Two hundred students sat down together at endless rows of tables in the cold refectory. Never had he tasted anything like the lumpy college dinners. Butter was rationed, foul-tasting marmalade made his eleven o'clock bread inedible. Hungry for the first time in his life, he stole a room-mate's biscuits. He thought his parents might bring some food but they didn't come on visiting day.

'That's some spring in your comb,' Tommy Moloney laughed. Push-penny, hurling outings and Monsieur de Regge's music lessons provided the only light relief. The push-penny wore out his trousers. His mother posted an oversize pair which dragged in the wet winter playing field. The legs froze at right angles across his bed; in the morning he had to force them back into shape again. He tripped as he and his classmates were herded through the streets to the cathedral. Tommy whispered opposite a sweetshop, 'We're like the fair-day cows. Oliver Twist was better off.'

He raffled his wallet and persuaded day pupil Pee Wee Deasy to buy a fruitcake with the proceeds. Their best precautions were no match for the dean. The door swung open as Tubby Hynes marched into the classroom: 'I believe that some students are having food brought in from outside. Hands up anyone who is defying college regulations.'

Silence filled the room. 'Well, a little inspection to make sure. Desktops up!'

The Dean approached his own desk. Under Peig Sayers, a paper bag rustled. 'What have we here? Fruit and nut cake. A proper glutton's feast.'

'Well, I'll give you fruit and nuts.' His pale jowls danced as he banged down the desktop. 'Where did you get this? And who is the wretch who brought it in? Tell me immediately, or I will scarify the place.'

'My mother sent it.'

'Flaherty's shop, Main Street. Lies as well, you little scoundrel.' The dean caught his jersey and sent him spinning across the floor.

Tubby marched Pee Wee and himself up to the front of the class. 'This is a college, not a holiday camp. We must have discipline. The food here is more than adequate. We will not have anyone disgracing our reputation by buying outside. I will make sure that nothing like this happens again. See me in the library after class.'

The dean waited beside his desk under a large crucifix. He anchored his chalky cassock with one hand and steadied his biggest cane in the other. 'Six strokes. Hold out your hand. Flat!' Tears shot out of his eyes at each stroke; chalk-dust filled the room. The burning pain was matched by guilt as the unfortunate Pee Wee was given four strokes. He was equally terrified a week later when he lost the diary, in which he had written: 'Sparta was a swizz compared to here. They are all monsters except Father O'Meara.'

'You are very lucky I found this.' Father O'Meara handed it back in the playground.

Mensa, mensa, mensam. Whack! His happiest Flannan's day was the one he left. But it was to be a long time before he forgot the kicks and rabbit punches of the teachers, the swish of cane and soutane in the dean's library, the lonely whistling of night trains across the adjacent Siberian wastes and the clanging of the six o'clock bell down cold corridors.

'The priests were a tough crowd,' he told Jack Hackett.

'You'll think twice now before signing up! Sure I heard before that that place was like the Black Hole of Calcutta, fit for neither man nor beast. You'll find the Nenagh Brothers a much more civilised lot.'

Nothing, however, would console his mother for his failure to continue to be a priest. She looked up from her book one rainy evening: 'We sacrificed a lot to board you. I'll be paying off the St Joseph's for many a long year. Why is it good enough for the O'Briens and so many students but not for the likes of you?'

'The priests and teachers were cruel. Would you like to be beaten every day?'

'They punished you because you were disobedient; it was for your own good. Only by suffering and discipline can we do anything in life. Bishop Rogers knuckled down in Flannan's and now he's our bishop. Why couldn't you be like him? I hope you won't disgrace us with the Nenagh Brothers. Poor Colm was a credit to them.' She ran out to the kitchen. One day, he heard his parents speaking about his brother but they stopped when he came into the room. Was his mother's final hope of a child in Holy Orders about to be dashed?

6

His mother cried after receiving a letter from Colm's Superior. 'What's wrong?' he asked.

'Your brother's not very well.'

His father went to the barracks to phone Dublin. His mother stayed in the porch until he returned. 'Colm's developed an ulcer and he has to rest. The superior says he should be all right after a few weeks.'

His parents made a special trip by bus to see his brother. When they came home, his mother added a new petition to the rosary: 'Dear Lord, please assist our son in his time of special need. But as always, Thy will be done.' He sped around the parish on his father's old bicycle, building up his strength for the long journey to secondary school. Originally, he had wanted to be a hurling star like Tony Reddin, who could score points over his shoulder without even seeing the goalposts. But after watching Irish champions Mick Christle and Frankie Baird at Nenagh Sports, he dreamt of being a cycle racer.

As he started out for secondary school, he felt that he was at last on the road to some new life, some assertion of himself as an individual. Finally on his way to escaping his parents and equally restrictive village. He enjoyed John Masefield and the poets introduced to him by his English teacher, Rodney Bent. 'It's good to be out the road, //And going one knows not where.'

He relished the freedom of the seven-mile cycle ride, even when the cold wind brought tears to his eyes and freezing fog thatched his hair with ice. Cresting Slevin's hill, he remembered the night the Toomevara band lorry overturned, scattering instruments and drunken bodies. 'Never mind yourselves, save me big drum,' Martin shouted. Stimulated by his *Eagle* motor-sport heroes, he dived down Lisatoggart. His schoolbag hopped up and down as he tucked in his head for extra streamlining like racing motorcyclist, Reg Armstrong. 'Jasus, you'll kill yourself,' shouted Martin Cummins one morning, as he swerved just in time to miss the farmer's cart. The flat stretch past Jackie Hogans sent the blood coursing through his veins. He fantasised about the people in the nearby Big House, as he passed Shanbally Cross and the watery Well Tree. He bridged seven hundred years of history with his first glimpse of Nenagh Castle's round keep from Phil the Sailor's cottage.

From the halfway house of Boland's forge, he slogged against the wind to the sheltered reaches of the Islandbawn flour mill. How constructively man and nature had harmonised here and at nearby Lisboney Abbey, whose monks had studied and harvested the surrounding fields and stream. Missing the convent departure of fairhaired Eileen, he left the local stragglers in his wake as he swooped across the nearby railway bridge and up the St John's Lane school approach.

'It's the Ice Man,' the townies laughed in winter, as lumps of frost fell from his head while he thawed out by the rumbling radiators.

How he envied the town boys, who were so advanced and who didn't have patches in their trousers. Tommy Irwin could sing Johnny Ray's 'Just Walking in the Rain'. They did not live in awe of their teachers and they spoke freely to the convent scholars. Some even walked out with girls after school. Seamus Cleary boasted, 'Sheila Kennedy's a lovely kisser.'

His childhood reading provided the launch pad from which Rodney Bent piloted him to the heights of Wordsworth, Shelley and Milton. His imagination soared, his heart exulted with unprecedented emotions as he wandered with *The Scholar Gipsy* and wept for Lycidas.

> Where were ye, Nymphs, when the remorseless deep
> Closed o'er the head of your loved Lycidas?'

His mother was mistaken to think he would not settle in Nenagh. She was unaware of how his new writers signposted him to life and thought outside of Ireland. He raced Seamus Cleary each evening to see the Dublin train. As the smoke swirled around the stone bridge, he felt a vivid sense of life's vast potential. But he was so puny and limited, how could he ever embrace it? His eyes followed the green train as it laboured up the ascent and out of sight. The last plumes of smoke dissolved in the distance.

'Wouldn't it be great to be on that train?' Seamus threw a stone over the curving parapet.

'I'll go one day to the great city of Hazlitt, Lamb, and Goldsmith.' He flung even farther. As the prevailing south-westerlies swept him homewards, he often shouted Shelley's 'Ode to the West Wind' or reached for Charles Lamb's essays. But these were stowed away before he rounded the last bend into Toomevara. Din Ryan touched his head: 'I'm telling you, Mrs Lynch, it's all dem high books that has Bill O'Meara half-cracked.' The farmer had shown him the site of Bianconi's staging post and O'Sullivan Beare's route, and lent his mother copies of *The Bell* literary magazine.

He was stirred by wonderings about girls. He admired black-haired Jane Dulanty and Nora O'Brien, whose hair fell over her shoulders like gold. But at the age of fourteen, he still did not know how babies were made. He laughed but didn't understand Seamus Cleary's dirty joke: 'She offered her honour. He honoured her offer. And now he's more on her than off her!' A Scarriff fishing mate jolted him into stark reality. Finbarr flung the weighted line into the water and sat down beside him on the grass and dockleaves. 'Babies are made by the father sticking his "thing" into the mother. The father's creamy pee makes the baby which is born nine months later, just like calves and foals.'

'Disgusting. Our parents never did anything like that.'

'I'll show you then.'

Their cork floats bobbed unattended and the river gurgled as Finbarr pulled out his thing. It stood up when he started to rub it. He suddenly shook all over and a jet of white fluid spurted out. 'God, that's a great one!'

It took him a long time to accept the practicalities of reproduction. He experimented like Finbarr until, one night, an astonishing sensation of pleasure heralded his first orgasm. He soon found that like all good things, his gratification would exact a high price. 'The devil's target is the young. Never forget that God's special wrath awaits those who indulge in impure thoughts and sins of the flesh.'

Now, he knew what the Passionists had shouted about. 'Bless

me father, for I have sinned.' Filled with a profound sense of shame and terrified by the prospect of hell, he confessed his repeated sins, hoping that Father Moloney wouldn't recognise him through the thin grille.

'You can kiss me,' convent student Patricia told him in the doorway of Jackie Whelan's Nenagh radio shop. But his fumblings were overshadowed by a nagging guilt. He sought practical advice in the chapel's Catholic Truth Society pamphlets. But *Blessed Oliver Plunket* and *Maria Goretti – Death before Dishonour* only lauded the mortification of the flesh and the sacrifices of those who had died for the Faith. No wonder that hunger strikes thrived in his country or that Mrs Reilly had run out on her wedding night.

There was a major scandal when an unmarried country girl became pregnant. The canon waved his arms: 'We will not have young couples walking out unsupervised and indulging in foul behaviour in barns and dark lanes. These sinners are giving scandal to the rest of the community and calling down God's wrath upon the country.' The girl and her family were in the congregation. His mother practised more Christianity. She regularly visited the girl's home and later brought clothes for her new son. 'We're all God's children,' his mother said to Auntie Hannah.

His mother often waited in the porch for the postman. 'Anything from Dublin this morning, Jim?'

His father came back early from the barracks one morning. 'Bad news, I'm afraid. The Superior phoned. He said that Colm's done his best. He thinks it might be better if he came home.'

'The poor boy, sure we can't have him suffering any longer.' His mother picked up her rosary beads. 'But it's going to be hard for him – and what are we going to tell the neighbours?'

Colm was no longer wearing his dark uniform when he stepped off the seven-o'clock bus. 'I shouldn't remain here long before I obtain a lay teaching position.' His brother's accent had become more sophisticated. It took their mother a long time to get over her disappointment. She cried again as she removed his soutanned photograph from the mantelpiece. 'It was a duodenal ulcer, God help him,' she informed Mrs Delaney.

'You're not to worry about anything,' their mother reassured

Colm. 'We've fixed up your own room for you and it will be just like old times to have you back again.'

But it wasn't to be quite like old times. His brother was now more knowledgeable. His return led to their home's first non-political argument. 'Would you mind if I changed stations to listen to the James Joyce anniversary reading from *Ulysses?*'

James Who? His parents knew little about the writer, apart from his recent castigation by a religious columnist. 'What station is it on?' their mother asked.

'Unfortunately, Radio Eireann is not doing anything; it's on the BBC.'

'The BBC? Well, doesn't that tell you anything? They're only broadcasting it because that fellow was a shoneen for whom Ireland wasn't good enough. He ran off abroad so that he could slander our country and our Church. Can't you see that's why the English are using him?'

'Many scholars regard *Ulysses* as the greatest book published this century. It's literature, a work of art, not a criticism of the church. We should be proud that Joyce is being acknowledged internationally. Surely we shouldn't have to go abroad to read him, I think you should give him a chance?'

Their mother's face reddened. 'There's no place here for renegades like him. We'll not have that filthy writer in our house.'

'That's your prerogative.' His brother went upstairs to his room.

Another day, Colm apologised to him after an argument over a dictionary. It was the first time he had seen someone act in such a civilised manner. He knew then that his brother was a real Christian Brother. While in the novitiate, Colm had developed a passion for classical music. Every fine day, he took a gramophone down to the garden, where he could play Beethoven and Mozart without being ridiculed. *The Barber of Seville* soared above the lettuce beds with the birds and butterflies, Pallas road passers-by paused in amazement. Their mother put the plates on the table one day. 'Will you go down and tell Figaro his dinner is ready. He can't hear with all that racket.' But even she derived an original anecdote from the music. The day before Colm left to teach in Wexford, Mrs Tierney made an appointment to discuss classical music with him. 'It will be like George Bernard and Gene Tunney,' their mother muttered.

She wasn't wrong. When his brother asked Mrs Tierney what her favourite piece of music was, she replied, 'I swoon at the thought of Largo's Handel!'

Brroom, Brroom. One Easter Saturday, the Circuit of Ireland rally roared into their village. Many of the drivers stopped for refreshments. His imagination went into overdrive at the sleek numbered cars and the accents and camaraderie of the competitors. 'I say, Alastair, can I have a dekko at your Silvermines map?' His friend removed his goggles. 'We nearly lost it and every other damned thing on that last corner!' The windscreens and bonnets sparkled in the sun; drivers made engine adjustments.

One driver felt a front wheel of a green Singer sports car. 'You'd better put a few pounds in that tyre.'

He hadn't known there were so many different makes of cars. He admired a rounded black Austin A40 Somerset and a flowing blue Bristol. He had never seen anything as exciting as the wire-wheeled red MGs and the big white Jaguar. He plucked up his courage: 'What's its top speed?'

'About one hundred and twenty – but don't tell that man in the uniform.' The leather-jacketed driver pointed to his father. His mother called him back to the porch. 'That's Cecil Vard – the Dubliner who nearly won the Monte Carlo Rally!'

'Is the Silvermines turn far from the village, Sergeant?' Cecil enquired.

'I'll stand at the corner and show you,' his father volunteered.

The competitors waved to his father on point duty at the Mines' Cross and rushed down the Grenanstown road. What power, what freedom! How he longed to go with them, away from his sleepy village. The crackle of their exhausts reverberated from the Gunner's furze-crowned hill. Din Ryan tapped his pipe against Kelly's window ledge: 'The best bit of excitement since the Emergency.'

'There's a lot of life outside Toomevara.' He kept his face towards the cross.

He clung to the sound of the fading engine notes, as the last of the cars disappeared like the travelling shows. The dust settled; a hen cackled; Looby's cat crossed the road with its tail in the air. He was overwhelmed equally with sadness and improbable dreams. He dragged his bike from the shed and sped down the Pallas road. 'I'll have a sports car one day too.' He took Robinson's Bridge with two wheels in the air.

The circuit provided his most exciting brush with the outside world and its fantastic possibilities, and sparked an insatiable passion for speed. Henceforth, when he cycled out the country roads, it was as Stirling Moss and Dublin racer Joe Kelly that he swooped around the bends and leaped over the potholes on his Sturmey-Archer geared charge. He constructed a speedway track in their backyard. The hens fled as he skidded around for ten-lap sessions. He skinned his knuckles against the shed door as he sought to reduce his times on the window-sill alarm clock. 'We need an expert, will I get the Timekeeper?' Chris Shanahan sheltered behind the old range. Tommy the Timekeeper treasured a pocket watch whose three protective covers he opened with elaborate ceremony. 'What would the time be, Tommy?' Villagers often said with a wink.

His mother surprised him with her knowledge of the Irish-born record-breakers Kaye Don and Stanley Woods, and Fay Taylor who had beaten all the men in the Leinster Trophy race. 'You can listen to the Curragh motor races on the wireless on Saturday, if you're a good boy.'

'I'm not a boy any more!'

Schoolmate John Tynan told him how engines worked. Each Sunday he admired the high-radiatored Rolls Royce, in which a New Zealand newcomer named McClelland brought his family to Mass. He extended his *Eagle* education by buying the weekly *Motor* and *Motorcycle* magazines in Ryans' Nenagh newsagency. He could now follow all the big races.

'Alberto Ascari will win the championship,' he predicted to his bemused mother.

She looked out to the yard one breakfast time: 'Those hens aren't laying at all, Paki.' Luckily, she never saw him sell the still-warm eggs to Peig Devaney for one-and-six a dozen, the price of the magazines. Summer telegram deliveries subsidised his requests to drivers for autographs and photographs.

Jim O'Rourke staggered to the door with packages from Modena and Stuttgart and letters from his heroes Mike Hawthorn and Rudolf Caracciola. 'You should open your own post office.' World Champion Ascari's photograph addressed to Signor Toomevara, Irlande arrived safely. Stirling Moss sent a signed photo in the Irish-stamped SAE from London (little did he dream that the great English driver would one day write a book foreword for him).

He relished the adult-like feeling of his first paid work. Whitethorn and woodbine intoxicated his senses as he raced out with tidings of exam results, impending visits and the deaths of emigrant sons or daughters. His favourite destinations were the Big Houses with their eccentric and frequently generous owners. 'You really are a fright on that machine; you should be a racer.' Mrs Carew smacked her boots with her riding crop. Inside the loose-puttied windows, rainwater dripped on to her mildewed furniture and mottled mirrors.

He found no door to knock on when he called to Mrs Regan. It had been used for firewood. His former teacher was clutching a Baby Power: 'It's for the circulation.' He declined the fourpence delivery charge. 'Well, you're not laving without a hot cup of tea and a slice of bread.'

A dark-haired tinker girl waved to him from an encampment near Knockane Castle. She was swinging her long fleshy legs from the stone wall, as he returned from his Brownstown delivery: 'Sit down and I'll sing you Ruby Murray's "Softly, Softly!" He slowed. 'How are you?' he stammered and pedalled away, his face as red as her swirling skirt. He was stirred by the strength of her uninhibited gaze. It seemed as if she were inviting him to be her travelling companion, to wander forever Ireland's winding roads and sleep together under dewy hedgerows and starry skies. Her image haunted him for months. But he was so backward; would he ever be able to speak to a girl?

He felt, however, that women were unpredictable and not easy to live with. His father was nearly always away from the house, patrolling the streets or cycling the countryside. But apart from their curdeeking to Hacketts, Loobys and Gleesons, his mother mostly stayed indoors or in the garden. One day she complained to his father: 'You are never here, morning, evening or night. Why can't you spend more time with your wife? This is your home. This is where you should be. Why do you call so often to Mrs Flaherty?'

"If I am out, you know it's always on duty. And I visit Mrs Flaherty just to see how she is since her husband's death.'

His mother continued her criticism. As he tried to defend himself, she ran upstairs to bed: 'You're a street angel and a house devil.'

'You've been overdoing it again, Mrs Lynch. You must have a good rest,' the doctor advised. Though his father was strict he was always fair. He felt that his mother was being unreasonable. Were all women like that?

'Getting married is like the priesthood.' Jack Hackett handed him a betting slip to take to Nenagh. 'Aisy to get into but hard to get out of. It requires a considerable degree of cogitation, as the Oracle might say.'

'Let the clutch in. Slowly!'

One great day, Jim Hickey taught him to drive a Baby Ford across the oily floor of Dick Williams's garage. Jim wiped the starting handle. 'The Circuit's next.'

Dick let him steer an old Vauxhall to Ollatrim. As he fought to control the wandering juggernaut, he dimly saw a cyclist on Maher's hill. Dick grabbed the wheel: 'Jasus Christ, we nearly killed the Sergeant!'

The garage owner received an official visit that evening; he himself was forbidden to drive until he had a driving licence. On the night before his seventeenth birthday, he counted out seventeen and sixpence from his telegram and egg money. He sped into Nenagh courthouse the following morning and bought his first driving licence. He dreamed with every homeward push of the pedals of one day driving a racing car. From purloining eggs, he descended to the depths of pitch and toss, against which both his father and the PP had campaigned. Five shillings was his best win in Shanahan's backyard school until, one Sunday, he found himself going for a thirty shillings treasure trove. The sweat rolled down inside his shirt. Eason's motoring encyclopaedia and the glittering watch advertised by Doré of Dame Street were within his grasp.

The crowd fell silent, the stone-anchored notes flapped in the afternoon breeze. He screwed his eyes against the dust and steadied the two coins on his Brylcreamed comb. As he flexed his arms for the final throw, a voice suddenly warned: 'The Sergeant!' He turned in terror towards the gate. Fortunately his father was not there. When he looked back at the ground, neither were the precious thirty shillings. He could hardly complain to his father. 'I hear you're recovering from a little addiction,' Jack Hackett chuckled the following day.

His parents celebrated his Intermediate Certificate results with a holiday in Dún Laoghaire and a trip to the midget car races in Shelbourne Park. He was intoxicated by the speed and the smell of castor oil and burning rubber. 'Come on, Leo,' he shouted with the crowd for Leo Manthorpe in his under-powered car. Fay Taylor introduced him to Charlie Norton and other drivers. He rashly informed Fay of his own speed dreams. Fay responded, 'You will do it, if you want it hard enough.'

He wasn't the only motoring addict. A week after their return, he discovered the nature of some mysterious business his father had conducted while on holiday. Billy Shanahan, who had a Dublin garage, knocked on their door. 'It's here, Paki,' his mother shouted.

They all rushed out to see a shiny blue Morris Minor. Billy handed the keys to his father. 'These are yours now.' The insurance policy, paid for over two decades, had matured and his parents had their first car. Each Saturday he helped his father wash the Minor. He cleaned the red leather and checked the battery and tyre pressures. 'If you go slowly, you can drive us part of the way to Scarriff,' his father said.

'Are you sure, Paki?' his mother asked. She held her rosary beads tightly as he steered them all the way to Scarriff.

But he found the driving tame compared to his more adventurous cycling. He chased laden lorries for the thrill of a fast sheltered ride from school, then sprinted past them up the incline to his father's barracks. The schoolbag straps caught in his back wheel as he followed a lorry down Clonolea hill one evening. The locked wheel swerved from side to side; it seemed like hours before it stopped and he could breathe again. His obsession with outspeeding fellow-students earned him a reputation as a daredevil. Officials of the Nenagh MacDonagh athletic club knocked one Sunday: 'Any chance of Brendan competing in our first race?'

'Come in, Dinny and Sean, and have a cup of tea.' His mother put the kettle on.

'Your son will make a great competitor,' Dinny O'Brien coaxed. 'Hasn't he cycled half way round the world already with that school journey of his?'

Dinny was a Dev man; an affirmative answer was guaranteed. 'We'll try one race, providing it doesn't interfere with his Leaving Cert studies.'

Mick Christle and Frankie Baird were supermen; he could never be like them. 'Strange you were never so quick with the homework before.' His mother watched from the gate as he rode out for evening training runs. The following Sunday he repaid the club's faith and rode Malachi Cardiff's red sportscycle into second place behind an experienced visiting rider. 'The discovery of the race,' said the weekend *Guardian*. 'That's the threepenny liar for you,' laughed Malachi.

Pride turned to apprehension as the club entered him for a twenty-five mile open race in Tipperary town. 'And so we'll go to fight the foreign foe…' He whistled Josef Locke's rousing hit as Sean Mounsey's Morris Minor swept him towards foreign territory. He wore an old hurling jersey, baggy shorts and sandals which looked like snowshoes beside the other riders' streamlined gear. A Clonmel rider laughed: 'You forgot your camán!'

He studied the other competitors. He rashly chased after anyone who attempted a break, before learning to conserve his energy. He couldn't match their experience or strength. He wouldn't win, but he was determined to give them a hurling. He knew how far he could sprint without weakening. If the field stayed together, he would be in with a chance.

'Watch Healy!' Several riders tried to get clear as the finish approached. But they all turned the final corner together, a hundred yards from the line. The leaders studied each other like hawks. None paid any attention to him as he gathered speed. The sprinting ability honed on overtaking those lorries didn't let him down. The wind tugged at his hair and voluminous shorts. He rocketed past his neater rivals.

As he stumbled over a victory speech, his mother was congratulated by the PP: 'He's the kick of a Toomevara Greyhound!' County selector Willie Hyland shook her hand. She hadn't seemed so happy since Dev won the general election. Once they were home, however, his mother ordered: 'Extra hours from now on for your Leaving. No cycling any night until you have shown me your completed home-work.'

Within a short time, he was picked to represent his county but he needed a bicycle with gears. He wrote with some press cuttings to his Aunt Bridget. 'You have a way with words, as well,' she replied with a fifty-dollar cheque. He won a race in Templemore and led the Tipperary team to success over neighbouring Limerick. His exploits provided a providential antidote for his adolescent diffidence. And heading for school one morning, he found Eileen waiting by her gate: 'Tell me about the racing.'

'Those shoneens are recognising the British border,' Dinny O'Brien fumed. Cycling and athletics were caught up in politics. His club was split, as ambitious members sought to enter international athletics by joining the rival Amateur Athletic Union which represented only the twenty-six-county Republic. But when Ronnie Delaney won an Olympic gold medal, he knew that the Dubliner had done more for Irish sport than his patriotic friends and himself.

Nothing seemed to change in his village, but now the funerals featured as many cars as ponies and traps. 'A factory on wheels.' Din Ryan walked around the village's first combine harvester. Guard Coleman died of a heart attack at Shelley's Cross, where he had found Mick Dalkey's body a year earlier. A few mornings later, the Gunner staggered into the Garda station. 'Sergeant, the Huns, the Huns! They're here again. I saw them with me own two eyes. The gaz is coming down the hill.' Guard Howard made the Gunner a cup of tea while his father cycled out to investigate. The little hill behind the house was covered in the mist which the Gunner had mistaken for poison gas. 'No wonder Old Mate's eyes always look so far away,' his father said when he returned. 'He and the Gunner must have had some terrible experiences.'

A few weeks later, the Gunner died alone. Unlike Bishop Fogarty's sister, the Mass featured no priestly guard of honour. He followed the funeral as far as the Gunner's deserted home, where the driver whipped up the horses for the long journey to Latteragh cemetery. A single mourner rode high in the wake of the hearse – his father, the sergeant.

He remembered the Rineanna tanker when villagers gathered again one night at the bridge. This time their gaze was heavenwards, as Toomevara greeted the space-age Sputnik, whose pips they had heard on the wireless. The Timekeeper unveiled his watch and right on schedule the first-ever spaceship climbed across the autumn sky. 'More reliable than your nags,' Tommy told the tipster Joe Ryan Cox, whose Woodbine glowed in the dark. As it disappeared behind the Long Stone hill, Din Ryan proclaimed through the pipe smoke: 'One in the eye for the Yanks and a fine yoke to be sure. But where do we go from here?'

After a lecture on how some parents had not yet paid their school fees and pointed stares in his direction, Brother Harris hit him on the head and knocked off his glasses. He closed his schoolbooks for the last time two days later. Bill Small knew of his interest in politics. 'Keep away from the professional patriots; enjoy the big wide world out there.'

The teacher was a political sceptic since his brother had been shot by the Tans in Templemore. 'You never see a private dying – only field marshals,' he exclaimed over the half-page obituary of an Independence veteran.

'Keep up the writing,' advised the stricter Rodney Bent, who strapped Seamus Cleary every morning as he strolled into class, late and bookless. He cycled home to the news that he had passed the CIE examination. 'You will take up your first position in September at our Thurles beet factory office,' the personnel manager confirmed.

His brother wrote, 'If you don't like the clerical work, you can look around for other opportunities. Our parents only think about good jobs and pensions. Work is scarce but it's also important to be happy at what you are doing.'

He had his long-dreamed-of passport to manhood. He was at last free of his oppressive parents and village. Despite her heavy hand, he felt sorry for his mother who could never leave but he knew very little about the outside world. Would it live up to his expectations?

7

Seamus Cleary joined him at the railway bridge for the last time. 'Loads of women there; you'll have your oats within weeks.' His mother had more elevated concerns. 'A big change for us too, now we'll have no one at home. Don't forget your morning Mass and evening rosary. Write each week. If you're short of anything, we'll help you.'

He felt lonely as the Morris Minor disappeared over the hump of Thurles railway bridge but he soon enjoyed midnight Suirside walks, vinegar seeping through the *Tipperary Star* wrapping of his salty fish and chips. So many streets to explore, he could go and come as he pleased. This was it, the experience for which he had so long yearned. Travel, money, independence. And, shortly, that first girlfriend. The outside world featured some strange characters. His cuckoo landlady couldn't cook; she frequently served up beet as turnip. No matter how gently he closed the door, neighbouring curtains twitched as she shouted from the middle of the road: 'Is it trying to bring my house down you are?'

He shared a room with an alcoholic cattle agent who never returned until the early hours. Johnny fell on to his bed one night. 'You're drunk again,' he protested.

The cattle man farted as he tried to heave his bulk off the divan. 'So what? What else can we do in a dump like this?'

He flinched from the beery fumes. 'I have to go to work at seven, I need my sleep.'

'Work? In an office?' Johnny laughed so much that he slid on to the floor. 'Women's shite. Why don't you have a drink and meet some real people? Have you had a woman yet? Jasus, there's nothing like a good ride,' he slurred, before starting to snore in his crumpled suit.

He didn't admit that he too was preoccupied by sex. But he would need to be careful. Fellow-lodger Declan closed his book: 'Women only want marriage. If one lets you do it, you can be sure you'll be marching up the aisle at the end of a shotgun. It happened to a friend of mine.' The Corkman lent him an eighteenth century edition of *Don Quixote*, in which the letter *s* was written as *f*. 'The books keep me sane. If I'd enough money I'd drink myself to death. I'd take the boat, but I've to keep the mother. There's nothing but repression in this priest-ridden backwater; even jazz is banned. Get to Dublin as fast as you can. There might be some life there.'

Once over the thrill of his four-pound wage packet, he resented the repetitive work which could have been done by a primary schoolchild. A driver shouted at the chief clerk: 'Covering your backs and clock-watching is all you wasters are good for.'

'Be nice to the boss and you'll get on.' A ponderous eighteen-year old colleague going on eighty prepared the chief clerk's tea. Cleary was right; the typing pool was full of women. He fell in love with the blonde and doll-like Marion but he was tongue-tied when he delivered her a traffic survey each morning. 'I'm too ugly for her,' he confessed to Declan across the dinner table.

'Women only respond to the look of your wallet.'

After weeks of planning, he clung to the survey a little longer one morning. 'Would you like to come for a mineral tonight?' he blurted.

'Oh, I'm sorry. I couldn't do that. Sure I've a boyfriend already.' Her colleagues tittered.

He sent her a letter, which she ignored. He avoided the typing pool thereafter. 'Singing the Blues' was Guy Mitchell's appropriate pop accompaniment. He would never get a woman. Neither school, home nor the books had prepared him for the quagmire of the real world. 'You cycled into me,' roared the lorry driver, who reversed over his pristine racer. From Thurles he progressed to Athy, where he trained nightly around the route of the great 1903 Gordon Bennett Cup, Britain's first motor race. The telephone wires hummed, the moon played tag with the windswept clouds. He felt the presence of the pioneer drivers as he rounded the Moat of Ardscull. French champion René de Knyff and racewinner Red Devil Jenatzy, first to travel at a mile a minute, had slid their monster machines around these very bends. How wonderful it would be to race a car! But Athy, like Thurles, seemed just a larger Toomevara. He pestered his buck-passing superior for a move to Dublin. There, he would certainly find more action, and a girlfriend. The transfer finally arrived, on the company's terms. For the first two years, he would have to work on a Kingsbridge night shift.

'Welcome to the East India Company. Another Charlie Lamb – but will you last the thirty years?' Billy Lane teased from the opposite invoicing high-stool. 'Long walks will help those troubled by impure thoughts.' preached the Adam and Eve's friars. He soon knew every corner of Dublin. The horror of nightwork, starting when everyone was heading for bed, was mitigated by the excitement of the cinemas, theatres, bookshops and busy quays. Men in caps licked stubby pencils and discussed form outside the betting shops. He wandered under clocks and shop signs, the Nassau Street umbrella, the Dame Street horse's head, Elvery's elephant and the golden balls of the ubiquitous pawnshops.

'The footpaths are so crowded, I've crashed into people twice,' he informed his mother. 'The city rings with bicycle and church bells. It's like medieval times when the peals ring out from St Patrick's and St Audoen's.'

Dublin was also a city of smells, from the low-tide Liffey and the decaying and teeming tenement houses. Old men looked longingly towards the distant brewery, as the west wind carried the tantalizing aroma of hops. He imagined *Les Misérables* as he crossed the river from Ormond Quay's cast-iron urinal. A local leaned over the parapet. 'They brought that from Paris for the 1932 Eucharistic Congress. Those culchies pissed like horses; 'twas like Niagara down there.'

He climbed towards Dublin Castle to see the tower from which Red Hugh had escaped the British. Cresting Winetavern Street, he brushed against the hanging clothes of secondhand shops in the shadow of Christ Church. A barrow-boy chatted to a shawled lady who was knitting on an upturned box. They both studied the man sketching the children who skipped and swung from lampposts beside the ruined city wall. 'Harry Kernoff, the artist. Did yous ever see such a wide hat on such a little leprechaun?' The boy wiped his nose with the sleeve of his jersey.

'Gee up there, or you're for the knacker's yard!' Carters with cigarette butts on their ears held the reins with one hand, as their horses clattered through the streets with drays of Heiton's coal, Dardis and Dunne seeds and barrels of stout, their din only drowned by the buses screeching, as they braked for the white-gloved Garda on his O'Connell Bridge podium. Pedestrians held their hats as they crossed over to Bachelor's Walk.

And he stopped the whole street with one wave of his hand. He met a Flannan's schoolfriend, Zimmerman, who was now a point-duty Garda on Capel Street bridge. His friend pointed between the hovering domes of the Four Courts and St Adam and Eve's to the chimneystacks silhouetted against the evening sky. 'Minarets – wouldn't you think you were in Contantinople?' Horses neighed, a horn tooted, the traffic backed up along the quay before they parted company, laughing at the jarvey's dismissal of the Liffey's hazards: 'With that smell, no typhoid germ that was ever invented could last more than a minute!'

'Sixpence a bunch the last of the daffies.' The exhortations of the flower sellers faded as he reached the top of Nelson Pillar's one hundred-and-sixty-six stone steps. It was the highest he had been in his life, the city spread out on all sides: over to his left, the gasometer, the mouth of the Liffey and the bay; ahead, he could almost touch the dome of Rathmines church and the encircling hills. Away to his right were the expanses of Phoenix Park, where he would soon race his bike. He felt he was walking on water, as the crowded mailboat slid past the mile-long finger of granite which brought him to the Pigeon House lighthouse. England and the world was that close now! He waved to the passengers. The keeper invited him up to the glass-laden platform. 'Did yous ever see such a view – and all the bay and the Sugarloaf for good measure?'

The port became his favourite part of Dublin. He followed the *Irish Press* shipping schedules, and was always the first to welcome the virgin-white *Leeward* and *Windward Island* fruit ships. 'Liverpool next, then back to the warm Caribbean. Man, I can't wait.' A West Indian sailor pulled up the *Leeward's* inviting gangway. He told his mother of his ambitions to travel. 'Go more often to church and thank God for your good pensionable job.' His right hand was tired from blessing himself, as he passed the city's churches and saluted innumerable priests. But he met some strange worshippers. A gaberdine-clad man tapped him on the shoulder as they left Adam and Eve's: 'A fine boy to be so faithful with your prayers. Are you new to Dublin? Be careful with the girls, they're heartbreakers. If you're ever lonely come down and see me in Talbot Street. Here's my address.' The man's warm breath stank of cigarettes.

His religious zeal was matched by his obsession with women. Even in church, he could not take his eyes off a shapely kneeling bottom. He frequently left overwhelmed with confusion and guilt. His older workmate Jimmy blew a thick black hair from his spectacles. 'Nothing wrong with sex, until narrow-minded gobdaws took control of the church.'

'The Ancients considered sex a truly spiritual experience. Anatole France was right – of all sexual aberrations, chastity is the strangest. Little wonder that priests' hands stray under altarboys' soutanes!' Known as the 'Professor', the stocky Clareman came from a long line of railway employees. Habitually blue-suited, his pace proclaimed that when God made time, he made plenty of it. He discoursed on everything from literature and current affairs to religion: 'Jews wailing at walls, Mohammedans with their bums in the air, Hindus harbouring cows in the parlour, Catholics obsessed with redemptive masochism – and each of them claiming the One True Faith. Could you invent anything more ridiculous? I'm a believer in life *before* death.'

'But you go to Mass every Sunday?'

'Leave my insecurities out of this!'

He envied his Southern-Hotel roommate who was doing a line. Willie gave him some good news one evening. 'I'll fix you up with my cousin. She's coming up for the weekend. But be careful; she's hot stuff!' With a tight black skirt and full white blouse, Philomena lived up to her reputation on their Sunday Capitol Cinema date. But a morning cycle racing crash had removed skin from his every extremity. Each time Philomena snuggled closer, he was forced to retreat farther into the corner of his expensive balcony seat. Her blouse tumbled over his armrest. 'Don't you like me?'

The eight-day Rás Tailteann proved even more hazardous. Thirteenth on the opening Newry stage won by Cecil Donoghue, he had hopes of lasting the distance. But director Joe Christle led the race into the Protestant hinterland with tricolours provoking from every vehicle: 'The National Cycling Association recognises no border.' They miraculously survived to Lisburn, where a unionist reception committee greeted them with a fusillade of stones and bottles. 'Up the Republic' shouted some of the riders, as one shinned up a flagpole to remove a Union Jack and ensure an even more exciting welcome in Cookstown.

Violence hung in the air like the summer heat. 'Papist bastard!' A middle-aged man dislodged him from his bicycle. A woman swung a rubber hose which curled around his green singlet and seared his back and stomach. 'Go back where you belong, you dirty Fenian.'

'My arm, my arm!' Dwarfed by helmeted RUC men, Nattie Fahy was spreadeagled across the bonnet of a Ford Prefect, his aluminium cycle pump bent at right angles, as he tried to protect his other arm which was in plaster. The earlier sloganisers were nowhere to be seen. He waded to Nattie's assistance through the swearing crowd and thudding truncheons. 'What sort of men are you, to hit someone with a broken arm?' he shouted at the RUC officers.

Astonished, they lowered their batons and, instead, kicked the pair of them up Cookstown's unending main street. 'That's it, boot the bastards. Next time, we'll have more than bricks for you.' One of the mob lobbed a bottle, which shattered just ahead of a startled policeman. Subdued Catholics looked on from the top end of the brick and bottle-strewn town. He lifted his singlet to see the red streak that encircled his body. Nattie put the L-shaped pump in his jersey pouch and remounted his bike. He held up his broken arm: 'They never signed my plaster!'

He couldn't resist a last backward glance at the RUC and the jeering populace. A Union Jack and Tricolour intimidated from opposite sides of the street. Pieces of cloth nailed to sticks, how easily the roles could have been reversed. 'We'll holiday somewhere else next year.' Obstinate tears rolled off the oily chain which he pretended to check. His burning midriff and aching shoulders became an irrelevancy a few miles down the road. He barely heard the warning shout, before a brakeless car launched him skywards and out of the race. The Orangemen had the last laugh. But it was one of his own: 'Jesus, Mary and Joseph. More holy water, he's coming to.'

'Brendan had to retire after he was injured while protecting the national flag, Tipperary should be proud of him.' Joe Christle addressed the Nenagh audience. His mother and the crowd applauded the fiction. Willie Heaney interviewed him for the *Tipperary Star*. 'What next?' Though he was interested in politics, he hadn't forgotten his motor-sport dreams. 'I'd love to race a car one day.' Willie was a serious man but his laughter followed him all the way to the railway station.

The shame of abandoning a snowy two-day race which he could have won was to stay with him for years. But despite his indiscipline and tactical ignorance, the cycling boosted his confidence. It also demonstrated that dreams could come true; maybe he would show Willie one day! Nothing matched the thrill of speed or the ecstasy of winning. Even the danger was exciting, despite shredding shorts and flesh in Maynooth and Limerick crashes, and a Mercer's Hospital incarceration for blood poisoning.

Thanks to an obsessive training routine, his final cycling spree proved to be his most successful. Twice weekly, he left the city behind and headed for windswept Sally Gap. Sitting well back, arms apart on the top of the bars, at one with his bike and the elements, he built up the miles, stamina and assurance, only up on the pedals for the final hundred yards, encouraged by the shouts of occasional turf-cutters. And the reward of the thrilling descent, momentarily staying a mouthful of raisins as he threaded the eye of a curving stone bridge at forty miles per hour. From being a challenge, he impatiently awaited the Sunday races. He relished the thrill of the breaks, the fading 'Up! Up!' cries of an indecisive pack, the joyous security of craftily conserved sprinting power. He won four prizes in two Phoenix Park events. 'Aunt Bridget's gift was well invested,' endorsed his spectating Yankee cousin, Cathleen.

Cathleen had even more to celebrate when he won the Cooper Cup race. With new tyres on tick from the Rutland shop, he initiated every break. 'What's in those canvasses?' teammate Mal Denny panted.

He led with a diminishing group for ninety of the 100-kilometre event. But they were caught by favourite Cecil Donoghue, who had trained with Tour de France star Shay Elliott. 'After all my hard work,' he spluttered to Mal. 'I'll be fucked if I'll give up now.' He reached down and tightened his toestraps.

They swept around the Phoenix monument. Two hundred yards, one hundred yards. Riders jockeyed for position. The grunting of rigid arm effort multiplied. Metal creaked, high-pressure tyres rasped against the tarmac. The wheels' whirlwind incited his coiled legs. Suddenly Frankie Baird sprinted. Like a spring released, he followed the veteran's wheel. The cheering started: 'The ould dog! Come on Frankie!' Mind that culvert, watch those riders. Remember Fogarty bringing you down in Kildare. Don't crash now! Where the hell was Donoghue? Any later, he would be uncatchable. Thirty yards out, a blur of blue swept past. He jumped on the pedals, one leg pushed as hard as the other pulled. His head went down to the bars. He'd done a good job on the straps; every ounce of energy went into those wheels. There would be no excuses. Every muscle strained, the line rushed towards them. Cecil didn't let up; he couldn't gain an inch. He willed his whole body into those pedals. Yards to go, his rival started to falter. He grabbed his own handlebars tighter. The cheers multiplied. They drew level. When Cecil looked over, he knew he had won.

'Up Tipp!' Joe Christle proffered a congratulatory orange. Teenage hero, Rás Tailteann winner Gene Mangan, shook his hand. He didn't want for anything more. Never had grass smelled sweeter, as he freewheeled home past Gough's poised equestrian statue. He would have some good news for Jimmy when he met him that night.

But his friend was unimpressed. 'All that huffing and puffing for a bit of tinware. It's only a substitute for a more natural form of riding. I think you're afraid of the women?'

His friend didn't know how hard he tried. He spent weeks and a fortune in Manelli's fish and chip shop. His clothes reeked of cooking oil.

'You like the fish and chips.' The girl smiled over the crisp white top which highlighted her rich colour. His legs weakened. Jet-black hair, olive skin, Mediterranean passion. How exotic compared to the dull Irish girls.

He pointed to the lustrous-haired mirror image on the Botticelli calendar. 'Head of Venus, I think that's you.'

While he plotted how to ask her out, he showed her some of his cycling photographs. 'Bene – you the same like Fausto Coppi.' Her warm hand touched his as she handed back the pictures.

'Would you like to come out for a walk with me?' he finally asked one evening. But he spoke too quickly.

'Inglese no good, what you say?'

It took him all his courage to try again a week later. 'OK! Tomorrow, we go Phoenix Park – I meet you bus stop at ten. And then maybe see Bill Haley film?'

It was summer. He would bring a couple of minerals and they would lie somewhere quiet in the long grass. He didn't sleep all night. The continental women were very advanced. She would let him kiss that lovely hair – and, maybe, even those Italian lips. But the following morning, he couldn't find his cycling jock strap. He paced up and down the room. It was nearing ten o'clock and he desperately sought distracting thoughts to reduce his tumescence. 'Sale today,' the auction-house bells rang out. Maybe some great book bargains? St Michael and St John's clock chimed the hour; he would be late. But not even the agonies of hell worked; her dark hair monopolised his senses. His irresolute erection prevented him from making even the bus stop.

'I was sick,' he lied, when he met her in Capel Street the next day. He was so embarrassed that he fled his cockroach-infested Ormond Quay room a fortnight later.

Jimmy helped him to pack. 'Chasing women is like your bike racing; you mustn't give up.'

'Why are you so restless, why can't you stay in one place?' his mother complained.

He shared wallpapered houses in Berkeley Road and Drumcondra and lonely bedsits on windswept North and South Circular Roads. His frustration grew in concrete Marino, where his flatmate Gallagher shocked him with stories of an actress named Marilyn Monroe. 'She posed for photographers – without a stitch.'

He celebrated Pat Boone's 'Love Letters in the Sand' hit by graduating to tree-lined Elgin Road. His landlady, Fiona Plunkett, discarded her fox stole to feed him when he caught the flu. She allowed him the freedom of her library, whence they appealed to the American ambassador to spare the condemned kidnapper, Caryl Chessman.

'Joseph Mary signed that book the year he was executed. But my brother wasn't just a bookworm. He also travelled, to France, Italy, Sicily and even Algeria. It was through his friendship with Thomas MacDonagh and Roger Casement that he became involved in the independence movement.'

He built up his own window-ledge library with treasures unearthed in Hannas and the quayside bookshops, whose trays bulged with the writi'ngs of patriots John Mitchel and Fr Kenyon, and gilt-edged Victorian editions of Addison and Tennyson. His most exciting discovery was the four-volume *Treasury of Irish Literature*, which he bought from the barrow of a whiskered pensioner's on Eden Quay.

> The glory of ould Ireland and a thousand buccaneers,
> And a terror to creation were the Dublin Fusiliers.

He was shocked to see a Union Jack draping the back room when he visited the man's little Ormond Market shop. 'We gave MacBride and his mates the fucking Irish Brigade at Pieter's Hill.' The Boer War veteran toasted the shredded banner with a Jameson. 'The only dacent man that ever came out of this town was Dr Barnardo. He saved London's homeless but you'll never hear about him because he was a Protestant.'

He went home to see his parents and his brother, who had completed his Wexford teaching contract. Toomevara now seemed so small and quiet. Colm confided: 'I have had a sufficiency of caustic remarks about the classical music and the *Irish Times*, I am off to London for a school interview. Later, I might try either Austria or Germany!'

'To be nearer to your deities Mozart and Beethoven?'

He was shocked that his brother was emigrating. What a disappointment for their parents, particularly their prejudiced mother. A row erupted when Colm returned from Nenagh with *The Irish Times*. Fired by an *Irish Press* feature on the burning of Cork, their mother reacted: 'The organ of the Protestant Ascendancy class, the landlords who starved our people, shot our leaders, torched our towns. Why can't you read an Irish paper and show some respect for those who gave their lives to win our freedom?'

'I admire the people who died. But I want to learn and get

away from hatred and bitterness. I want to be informed. The *Irish Press* favours Fianna Fáil and constantly relives the Civil War; the *Independent* promotes the Fine Gael view. Only the *Times* provides objective opinion, news from the outside world, columns on art and music.'

'Objective all right, because it doesn't care about Irish history. It's for the Big-House robbers with their heads in the clouds and the West Britons who ape their ways. Where did they get their art only from the sweat of tenants? I'm ashamed to have a son who supports such a gang and their rag.' Edna O'Brien got similar short shrift. 'Many a time you played with her and the rest of the family in Drewsboro. But she let them and Scarriff down with those scandalous books – though I wouldn't be surprised if that foreign husband of hers wrote them.'

His parents feared that he also would emigrate to escape the night work. They contacted an influential family friend. 'I'll be delighted to help,' wrote Mr Treacy.

High in his Customs House eyrie, the senior civil servant stirred his afternoon tea. 'Sure that work's only for donkeys. The chairman's my friend. I'll get you out of there in no time. One thing, though' – he gazed out Gandon's windows – 'you'll have to steer clear of that subversive Christle family. Last week, a man I arranged to be made a peace commissioner got six months for possessing explosives.'

He had discussed political action with Joe Christle, before Cookstown revealed the bankruptcy of slogans. Violence was a defeat. If his mind had been made up, however, he still resented someone telling him who his friends should be. No job was worth that. But how could he face that night work for another year?

He left Mr Treacy with his cup in mid-air and waded past the card-schools into the bustle of the quays. The freed ropes splashed in the water, as the cream and blue *Lady Miranda* prepared to sail for Liverpool with its cargo of stout. In England, he would not have to work all night for a pittance.

8

He still hadn't found a girlfriend. Unaware of his main preoccupation, his mother wrote: 'Be patient and soon, with the help of God, you'll be working more normal hours. Why don't you try to do something worthwhile, like joining the Legion of Mary?' For once, he took her advice. A tin of beans dressed the newspaper-covered table of an old man's Inchicore railway cottage. Legionaries prayed under the only wall decoration of a Sacred Heart print: 'Dear Jesus, guard us constantly and enable us despite our trials to live a pure and righteous life.'

'Over-fed shitheads chasing indulgences,' Jimmy rubbished his do-gooding activities. 'For Jasus' sake, let the politicians sort out the social situation. Concentrate on your own more pressing problem of finding an amenable woman.'

Noël Browne asked a Dáil question about a woman who had been found dead from malnutrition. 'She had an allowance of twenty-two and sixpence per week; the state did its duty,' a government minister replied. He joined the National Association for the Aged, which collected food for pensioners. 'A little tea and sugar would be a great help for me and Mrs McDonnell on the same landing. Mind that hole.' Mrs May led him along the stairs of a buttressed Mountjoy Square tenement, whose fanlight gaped. Lonely men and women despaired under leaking roofs; the smell of decay and carbolic soap permeated his clothes. The window cardboard failed to deter the chill as Mrs Kane grasped his arm: 'I can never go out to the lavatory at night because of the rats.

Dublin can be heaven, with coffee at eleven…

'Noel Purcell would sing a different tune if he lived here.' Two hundred yards away, he passed a couple outside a Wicklow Street window. 'Jonathan, that salver, perfect for the new tureen.' The woman tugged at her husband's crombie. His Christmas appeal appeared among the *Evening Mail's* mixed marriages and Nelson's Pillar effusions. 'We do not ask for money. Only for food and, maybe, a gift to brighten the holiday for those who are without a family.' Boxes and bulging packages poured into the Parliament Street office and soon outnumbered the list of supplicants. But who would better know what needy people he had missed than the local parish priest? Images of Yeats's 'old priest Peter Gilligan' ran through his mind as he took the six granite steps two at a time to the multi-windowed presbytery of St Michael and St John's, where the bells had rung for Ireland's first Emancipation Mass.

'Wait here. I'm not sure if the priest is available.' The housekeeper resented his intrusion. She eventually ushered him into the sitting room. Hands in his pockets, the priest stood with his back to the full fire whose flames danced in the bookcase glass. 'Sure we don't have that many poor folk living around here at all, thank God,' he disabused in a broad western accent. 'By the way, do you have ecclesiastical approval for these activities?'

'The padre never knew how close his arse came to an ecclesiastical roasting,' Jimmy laughed that night. As another nail was hammered into the coffin of his Irish faith, his mother urged him to show more understanding for the PP. 'Priests can't solve every problem. They have difficult enough lives, with no one to help or console them.'

'They live like lords, compared to those in the tenements.'

A Summerhill widow limped into Parliament Street and restored his humour. 'Mister, I'm going the national colours from all dem Bachelors peas. But I'd be in Kevin's or Glasnevin without them. Here's a pair of gloves I knitted for you.'

Joe Christle found him studying the Swiss Chalet menu on Merrion Row. 'Why don't you try the Uni?' Finally transferred to day work, he decided to improve his mind.

With a ten-pound loan from Jimmy, he enrolled for an Arts degree night course. 'I'll find an educated response to the issues of our time and how to make the world a better place.'

'You'd be better off learning how to attract women,' Jimmy reiterated on a Stephen's Green walk.

Crisp cracks reverberated around the pathway, as an old woman broke a fallen branch by levering it through the railings. 'Me father's up there.' She pointed to the Boer War arch.

'That's a place that shows the mentality of the people you want to change.' Jimmy stopped under the Dublin Fusiliers monument. 'Calonso, Talana… Who gives a monkey's now? But the patriots who call this Traitors' Arch are the real shitehawks, cute whores who wouldn't have the balls of those who died, cannon fodder or not. Do you know that an uncle of your hero Behan is named up there too?'

The dark continent came to Grafton Street. Pursued by a hail of stones, two bloodied African students raced across the street from a nearby dance hall. 'Fucking black Balubas coming over here and stealing our women.'

'Behold the welcoming natives of Christian Ireland, the only country where violence is more acceptable than sex.' Jimmy pulled him into Peter's Pub.

UCD proved to be well insulated from such exterior problems. 'Shakespeare is alive; life is for living.' Roman-browed lecturer John Jordan looked up at the crowded auditorium. One memorable night he wished he were Patrick Pye, that he could immortalise the stately progress of gravel-voiced Patrick Kavanagh and Cork-accented Sean O'Sullivan. Ascending the broad stone stairs as if to heaven, Dante in hobnails and the mellifluous Leonardo, who declaimed in French and Gaelic as he painted. But these were among the few nuggets he found in Earlsfort Terrace. 'Where will reading that West British rubbish get us?' remonstrated two fellow-Tipperary students, when he enquired if they'd read Honor Treacy's *Mind You I've Said Nothing*.

Jimmy nearly fell off his high stool. 'I told you you'd only find the sons of gombeen men chasing the means of acquiring even more spondulicks. Ideas my arse.'

'*Catholics at Trinity?* Debate Wednesday Night.' There was no dissent when the event was banned, as was Brendan Behan. 'And my address was to be through the medium of the official national language! All those gobshites understand is my drinking. I'm banning them.'

Classmate Conor Leahy took early retirement. 'Ireland's standing still. People will accept anything. It's Londinium for me. More debate, more opportunities and, certainly, more agreeable women. Why don't you come?'

'Stop the massacre of Algerians!' Neither the republicans nor any other group would support his picketing of the French warship which visited Dublin at the height of the Algerian colonial war. Only three others joined him, two South Africans and a Belfast Presbyterian.

'Pampered students, why don't you do a day's work?' A dozen dockers crowded them close to the water into which they had previously thrown an Animal Rights protestor.

He sought the protection of a tall crane. 'I'm working by day and night.'

'Your hands are as soft as your brain.' They jammed him against the flaking metal, beneath which French ratings made throat-cutting gestures. The Gardai dispersed them and took the South Afftricans' placards. 'Do this again and you'll be on the next banana boat home.'

To his mother's embarrassment, the protest was recorded by an *Irish Times* photographer. 'Put your own country first, don't be getting mixed up with these foreigners and their strange ideas.'

'Algerians are being slaughtered every day. Christ and Gandhi were foreigners with even stranger ideas.

'Tell Laura I Love Her'. He developed a lofty affection for fellow-student Laura, whose alabaster perfection put Leonardo's *Virgin of the Rocks* to shame. They held hands beside the Clog coffee-bar's fire, where they were admired by the artist, Leslie MacWeeney. But on a fiver a week, a cappuccino was all he could rise to. One night, the unattainable one confessed that she had fallen for a Guinness executive. Jimmy held his sides: 'Pure love? All the women want is a wage slave, so they can spend the rest of their lives listening to *The Kennedys of Castlerosse* or *Mrs Dale's Diary*. They're all prostitutes.'

Hitch-hiking provided a healthy diversion. Gallagher, his workmate, introduced him to the Pine Forest and lonely Fraoch Halla, where Synge had also supped. Looking down from the resin-scented wilderness to the distant twinkling lights, he remembered the poet's Paris loneliness:

There's snow in every street
Where I go up and down,
And there's no woman, man, or dog
That knows me in the town.

'Give those books a rest and do some travelling,' Gallagher advised across the disappearing brown bread. 'And when we garner a few bob, we'll chase the women in earnest.'

He followed in Synge's western footsteps. Swans flapped their wings beside lakeside Ballinakill cemetery as he paid his respects to another racing cyclist, Oliver St John Gogarty. Bog insects swarmed around Derrygimla's Marconi station ruins, where Alcock and Brown had landed: 'Yesterday, we were in America.' He was shocked to hear that the station had been burned by republicans, together with a nearby orphanage. Smoke curled from a fire behind a rock on Inis Iarc. 'We knew you weren't a Garda with those glasses.' A woman proferred a sample from the focal still. Connemara cast a spell. Voices of children carried across the seaweed pools. Everything seemed to have grown from the earth: crags, hillocks, stonewalls and thatched cottages. Roads bent to nature's way; even the disused railway cuttings, rusting bridges and overgrown embankments all now seemed organic. Gentle light soothed the towering Maamturks. How lovely it would be to live here, away from that dead-end office. If he emigrated he could work and save the money.

He met the Griffins with whom Brendan Behan stayed in Carraroe. 'Brendan said the *poitín* gave texture to his Gaelic!'

A little boy ran after him from a listing cottage. 'Will you buy an egg, sir?' Remembering his own egg escapades, he wanted to help but funds were low. A few bends later, the panting boy caught up with him again. 'My mother says you're to have it anyway and may God bless your journey, sir.' The egg and threepence changed hands and they walked together for a while. He told the boy about Dublin. 'So many houses?' his companion looked up at him. 'I saw a train once going to the big city. A long curling thing with lighted windows and it could see its way across the countryside – even though it was night!'

The rain ran down the inside of his jacket as he waited

near Craughwell. A vintage wooden-partitioned Rolls Royce approached. It certainly wouldn't help a sodden hiker. 'Stick the bag in the back and you keep me company here in front,' invited Patrick Lynch, John Huston's chauffeur. Motionless, they purred along at fifty miles per hour. 'Do you know who sat two days ago where you're sitting now? The most beautiful girl I ever saw in my life – Marilyn Monroe.' The film star had flown over to visit John Huston for a week. He remembered Gallagher's midnight stories, as Patrick peered through the swishing windscreen wipers and mused: 'No airs and graces, a lovely, simple, friendly girl.'

'Did you lose your Pioneer pin?' his mother wrote, after an alert villager had spotted him in a Dublin bar.

'Have a real drink and loosen up,' Gallagher tempted him one night into the Old Stand. 'This is the way you'll meet more broadminded women.'

'If you call drinking this horse's pee exciting, you can have it.' He grimaced over a cider. But before long, a relaxing feeling of well-being coursed through his veins. His inhibitions and seemingly invincible shyness vanished. 'Is this really me?' he wondered, as he heard himself enunciate in divers tongues. And the democracy of drinking! Young and old, resting actor and bank clerk laughed together under the curtains which kept the world and its problems at bay. He had a civil discussion with an equally happy Orangeman who touched his glass: 'I'll join any bloody republic, as long as the pope in Rome doesn't tell me what to do with my private life.'

He found seven tempting pound notes down the toilet's conning tower descent. Louis put the money in a jug on the dresser. 'Ah, I know the fella well.' A few nights later, the man who pulled the best pint in Dublin handed him a three-pound reward. 'Drinkers are civilised people,' he assured Gallagher, as he spat against the subterranean porcelain.

'Sure things,' Gallagher celebrated, after they chatted up two Jacob's factory girls. He left nothing to chance for their subsequent date. A new red tablecloth for five shillings at Arnott's sale, extra briquettes to raise the temperature, an Easy Listening record from the International Record Library and no fewer than four flagons of Bulmer's cider. Why did he get the agricultural girl? But with his dismal record, he could hardly be particular. The drink flowed. Perry Como crooned. The warm fire enhanced the mood and expectations. Gallagher's companion was kissing him. But his stouter partner firmly rebuffed his chaise-longue gropings: 'Will yous lave off the maulin' and open another cider.' The cider ran out; his companion stood up and smoothed her voluminous frock: 'Come on Bridie, we'll miss the last bus.' The expenditure ensured a week's porridge-only diet. Was he ever going to get a woman? Bartley Dunne demonstrated his Stephen's Street wine racks: 'Malaga wine for the young ladies!' Lauri Dunne lent him Dale Carnegie's *How to Win Friends* but it was lacking in romantic content.

'We'll get the real thing.' Jimmy encouraged him to share the cost of a mail-order sex manual. He spent nights fantasising about the blonde English student, Muriel, who lived upstairs. 'She's an arse to die for,' fellow-lodger Ted Sinnott endorsed.

> When I play on my fiddle in Dooney
> Folk dance like a wave of the sea.

The major annual social event was the Whitsun Fleadh Ceoil, which attracted musicians from the four provinces to such towns as Boyle and Swinford. Rich and poor, young and old, flocked to celebrate their country's musical heritage. Four glorious days during which daylight and darkness, drink and music fused in one unforgettable Bacchanal. 'A great time to be solvent; you did the right thing pawning the green suit.' Gallagher opened a baptismal bottle as the train pulled out of Kingsbridge. A shy provincial sat on a pub window. Two drinks later, he reached into his breast pocket. A tin whistle emerged glinted in the sun, notes as clear as Hemingway's words released 'The Blackbird' into the weekend air. A passing fiddler joined in. Accordeon straps slipped on to well-grooved shoulders, spoons and a bodhrán completed the final tribal flourish. 'Me life on ye, lads. There's more where that came from,' the publican said, as he carried out a tray of pints.

A northern Presbyterian touched glasses with Jimmy. 'Isn't music great, the way it brings us all together.'

'The Humours of Clare'. 'The Jolly Tinker'. The transfixed audience tapped their feet and swayed with the players, as if responding to memories of some deep-rooted communal past. 'Listen how the air vibrates. Ghostly approval from times and clans long flown.' Pint-sized Larry Hussey offered his brimming glass to each of the four corners. 'From the courts of Tara and Kincora, and the ruder settlements of early Celts and forgotten Firbolgs. A scene two Yeatses would have competed to record.'

"Twould stir the roots of your balls,' Jimmy conceded through the froth of a fresh pint. Harry O'Toole-King, something of a student agitator, stirred on his pavement bed: 'I need my beauty sleep. Would yous ever fuck off and play somewhere else!'

> In the female prison
> There are seventy women,
> I wish it was with them that I did dwell...

Emboldened by cider courage, he himself shocked *fáinne*-laden traditionalists with Brendan Behan's as yet unfashionable 'Ould Triangle' and 'St Kevin' lyrics. High on drink and low on funds, his friends encouraged him to solicit a half-crown loan from Garech Browne. The Guinness heir adjusted his *crios*: 'I never carry cash.'

'Give him a cheque, then.' Jimmy waved his glass.

Another shameful night he reprimanded a Dublin guitarist for playing flamenco rather than Irish music. 'I'll manage the bloody machine next time myself,' growled beardless Ronnie Drew, whom he had helped shortly before when a sculpture had grounded the musician's Merrion Square barrow.

'The train left two hours ago. Try Claremorris.' They all trekked the Michael Davitt country from Swinford to Claremorris. Every breeze, curlew call and humming telegraph wire reverberated with the fleadh music and haunted their semi-intoxicated progress across the boggy landscape. 'We're under a spell,' Hussey said, looking around.

For days afterwards, the city sounds, from flowing tap water to braking buses, were likewise transmuted into a Seán Ó Riada symphony of wild pipings and bodhrán throbbings. And his heart would turn towards Connacht, where he had experienced such a stirring manifestation of his country's complex soul. Boyle Fleadh Ceoil almost provided an even more memorable experience. He came closest to losing his pent-up virginity. 'I'll stay for a minute only,' a red-haired Dublin teacher said, looking tentatively around his room. In the fever of the Fleadh, Rita and he soon lay starkers on the bed. Bliss! The first time he had seen a naked woman. Her hair touched her bottom. He was wildly excited. A band marched across the nearby bridge. Drums rattled, pipe music swirled, the universe stood in abeyance. Romance, music and long-thwarted desire were poised to fuse in one unforgettable climax.

But as his staff poised itself for its long-delayed baptism, the Catholic girl spotted the bearded hypocrite's bedside missal. 'No! No! No! It's a sin, a sin, a sin.' She brandished the holy book in all her uncovered glory. Dracula repulsed by Gertrude Stein, he wilted before the missal, his manhood retreating in doleful time with the fading bagpipes.

From a funeral to a feast, he progressed on his Dublin return to another fleadh contact. Dispensing with formality, the American actress bared her swaying breasts in her parents' Jury's hotel room. The wait had been worthwhile; nothing could go wrong now. He was mesmerised. He didn't know what to do but emboldened by cider and lust, he grabbed and kissed her breasts alternately. His organ leaped out of his trousers. 'Oh! that's cute,' she gushed. 'Take off my pants.' At that very moment, there was a knock on the door. Her parents had returned from an early–ending Abbey play. Mortified but unbowed, his condition ensured an ignominious and hazardous navigation of the hotel's revolving door. 'Had it been a Eugene O'Neill marathon, you'd have been on the sow's back – in more ways than one!' Jimmy commiserated.

He finally succeeded in surrendering his virginity in Upper Mount Street. He was reading his green Penguin *Germinal* in the doorstep sun, when Muriel came home from Trinity lectures. His face caught fire as he wondered if she knew about his fantasies. It reddened even more when he couldn't remove his eyes from her equally inviting breasts.

'That's all right, many men like my figure.' She poked his own less well-endowed chest. God, how frank English girls were compared to their Irish sisters. 'I heard you might have a copy of *Dubliners*. Could I borrow it for a few days?'

His trousers moved as he invited her into his room. He was

mortified. Did she notice? She went down on her knees before his bookshelves. Her skirt tightened around those lovely curves; he could see the outline of her underpants. Simmons was right. His trousers heaved even more. 'You can tell a person's character by their books. George Moore's *Confessions* – do you have anything to confess?'

'I wish I had,' he said, sitting on on his virginal bed. She extracted the Joyce and sat beside him. 'Life's too short to be shy. Tell me all about it.' Her candour encouraged confidence. 'There's not a lot to tell.' He sat on his shaking hands. 'I'm afraid I'm the most inexperienced man in this house.'

'Well, we can't have that, can we?' She moved closer and kissed him on the cheek. 'Oh my! What's that moving down there?'

'Where do you mean?'

'Here.' She stroked his groin. 'Let's release him – and give him something really naughty to confess.'

She pushed him back on the bed and unbuckled his trousers. She unzipped her skirt, it fell to the ground. 'Undo my bra, like this.' She turned around. Her bottom was even more alluring in pink.

'My! What a hungry boy.' She stroked his penis. But they were both shocked by his sexual ignorance. Foreplay was something he apparently thought applied to a whist drive. She had no sooner removed her knickers than he was on top of her. Incapable any longer of restraint, he sprayed her as his organ touched the blonde tufts he'd fantasised about.

'You've come? Already?'

Jimmy placed a compensatory cider under Nearys counter lantern. 'Selfish bloody woman, no consideration. But you've finally broken your duck. A bit more practice and you'll be giving lessons. And that manual will seal your reputation; they'll be queueing up.' But, despite its guaranteed plain wrapper, the customs winkled out the expensive book. 'Another conspiracy by the church and its capitalist lackeys,' Jimmy mocked.

He thought of Conor Leahy, who was able to read anything he liked in London. Who didn't have to pawn his suit and who probably now handled women like a professional.

9

Muriel and he agreed to be good friends only. 'Come for a picnic. I've made salad and bought this with my allowance.' She proffered a bottle of Riesling.

'My very first alfresco.' He cradled the wine as they walked past Baggot Street's Doric-columned temple and turned right by the canal.

'Steady with the glasses.' She waited as he swayed across the unprotected Mespil footbridge.

'"Once more to walk in summer along the canal",' he quoted.

'Patrick Kavanagh – a rare species, an honest Irishman!'

Muriel laughed, as she sought a likely picnic site. A tarred mooring post stood sentry, its phallic corrugations proclaiming a proud apprenticeship. Water hens explored the green-bordered expanses; a betting slip bobbed gently. Opposite was the mews garage where Alfie Hinds, the Cockney jailbreaker, had been rearrested. 'Finished in 1791, seven years before the rebellion, one of the industrial revolution's more benign legacies.' He dangled his legs over the edge of an old subsidence inlet.

'Everything here is related to history.' Muriel removed the cork from the domed corkscrew which he didn't know how to use. 'So much time and intelligence squandered on retrospection. Ireland will go nowhere until it ends its obsession with the past. Those bombs on the border, what a waste of energy.'

'There's a snobbery about bombs.' He munched. 'You and the Yanks have an arsenal which could destroy the planet. Don't be criticising Ireland's modest contribution.

'Ahead of your time! Nuclear war is the biggest threat our species has ever faced. That's why I admire Bertrand Russell, who was imprisoned for organising the big London protest. A real hero of our time.'

The author whose book he had seen on that Dundrum holiday! 'Saving humanity sounds more sensible than splitting hairs over the

Irish border,' he said by way of a toast, as a pair of expectant ducks scattered the blue reflections.

Muriel had been to Paris for Easter. 'Art and culture inhabit every corner; it makes London seem deprived. Many Irish writers lived there too: Joyce, Synge, Oscar Wilde.'

'Paris, the city of my idols, Hemingway, George Moore, Modigliani.'

'You know more about it than I do! But don't let it remain a book interest. Don't complain like your friends about your lack of freedom. Go and express yourself before you succumb to suffocation or cirrhosis.'

'All I need is money!'

Muriel topped up his glass. 'Making decisions is harder than making money.'

Muriel was right. It was entirely up to him. He had command of his destiny. Possibilities suddenly opened up before him. There was a big, wide world out there to be savoured and see it he would. Tree patterns danced on their rug; it was a day to be alive. A familiar figure approached the opposite bank. Frank O'Connor studied the 'In Memory of Mrs Dermod O'Brien' inscription on Patrick Kavanagh's favourite throne of modest bricks and wood. The sun glinted off his white head as he turned left for Parsons Bookshop.

'I pronounce this place Paris Bay, from which my great voyage will soon commence.' He drained his glass on their picnic site. He loved Dublin and he still wanted to save the world. But for how much longer would he resist the temptation of England and travel? Someone would soon have to make a sacrifice, his mother or himself. His final Dublin address was the singularly beautiful backwater of Upper Mount Street, whose canal entrance was flanked by the Pike Theatre and Liam Miller's Dolmen Press, a light-reflecting symmetry of graceful windows, fanlight tracery and mellow brickwork, girdled by wrought iron railings and crowned by swan-neck streetlamps. 'We can thank the English for our architecture.' Jimmy pointed towards the echelons of lofty chimney pots.

Nestling between the Pepper Canister Church and Merrion Square, where Æ, Yeats and Le Fanu had sojourned, he woke each morning to the horse's clip-clop and the glockenspiel of milk bottles. Jimmy met some of his student neighbours, including Mr Cole from Sierra Leone. "The bloody United Nations, your man's aptly named.

'I didn't see him in the dark.' Harry O'Toole-King marred the housewarming when he smote the African with the toilet door. Actors and artists such as Patrick Pye also packed the throbbing Bohemia, which matched his Murger mood and smuggled Henry Millers. Coal-streaked dockers and their flocks of children inhabited the adjacent laneway cottages, whitewashed each Corpus Christi when ribbons replaced the flapping washing. Owen Walsh sketched the stevedores as they argued in Phil Ryan's bar.

Jimmy looked out the window. 'Jasus, it's Myles na Gopaleen under that hat!'

Instead of being authors he read, writers were people he met on the expansive Georgian shores. John Montague, Jim Fitzgerald and Petronella O'Flanagan regularly floated by. And once, a reflective Patrick Kavanagh. Soulmates he and Behan never could be. Hirsute Nevill Johnson, 'the Lion of Leeson Street', beat a well-trodden trail to Doheny and Nesbitts.

The unassuming balustrades of Huband Bridge and its eternal cataract buoyed him on many an evening. And to complete his joy, Parsons redbrick bookshop beamed culture from the crest of nearby Baggot Street bridge. Paint had never desecrated its creaking floor nor wooden counter. Sunbeams spotlighted the dust which danced on such regular customers as Behan, Kavanagh, Ben Kiely, O'Connor, O'Faolain, O'Flaherty and James Plunkett. And short story writer, Mary Lavin: 'Parsons is my parlour!'

Paris on the Grand Canal: his imagination soared. Under the mantelpiece he had placed portraits of such incompatibles as Socrates, Martin Luther King and Albert Schweitzer. He happily replayed his single Mozart and Beethoven LPs. The fermenting maelstrom of Jack London, Hemingway and James Connolly renewed his desire to change the world and explore its endless horizons

> I will give you a golden ball
> To hop with the children in the hall.

The two little basement girls raced up every time they heard the bumping of his bicycle on the wooden stairs: 'Give us a spin, mister! Skinny legs dangled high above the pedals, as he gave them each an arm-protected ride to the corner and back. The brick walls radiated the heat of the day; the Garda stroke survivor smiled on his evening constitutional. The girls' mother stood by the door, looking across Merrion Square for her emigrant husband who seldom returned. 'That London can be a snare,' his own mother had warned.

But she could not deter him from his new socialist faith. James Connolly's writings, Sean O'Casey's plays and Dr. Noël Browne's example had ensured his conversion. He finally understood that the poverty around him was as unnecessary as it was unjust. Mrs Scott, who lived underneath, conveniently reinforced his new philosophy. 'A lifetime polishing floors for the Merrion Square gentry and all I've to show for it is the bloody rheumatics.'

Each pension Friday, her best hat restored, the World War One widow limped back from the pawnshop. 'The prices is gone mad; seven and a halfpence for that turnover.' She rummaged for her room key. Her alarm clock ticked like a time bomb between the moulting basket's cargo of cauliflowers and stout. She sang into the early hours under a fading sepia study of her Victorian parents. Her pension was twenty-eight shillings a week, compared to the forty-two enjoyed by those enslaved in the Black North. Another slogan undone.

'I'm here since nineteen and fourteen, son. All me ould mates is long gone. I'd a wireless but it broke down.' She polished the door knocker and letterbox.

'She pawned the set for drink,' the caretaker revealed one rent day.

Outdoing each other in style and self-absorbed sanctity, a congregation of missal-carriers tripped across the street from Sunday Mass at the Convent of Perpetual Adoration. Shining emblems, glowing faces that knew neither hunger nor pawnshop interior. 'Perpetual humbug, why don't you *do* something Christian?' he shouted as they passed Mrs Scott's window.

An outraged worshipper wheeled around. Thinking he was English, she brandished her silk scarf: 'Take your filthy ideas back to where you belong.'

He pulled a high stool to Phil Ryan's counter with Ted Sinnott. 'I'm not part of it any more. A whole apprenticeship gone for nought.'

Bereft of half his life, he felt only half a person. But what could he do? He either sat back and lived a lie like everyone else or he summoned the courage like Leahy to seek a better life elsewhere. And what answers did that guarantee? His whole life hung on what he decided now. All change for Paradise.

'Beware of the Antichrists who exploit the naivety of young people,' warned Tipperary's *Skibbereen Eagle*. The sole aim of the Socialists is the destruction of the Church. If there are poor people, it's God's holy will. He works in mysterious ways; it's not for mere mortals to be questioning His intentions. Justice will prevail for all on Judgement Day.'

'I've seen enough prematurely aged workers and those swanning around Dublin on the fruits of their toil, to know that social injustice has earthly roots which demand earthly cures. It is unChristian to stand idly by and see decent people being exploited,' he replied.

'Those blacks are savages,' a colleague spat, as Chopin's 'Dead March' for the Congo peacekeepers echoed back from thronged Dublin streets.

'It was European greed that killed them,' he expostulated in the shadow of the seventh coffin. His pride in Conor Cruise O'Brien's exposures hardly mitigated the frustration. Even Jimmy reacted to the killing of nationalist leader, Patrice Lumumba. 'The Belgians and the CIA are murderous bastards, and our government doesn't say "Boo!" Neutrality, my arse. We're just another little Hawaii.'

Ted Sinnott had his own recipe for change, after the censor thwarted his efforts to read *The Country Girls*. 'Bless me father, for I thought of enjoying Edna O'Brien. It's a quare fucking place where we can't even read our own writers, let alone Ernest Hemingway.

'Instead of taking over the North, I think it's time they commandeered us. Then we'd have literature – and condoms and divorce!'

He felt increasingly stifled. Unable to read the books he wanted, scarcely existing on his weekly fiver of which a third went on rent, surrounded by social injustice about which Church nor government nor anyone else cared. There was no hope; only England offered freedom and the opportunity of a decent life.

His parents arrived unexpectedly. His mother was quieter than usual. 'I can see you're still discontented.'

His father looked around the bedsit. 'We all have to put up with things we don't like. It's not easy for me, keeping order without favouritism among people I see every day. I could have gone to America with my sisters but I felt I had a responsibility to stay. There's more to life than money. You have to make your own decisions but think carefully before you do anything rash.'

Jimmy disinterred his *Irish Times*. 'Did you see Myles taking the piss out of the Corporation over that Henry Moore?'

Despite the medieval inertia, Dublin had spirit. Sean O'Faolain and Patrick Kavanagh fulminated against censorship. Myles na Gopaleen's *Irish Times* column was irradiated with fantastic satire. Crippled Christy Brown painted pictures with his left foot. The Behans were wordy spendthrifts rarely out of the headlines. The Christles invested their vitality in study, sport and politics. Early school-leaver Seamus was a champion fiddler, boxer, county hurler and footballer.

Seldom off the streets or without his portfolio, wide-brimmed Harry Kernoff flitted from pub to pub before settling down for a Nearys nightcap. By cutting down on winter briquettes, he managed to buy some Dublin studies from the equally impecunious artist. The same woodcuts got bar manager Paddy O'Brien into trouble. 'Mr McDaid was doing the books one evening. When I told him that the two and sixpence entry was for *A Bird Never Flew on One Wing*, he went bananas. "Haven't we got a flock of Kernoff's bloody birds upstairs already?" he said, banging the counter.'

At an Eden Quay cinema queue, sports-jacketed Brendan Behan went around with the hat of an ageing busker. 'If yous don't contribute, I'll sing myself!' And sing he did anyway, a traffic-stopping Gaelic rendition of the 'Cúileann'. A bus conductor leaned out as the playwright padded in with Beatrice to Bergman's *Wild Strawberries*. 'Me life on you, Brendan. You never lost it.'

He witnessed Brendan in full flight at the Gaiety premiere of his brother Dominic's *Posterity Be Damned*. The playwright shouted at departing Legion of Mary protesters: 'The only book you gobshites ever read is the Bible. And that's more erotic than any modern play. Fucking crawthumpers.' An emperor in his gilded box, Brendan gave a boxer's salute to the curtain call cast and bellowed into the national anthem with his parents and Beatrice.

Mr Hegarty, the chief clerk, looked across the timesheets next morning in untheatrical Kingsbridge. 'I see your friend Behan's disgracing himself again with drink and blasphemy.'

Mary King of Parsons knew the playwright better. 'Brendan was weaned on drink. The wonder's not that he drinks so much, but that he can find the discipline to refine his column, plays and poetry. A punishment for such a gregarious person! Hopefully Beatrice will save him from the dangers of the drink, the diabetes and those hangers-on.' The Galway lady dusted her corner bookshelves. 'Unlike others with literary pretensions, Brendan has no airs and graces. His heart's on his sleeve, his writing's part of his great need to communicate. Thanks to his parents, he's remarkably well read. His Paris adventures have kept him abreast of the latest movements. His understanding of modern literature would put many academics to shame: he's the only one directly in the tradition of Joyce. Brendan takes his writing seriously and he was very sad when *Borstal Boy* was banned. He told us that he'd returned the taxman's demand: "You cannot tax me on books you have banned!"'

The Parsons lady was understanding of his own impecunious condition. Unknown to proprietor May O'Flaherty, many an unaffordable volume spent a night in Upper Mount Street. Little did either of them know that one day he would repay her and the Parsons staff with a special treat. Not only was Mary friendly with all the writers, she knew the identity of their books' characters. He enjoyed a singular advantage when the discussion turned to literature in Bartley Dunnes.

For all her Catholic decorum, May O'Flaherty could not conceal her crush on Patrick Kavanagh but it was Mary who knew him best. 'Patrick and Brendan, what a contrast! But no one did any favours for poor Patrick when he came to town wearing what Brendan unkindly described as seven-league boots. His seriousness and rural reticence also denied him Brendan's easy access to the journalists. It was his brother, Peter, who kept Patrick going, though I always thought that *Kavanagh's Weekly* and the court case were expensive diversions. For Dublin, that *Leader* story was harmless enough; it wasn't worth the action which wrecked Patrick's health. If he hadn't got that university lectureship I don't think he would have survived at all. Patrick's never received the credit his work deserves. There's a lot of talk about culture but it's always about the past. He and Brendan may have to die before their worth is acknowledged. But maybe things are changing! Last week, Patrick rushed in to borrow five shillings for a taxi. "I'm going to the Archbishop's palace, I must arrive in style." Nothing could hide his pride at this unexpected recognition.'

The Monaghan poet was one of his mother's favourites. But her *grá* sprang from political rather than literary criteria. She sympathised with Patrick since the libel trial in which his cross-examiner had been the Fine Gael leader, John A Costello. 'May God forgive him; poor Patrick was never the same after the grilling that Free State philistine gave him.'

He discovered that heroes have feet of clay when one night he met both literary protagonists. Emboldened by wine, he sought out Brendan Behan to sign a *Irish Press* photograph he had specially purchased. Patrick Kavanagh nursed a counter pint in high-ceilinged McDaids. 'What are you going to see him for, he's a quare fella?' he eyed him through a broken spectacles lens. 'Stay here and have a drink.' He was surely the only person in the world who would decline a drink from Ireland's best and poorest poet. But, on Paddy O'Brien's advice, he headed through Baggot Street's flying cherry blossoms for Mooneys on the bridge. The playwright was on full song. 'Come back in an hour, can't you see I have an audience to attend to? Now, angst is boring and played out.' He turned back to his wife and two English reporters. He waited under the clock at closing time, when Brendan emerged with Beatrice. The playwright gave him a brown paper bag of stout to carry, while he himself cradled three bottles of spirits. Beatrice superintended them across Baggot Street bridge, where Brendan stopped to serenade Parsons deserted shop:

God bless you Mary King and Miss O'Flaherty too.
If it wasn't for the lovely Beattie, I'd marry the pair of
you.

When they reached Herbert Street, Brendan was in an even more romantic mood. He took his arm and tried to divert him down the lane. 'Where will we do it?' He realised then that Patrick Kavanagh had not been referring to the writer's play. Beatrice caught her husband's sleeve. 'Enough of that, now. You come back to-morrow when he's better behaved.'

A grazing pony surveyed him from the convent paddock opposite, as he gingerly traversed number fifteen's steps the following afternoon. Instead of the wild man of the previous night, a sandalled Benedictine opened the heavy door: 'Oh, it's yourself, come in.' Flanked by marble reliefs of classical males and females, a long remove from Walton and Mountjoy gaols, Brendan padded ahead into the book-strewn back room. He had been checking his *Irish Press* column under a calendar inscribed by Liam O'Flaherty: 'Long live the Workers' Republic.'

'We'll be multilingual, I'll write in both Irish and English!' He sat down at the writing desk and picked up a fountain pen.

Light flooded in the generous window; a mews house teetered at the end of the garden. 'Could Beatrice sign too?'

'She's taken Beamish – that's the cat, not the drink – to the vet. Call back again. Sure we're not going to America.'

'*Do Bhreandán ó Bhreandán eile*' took pride of place on his mantelpiece but the manner of its acquisition was never completely ventilated. A patriot rashly disparaged the photograph: 'Behan's only a drunken guttersnipe. He disgraces our country wherever he goes; he deserves to be banned.'

'Bloody typical.' He replaced the photograph. 'Too lazy to study his work, all you understand is his gallivanting. If you read his 'Last Grey Eagle over the Blaskets' poem, you wouldn't talk like that. While all you greenies are hanging on to revolutionaries' frayed coat-tails, he's changing the consciousness of our race with plays like *The Quare Fella* and *The Hostage*. He's built bridges between us and the country he first went to blow up; he's shown us how to throw away the shoulder chips and crutches of dogma and xenophobia. His humour and talent are enlarging our lives and giving us the courage finally to think as individuals. He's a civilised and humane man. Read him, for Jasus' sake!'

His acquaintance hastened away. 'Next, you'll be a bloody

beatnik. You'd be better off over the water,' he shouted from a safe distance.

He harboured his own artistic dreams and wrote every morning before going to work. He discovered that composing was more difficult than criticism. But twelve and sixpence each for some *Ireland's Own* stories led to Jack White's acceptance of a Dublin feature for the *Irish Times*. In the same paper as Myles! *Gaieté Parisienne* stimulated the three pounds celebration of his thirty-shilling cheque in Bartley Dunnes.

Politics, however, took precedence over literature. He wrote an *Irish Socialist* series on how the idle rich grew even wealthier on the profits generated by the exploited workers. 'I'll tell you what an Irish socialist is.' Jimmy banged his glass on Sinnotts marble counter. 'His motto is "What's yours is mine and what's mine is my own." And who's exploiting who? Have these fuckers paid you yet?'

Ireland was getting him down. Another book by Frank O'Connor was banned; nothing would ever change. He would have to make some major decisions, sooner rather than later. 'There is not one party here of the Left,' he complained to Joe Christle, who had helped him with his Algerian placards.

The man whom he regarded as Ireland's Castro tossed his black quiff. 'You're just looking for an excuse to leave. But don't go. I may have important news one of these days.'

10

Joe Christle's conversion to peace wasn't an overnight event. He was arrested for misappropriating explosives, allegedly used later in the destruction of such British relics as the Gough monument and Nelson's Pillar. While invoicing at Kingbridge, he himself had heard the crump of Gough's early-morning demise. 'I fear the horse has lost more than his appendages this time,' Paddy Condon, the foreman, called in from the door. He went down to the Bridewell for his friend's court appearance. There was an unexpected bonus. It was the morning that the Pike's Alan Simpson was charged with indecency for staging *The Rose Tattoo*. Shouts and singing charged the air, as the anti-Establishment groups joined forces outside the grey building. 'Up the Republic! Down with censorship!'

Joe's high cheekbones dominated the courtroom. But despite looking more magisterial than the judge, he was remanded in custody. Key witnesses later developed amnesia and the charges were dropped. Like compatriot Pamela, wife of earlier revolutionary Lord Edward Fitzgerald, there was little singing for Joe's wife. 'Entrez, but careful of the baby – and the water.' Mimi's enchanting accent seemed sadly misplaced, as she swopped buckets under the leaking Raglan Road roof.

Forsaking violence for left-wing politics, Joe sacrificed his ESB promotion chances to organise its underpaid manual workers. He set up the National Students' Council, whose members underlined Ireland's Hugh Lane Collection claim by relieving the Tate Gallery of Berthe Morisot's *Jour d'Eté*. A consummate political animal, Joe turned to him following a discussion with some farmers' sons: 'In all our argument, did you once hear me use the word "socialism"?' He would hardly have been as diplomatic had he heard Brendan Behan's disparagement of the Gough monument destruction:

> This is the way our heroes today
> Are challenging England's might.

With a stab in the back and a midnight attack
On a horse that can't even shite.

Great was his joy when Joe summoned him to Bewleys one summer morning. 'I'm standing in the election!'

'You're joking?'

His host fixed an eye on him. 'I don't have a reputation for comedy.'

Never had butter balls looked so sweet, nor roasting coffee beans smelled so appetising. Hope replaced despair, James McKenna's *The Scattering* could still be about other unfortunate emigrants. An intervention from above: he could stay to work for a better Ireland. 'The mother's been working overtime,' he informed the bemused candidate. They discussed the publicity and letter-writing campaign. One of the leaflets included Joe's photograph with the Bishop of Kerry. His mother, who knew Joe through the cycling, was impressed. 'A fine Irishman, with great energy and a powerful mind, God bless him, but isn't it a pity he wouldn't join Fianna Fáil? Maybe you'd tell him that instead of squandering his energy on the outside, he'd have a great future within the party. He'd be a minister in no time. Then he could make all the changes he wants.'

The candidate permitted a rare smile. 'Remind your mother what happened to Noël Browne.'

Headlined by a rising sun motif, Joe's manifesto proclaimed: 'No country can be ruled from the grave. The Civil War, which formed our main political parties, belongs to the dustbin of history. Those who try to keep it alive have lost touch with the interests of the people. While our rulers argue about history, unemployment is at record levels. Education and health care should be a right for everyone but only one in 20,000 working-class families progresses to university. Practically every street and family has been hit by the scourge of emigration. The equivalent of the entire population of Dublin has left in the past fifteen years alone. It is time for political action by our younger generation. The vested political stranglehold can be smashed by your vote!'

Joe stood in Crumlin and Drimnagh, where his family still lived. 'Crumlin has over 40,000 people, yet there's neither general hospital nor public library nor park,' he himself reminded voters, before cycling back nightly to his more elegant Georgian quarter. 'And no secondary school, swimming pool or playing field for your children! When did you last see your TD? Why vote for someone who only appears at election time and then disappears for four more years to his own comfortable suburb? Joe lives here, he'll always be available.'

He had a falling-out with Jimmy over the election. 'Pissing against the wind. Do you think those fuckers in power will let your man even have a whiff of the Dáil? They'll destroy him; wait and see. And should he by any chance get in, you can rest assured he'll soon turn out to be just the same as them.'

The householders proved more receptive. They were inspired by the scholastic achievements of the candidate from their own background. Window posters sprouted throughout the constituency. 'For the first time, one of our own who cares. Someone who knows about our problems, someone who's not afraid.'

He was uplifted to be involved in something so practical, at last living a life he believed in. A campaign which would finally pave the way to social justice, in contrast to the empty pulpit and political rhetoric. Hopes and feelings ran high, placarded heads of opposing factions tumbled in unity into the canal. Framed in yellow and black, Joe's confident profile soon lined the waterway.

'Noël Browne was just one man. We're organised. We've the bastards on the run,' growled UCD's longest-serving student, Harry O'Toole-King. The Bogart lookalike was rumoured to have taken part in the raids on RUC stations.

'Were you in Armagh?' he asked Harry one night.

'I went there on a pilgrimage.' He lit a cigarette from the one he had just finished.

He tried again. 'Why did you do it?'

Harry did his impression of a laugh. 'For kicks – shag-all else to do in this dozy town.'

The *Emperor Concerto* alleviated the exhaustion of canvassing and debate. Billy Fogarty, who had been involved in the Tate Gallery heist, poured tea in Carrow Road: 'Beethoven's the boy for reformed hard men.'

'How now brown cow?' mocked Harry.

Seldom without a volume of poetry and always impeccably

attired, Byronic Billy attracted many females to their camp. He dusted a fireside chair one night: 'Sure, I was merely a minder at the Tate that April morning. Hogan was the brains. We'd studied the form and knew the movements of all the attendants. As we weren't sure how the picture was secured, we became the first Tate aficionados to pack both a screwdriver and hack-saw! But it was only hanging from a hook. Hogan simply lifted it off and walked out with it under his arm, while I took up the rear. I lit a fag outside, like Jimmy Cagney, and stood ready to anchor the revolving door should any guard come racing out. But there wasn't even a whisper of commotion. It was surreal, you might say. I was tempted to go back for a Dali! We were so disconcerted by this inactivity that when the cab driver asked: "Where to, guv?" we couldn't think of a destination. Our efforts led to the Lane pictures being returned to Dublin. Four hundred politicos and arties sipped bubbly on the unveiling night, but that proved more difficult to crack than the gallery. "Where's your official invitation?" a guard asked me. "I didn't need one for the Tate, I reminded him.'

As election day neared many were convinced of the new candidate's imminent success. But Joe's mushrooming popularity proved to be his downfall. The Fianna Fáil party activists hated him for hijacking their republican credentials. He overheard a Fine Gael official: 'Forget about the Fianna Fáilers. It's Christle and those young boyos who are the real danger. They mean business.'

'Better dead than red.' A whispering campaign commenced. The local hierarchy rose to the occasion. On the Sunday before the election, the parish priest turned to his congregation: 'You know we do not interfere in political matters. But it is our duty to advise you that there is a communist-inspired individual running in this election. I know I need hardly remind you of your Christian responsibility to reject any Godless political philosophy.'

With only one new candidate standing, the identity of the guilty party was obvious. Two days later, Joe polled almost as much as the regular TDs but the timely pulpit intervention succeeded. He failed by three hundred votes to take a seat. There would be no TD. No celebration. No future. Hermetically sealed Ireland would never change. The *fáinne*, Pioneer pin and dark suits were invincible. It was time to head for Dún Laoghaire pier.

Cliff Richard's 'The Young Ones' enlivened a Stephen's Green basement party a week later, before an argument erupted. 'Fucking Red!' were the last words he heard, as a bottle smashed into his head. On the street outside, a Garda helped him pick broken glass from his bloodied hair. As he staggered past the Merrion Row corner houses, the whispering ivy seemed to confirm that it was time to leave.

'How ironic that your mother's two sons have to flee to satanic England to escape her heroes' ineptitude,' Jimmy chortled.

'It's hardly going to be easy for me: the first major decision in my own life.'

There was also the social embarrassment. Emigration, like tuberculosis in the forties, carried a stigma. 'How's Brendan doing? Is he moving up the ladder in Kingsbridge?'

Jimmy treated him to a ticket to *La Bohème*. They met Ronaldo outside the Gaiety afterwards. The singer slapped Jimmy on the back. 'I need a woman.'

'By God, you've got to hand it to the continentals. We're just serfs here, always waiting to be told what to do, with limbo, purgatory and hell just around the corner. Maybe you're doing the right thing, escaping the land of guilt while you're young. At thirty-five, I've left it too fucking late. Let's try the ATS Club, we might meet someone amenable there.' A face peered through the Nassau Street grille. 'Holy Jasus! A dollar for a drink; the last time I'll bring you here.' Jimmy headed to the toilet. A slim blonde in a low-cut blouse emerged from the shadows. 'You look like a fella who knows how to handle a girl.' She put her arm inside his; it was like a French film at the Astor. He proffered his last five shillings for another Martini. He wondered if she was blonde all over. But as his hopes rose and she lit a cigarette, two sailors staggered in. 'Ah Jaysus, me ould mates! I must go and say hello.'

With nothing left for cider, he kicked the autumn leaves on a Ranelagh evening walk with Gallagher. 'All You Need Is Love'. As they passed the lighted suburban windows, they met the daughter of a band leader. They walked her to her door. To his embarrassment, she kissed him: 'Happy trip!'

'If he'd more kisses, maybe he wouldn't be going at all.' Gallagher offered his own cheek.

'Ah, mister, stay here!' cried the basement girls on the evening of their last spin. 'When are you coming back? Our daddy's over in London. Will you bring him back with you?'

'I'll try, though I can't promise. But how would you like an extra ride this evening?'

Their shrieks rang through the quiet street and shook the fanlight's bones to life. Mrs Scott hobbled to the door to investigate. 'What about me?' He sold his racing cycle and brought Gallagher and Jimmy to Nearys for a farewell drink. Harry O'Toole-King and Colm Christle were leaving. Harry wagged a yellow finger: 'None of that political gunge. Admit you're going for the floosies and not Karl Marx. Don't forget to practise safe sex. Don't tell 'em where you live!'

Harry Kernoff, his wide brim and portfolio were in their usual Gaiety corner. A halo surrounded Stephen Behan's hat as he puffed his pipe at the Chatham end. 'If I'd my fiddle, I'd play you a nice going-away air and my wife would sing it.' Dublin's Dr Gachet insisted on buying him a drink. With a thumb in his waistcoat pocket, Stephen gave them his definition of Ireland: 'A place or state of punishment, where some souls suffer until the time comes when they can emigrate.'

Stephen accompanied them down Grafton Street. He had earlier had an argument with a Legion of Mary man. 'Morality here is confined to the erogenous zones.

'I've the greatest respect for unmarried mothers. What can any priest or Legion man know about a mother's responsibilities? If I ever hear anyone giving out about a poor girl again, I'll set one of the sons on him. But I'd better be getting on myself or a strong woman at home will be making an unmarried father out of me.' He tipped his hat and turned into Suffolk Street, leaving a fragrance of pipe smoke in his genial wake.

He hired a car and loaded everything he would not be taking away with him. Clothes, blankets, cycling trophies and most of his books. His mother came to the porch. 'You're going after all?' She forestalled his well-rehearsed speech, as if she had known all along. How simple everything seemed, once a decision had been accepted. For the first time, he sensed a distance from her. His father was mopping up the crumbs with a piece of crust after finishing his boiled egg. His mother fetched a third cup from the dresser. 'He's leaving.'

He sipped the last tea he would ever have in their Toomevara home. 'The London Underground office is a step up the ladder. The experience will guarantee something much more rewarding on my return.'

He went down the garden to give his parents time to talk alone. November greyness had taken root. He could see the birds nests through the bare hedges. The ash tree retained the kink he had made years before. In the far corner lay an earthenware pipe. A ghostly Chum commanded: 'Surrender, Gunner, we've got you covered.' He stopped at the skeletal lilac tree. No more May altars! One day when he had sorted out his life, he would return to savour its scent and this oasis of beauty and toil. He most certainly would. He closed the garden gate.

'You'd better go; 'twill soon be dark.' His mother wrapped up a brown loaf, together with a medal and some prayer leaflets. He took the parcel; the bread was still hot. 'I'll write immediately before and after I leave Dublin.' His father seemed older as he hung back in the porch: 'If things don't work out, you'll always have a home here.' It was the first time he had seen him cry. A mile outside the village, he was forced to steer the Anglia on to the grass verge. Floods of tears drowned his shirt and jacket. Convulsions of grief and rage gripped his body. In the quicksand of his frustration, he pounded the steering wheel, oblivious of passing traffic or former neighbours.

'Fuck Ireland!' He wept for the pain of parting and the infliction of such sorrow on his parents, even if he didn't love them. He cried for the lack of that love, and for his isolation from Church, state and indifferent compatriots. 'Fuck Ireland!' he shouted. He loved every blade of his country's green grass. Every flower, every river, every hill, valley and monastic ruin. Maybe, like those monks who had also left, he would discover and experience some real truth. Maybe he would find love. He could only hope. He could only go. He wept for his lack of courage; he was afraid, going alone into his new life.

How long he lay across the steering wheel he never knew, before he finally pulled the car back on to the road. He raced up to third gear at Ollatrim Cross, to which his mother and he had often walked for Cleary's buttermilk. Mikey Troy and Mattie

Shinnors waved from the shadow of the old mill. Two kindly men, whose decency illuminated their sometimes dour and distrustful village. As he sped past McClellands, he thought about what else he would have to do before he took Tuesday's boat train. He wiped his eyes. The radio played the space-age hit, 'Telstar'. Rain bucketed down the chimney and drenched the bonfire of discarded notes and aborted stories. He unstuck the photographs of Fidel Castro, Gamal Nasser and Henry Moore, and carefully packed the signed Brendan Behan.

'You're doing the right thing. Have courage!' Muriel kissed him as she left for a Trinity lecture. Mrs Scott knocked. Johnny the postman had delivered a final letter from Tipperary. 'I'm sending ten shillings to buy hankies and a collar. I hope you will be happy and settle down quickly. I hope I was a good mother and that you'll realise that everything I did for you was meant for your good.' The caretaker's teenage daughter hummed 'What Do You Want if You Don't Want Money?', as she returned his deposit. 'You're going the wrong way. Adam Faith's over from London, I've a ticket for Friday.'

Gallagher helped him to carry the two suitcases, one loaded with clothes, the other with his wireless and favourite books. Jimmy held an umbrella against the rain and flying leaves as they trudged down Merrion Square and into Westland Row. Was it a gateway to heaven or to hell? Too late now.

'The bloody boat will sink, I've never carried such weight.' Gallagher paused opposite Wilde's birthplace. He surveyed the broad steps to the train station: 'This is where the bands greeted the returning 1916 prisoners.'

Jimmy furled the umbrella. 'Since when a million have gone in the opposite direction.'

City and rural accents blended, relatives and friends shuffled around the fogged-up windows. Late arrivals hoisted aboard cardboard suitcases secured with leather straps and binding twine. Parents said goodbye to sons. A young mother held up two children for a final kiss: 'You'll come back with Santa Claus, daddy?' Some had no one to see them off. Weeds sprouted from what could have been beautiful brickwork opposite. He leaned out of the carriage window. 'Moths galore and enough for vino every night; we might be over soon ourselves,' Gallagher encouraged them above the hissing steam.

A shrill whistle reverberated around the cathedral-like station which boasted a new congregation each night. The dark crowd stepped back; pigeons panicked from their lofty perches. 'Good luck!' Jimmy sent drops flying from the umbrella. With a succession of jolts, the train lurched into the darkness. The reality of flight hit him like a punch to the stomach. Now, there was no turning back! Was he mad to be leaving? Had he made a horrible and irreversible blunder? What right did he have to inflict such anguish on his parents? Would the English prove to be as awful as his mother had described them? Remembering that this was how Æ and O'Casey had also flown, did little to alleviate his loneliness and anxiety. He saluted his friends until they and all those parents were matchstick figures on the receding platform.

The train accelerated past the canal basin and the jutting mast of a long-submerged ship. He pulled the leather strap and closed the window. Dust rose as he sank into his seat under a sepia picture of the Meeting of the Waters. A man looked down on him from the corner: 'Twill be a good crossing this night. Your first going away, is it?' Listening to the Connemara giant who had been forced to flee for work, he cringed at the indulgence of going merely for freedom and new ideas. Other passengers sat silently, big-eyed cows for the slaughter.

It was seven o'clock on a November evening. But a twilight like any other down in Tipperary, as his village prepared for another night around de Valera's turf fires. Just about now, his parents would be getting on their knees for the rosary. Tonight, he and his fellow-traveller would be included in those prayers for the emigrants.

11

'I know you are not a fence-sitter. But under no circumstances risk prison with those Ban the Bomb weirdos,' Joe Christle wrote. It was the height of the Cold War and nuclear stockpiling; Armageddon beckoned. Bertrand Russell's seemed to be the only voice of reason. The philosopher who had sacrificed both freedom and position for his pacifist beliefs launched a campaign of civil disobedience to highlight the dangers. 'Every day, a trivial accident, a failure to distinguish a meteor from a bomber, may cause a nuclear war which, in all likelihood, will put an end to man and all higher forms of animal life.'

Two months after arriving in London, he joined the Campaign for Nuclear Disarmament. He rashly informed his former mentor that he would embrace its protests. 'Your loyalty must be to Ireland. Keep your feet on the ground. Waste no energy on such ineffectual action.'

High on distance, he retaliated: 'If the world goes up in smoke, there will be no Ireland.'

'This is a Circle Line train, stopping at Sloane Square, Victoria, St James's Park and Westminster. Mind the step.'

London at first alarming sight was a jungle. An impregnable overcrowded maze from seething London Bridge to pin-striped St James's. People stared at him as he whistled 'The Blackbird'. 'It's difficult to settle down; women are the least of my worries. This place is a colossus, a merry-go-round whose speed repels all boarders. They even have moving stairs. The Central Line is thirty miles long, Ballybrophy did not prepare me for the perpetual motion of Clapham Junction,' he wrote to Jimmy. 'Misery-go-round might be more appropriate, with the preoccupied pagans of my mother's nightmares and their hardly understandable accents: "Watcha' mate, Steady on guv." Well-programmed ants, they cram the red buses and dusty Tube as they rush to and fro from early morning until late at night.'

Night-time was equally intimidating, despite the irridescence of Piccadilly and Leicester Square. Looking at the relaxed faces inside pub and restaurant windows, he wondered how he could ever crack that social life. The calm superiority of the English deflated his high hopes; he felt a conspicuous outsider with his thick brogue, unfashionable clothes and clumsy Irish ways. Taxis took couples to assignations or home, Acker Bilk's 'Stranger on the Shore' rang out from all the coffee bars. 'No blacks, no Irish.' It took a week's wading through the advertisements before he found his first wallpapered Earl's Court bedsit. Through the wafer-thin partition, he heard the next-door lovers: 'Rupert, push harder.' His landlady compounded his frustration by purloining the *Ireland's Own* pen-pal replies.

The lingering evidence of the city's war wounds shocked him. Craters and crude buttresses mutilated terraces, a row of pre-fabs housed Blitz homeless at the end of his road. Lonely widows peered over bare aspidistras; disfigured men busked outside tube stations. Bombs had obliterated the area around St Paul's. The elderly caretaker of St Giles's church limped across the weed-covered rubble: 'A few seconds destroyed the culture of centuries; there's all that remains of Milton's grave.' As he picked his way through the ruins, he guiltily recalled his anti-British mother. In blissful ignorance of Belsen and Auschwitz, and with selective amnesia as regards Germany's occupation of most of Europe, she had not mourned at Britain's Dunkirk retreat. 'The Germans never did us any harm, didn't they help Roger Casement in 1916?' But his life jumped up a gear, as he grappled with London's fantastic diversity. Stirred by the roar of the printing presses, he felt the presence of Charles Lamb and Dickens as he watched the human tide flow by in Fleet Street. He remembered Nenagh railway bridge, as he paid his respects to Oliver Goldsmith in the oasis of the Temple churchyard.

The city pulsated with possibilities, political organisations, attractive women. No one enquired about his business. The floodgates of enlightenment opened wide. Mr Scudamore of the Earl's Court Bookshop reached into the window for *Borstal Boy*: 'Indifferent cash flow is the only censor here, old boy.' He revelled in unbanned de Maupassant, O'Faolain, ascetic McGahern and new acquaintances Hermann Hesse and Arthur Koestler. '*Borstal*

Boy is mighty and the women are willing,' he boasted on a postcard to Ted Sinnott.

At a tanner a paperback, his library mushroomed. Bent over the single gas ring, he finally discovered James Joyce. 'I will not serve that in which I no longer believe.'

'Tara via Holyhead indeed,' he laughed through tears of joy for the writer's courage and translucence. He was no longer alone; how right he had been to reject phoney answers. 'To live, to err, to fall, to triumph, to recreate life out of life.' Socialism was not a dirty word in London. From clear-visioned Connolly, he progressed to Marx and Engels. 'The history of all hitherto existing society is the history of the class struggle,' he educated Jimmy. 'Peace, universal brotherhood; it sounds more like Groucho Marx or a bottle you'd buy at Nenagh fair.'

'You and Ireland will never go anywhere. I am trying.'

A postcard of Blessed Oliver Plunkett arrived. 'You share your mater's inordinate need for faith. Get a long wick for your lantern. Regards, Harpo.'

His mother persisted: 'You won't find many churches over there. But at least say your rosary every night, and don't let yourself be used by the persecutors of Cardinal Mindszenty.' She would have been appalled as his last scapular lifeline to Rome was replaced by the new voodoo protection of a communist-party card. With all the convert's conviction, he braved the South African rednecks outside Earl's Court station each Friday night. He paraded his paperware like the barefoot *Herald a' Mail* urchins of his first Dublin visit: 'Peace and Socialism – read the *Daily Worker!*'

As the Queen left the motor show, a passer-by shoved a pound note in his hand: 'You're a brave lad.' He felt anything but courageous when four Irish-Americans surrounded him. 'You're a disgrace to holy Ireland. Peddling Soviet propaganda while enjoying the benefits of the Free World. Why don't you go and live in Russia?'

'This is about economics, not religion, America or Russia. It's your government which is disgracing civilisation, abusing all that technology and energy to slaughter Vietnamese peasants.'

'You're just a brainwashed lackey.'

'You're the ones who don't ask questions. Why don't you stand back and reappraise the opinions you were reared into? Read Marx or Engels, you might just think differently.'

The Yanks were not in a mood for change. The biggest of the group grabbed the papers. 'We're saving Vietnam from the Reds. We don't have to read anyone; we've seen the Berlin wall. You're just a traitorous Soviet stooge but you won't pervert anyone else tonight.'

'Help me,' he shouted at a group of passing youths. But in London people minded their own business.

At last, he would have some exciting news for Jimmy! Fellow-comrade Jennifer invited him back to her bedsit after a party meeting. 'I'll change into something more comfortable.' She left him to sip wine under her posters of Yevtushenko and the Beatles. Jennifer reappeared in an appropriately red and revealing nightdress. How could someone so elfin have such enormous breasts?

When he put his arm around her, she opened his trousers. He immediately tried to remove her pants. 'You're not very experienced, are you? You've got to prepare a woman for sex. You don't rush in like a navvy. Now, touch me here. That's it. Gently first.'

'Don't touch *me* there.'

'Crumbs! You haven't done it for a long time. It's like a fountain.' She tried to stem the flow. 'But don't worry. We'll have you big again in no time. Patience is the first requisite of a good lover. You must go slowly with a woman. You build her up. Now put your hand here. Oh, that's nice.'

A comprehensive sex manual completed his education. He soon confidently chased au pairs with fellow-lodger Alief. French divorcee Danielle took him to the heights of Bizet-accompanied ecstasy and afterwards introduced him to Sartre and de Beauvoir. With his mind-expanding books, his new faith and his growing boudoir skills, he had at last arrived. Vladimir Jean Paul Don Juan, late of Toomevara American papers please copy. But he had his come-uppance in a nocturnal Cromwell Road establishment. The Tipperary-accented receptionist tugged at her shorts: 'Aren't you the fella that won the big bike race in Templemore?'

And nemesis swiftly followed the realisation of a favourite fantasy. A slim girl introduced herself at his ticket office. Rush hour was over; her spectacles tapped against the glass as they chatted.

The grille framed her dark hair again the following evening. 'Where to?' he joked.

'How about your place?'

A few nights later, a thickset Cockney appeared at the window: 'Are you Brendan?' London was a great place; people were getting to know him already. 'Yes, but who are you?' The man reached in, grabbed him by the tie and almost pulled him out through the aperture. 'I'll fucking tell you who I am, you Paddy cunt. I'm the geezer whose fiancée you slept with.'

'I don't know you or your fiancée, put me down.'

'You know Mary?'

'Mary O'Brien?'

The man gave his tie another yank; his head hit the window again. 'That's my fucking fiancée. I'll fucking kill you, you four-eyed prick.' Mary's Irish-born mother arrived at speed. 'Are you a Catholic, you bastard?' she shouted through the grille. A London Tansport policeman heard the commotion. 'Now you know what it was like at Tyburn, Pat.' His protector helped undo his tie, before ensuring him a safe passage through dusty platforms to the Earl's Court line.

He didn't neglect his responsibility to save the world, joining Bertrand Russell and fifty thousand others on the annual three-day Aldermaston March. His guru's white hair was tossed all ways as he towered over the sea of banners in Trafalgar Square. 'If the world could live for a few generations without war, war would come to seem as absurd as duelling has come to seem to us. I say to the Big Powers, remember your humanity and forget the rest. If you do so, the way is open to a new paradise: if you cannot, nothing lies before you but universal death.' He pushed his way to Nelson's plinth to pay his respects. The octogenarian clutched his papers: 'One of my few Irish disciples!' When the police later charged a group of marchers, he was thrown to the ground under a heap of bodies. As he regained his feet he was arrested and thrown into a police van. 'Red Bertie won't help you now.' A constable removed his helmet.

True to his Leftist faith, he affirmed rather than swear on the Bible in Bow Street court. 'You believe in Canon Collins and Bertrand Russell but not in the Bible?' Judge Barraclough raised a benevolent eyebrow.

'I haven't done anything wrong, I cannot pay any fine.'

'You're like your mother; all your idols are jailbirds. I think you won't be happy until you become one yourself,' Jimmy wrote.

As he awaited his court appeal, it occurred to him that he still hadn't found a compatible companion. And this in the land of such forward women. He longed for a real girlfriend, someone to share his life with and not just his bed.

'Jasus! You're in paradise. Enjoy the fruit. Sign nothing,' Jimmy advised.

But one spring afternoon, the girl of his dreams unexpectedly materialised in an Earl's Court coffee bar. 'He's from my country.' A young brunette leaned over the article on Nelson Mandela and the Treason Trial. 'Of course, I hate the way the Africans are treated. That's one of the reasons I left. I'm not as tall as you,' she observed, as he stood up to shake hands.

'But you're much better looking and you have very nice dimples. Will you stay for a cappuccino?'

Divina was a refugee from a South African step-parent relationship. 'You're very pretty. Are you quite sure you're not engaged?' He supplied a censored version of his last romantic encounter.

'Where Have All the Flowers Gone?' Divina and he were soon inseparable. His spirit soared with the joy of sharing and communicating, and of sex without guilt. In the nearby Odeon, they savoured Cecil Parker, Peter Sellers, Alec Guinness: 'Mrs Wilberforce, I believe you have rooms to rent.' They held hands and marched on all the anti-apartheid and anti-war demonstrations. He took her to Brighton and to the Crystal Palace motor races. He introduced her to Irish literature and showed her where the Yeats family had lived in nearby Eardley Crescent.

'Would you like to move in with me?' he stammered one day.

'I thought you'd never ask!'

Divina transformed his drab room into a home. As well as exotic African dishes, mouth-watering mango and guava, she introduced him to Mediterranean cuisine. 'My father brought many recipes back from the war in Italy.' His life blossomed. Divina jettisoned his studs, detachable collars and darned socks and introduced him to the casual freedom of jeans: 'We're in the twentieth century now;

men don't wear braces any more.'

Previously alone with his books, he had envied the Sou Sol teenagers who chatted so confidently as they listened to 'Bobby's Girl' and 'Let's Dance'. Now he had someone to show off and talk with in the Earl's Court coffee bar. 'The Beatles or Billy J. Kramer?' he shouted ostentatiously, as he inserted a shilling in the rainbow-hued jukebox. He informed his mother that he had met a nice girl and was thinking of getting married. 'It takes a long time to get to know someone. Wait for a while, before you think of bothering a priest.' Fearful that she might attempt to stop them, he and Divina made a booking at Kensington Registry Office. The omens were good, the registrar revealed: 'Your compatriot James Joyce married here in 1931.'

They didn't have many friends in London. Alief was the best man and their landlady the other witness. They opened a bottle of wine in the Abbott Arms. 'What's a lovely young bird like you doing, marrying such an ugly Irishman?' Two Cockney builders rolled their eyes, before contributing another bottle. They took the night train from Euston to a Dublin mini-honeymoon. He made sure his new wife wore a nice suit and not jeans. 'I'm glad you're a Catholic.' After a close inspection, his mother led Divina into a church.

His father congratulated him. 'She's a very nice girl, I hope you'll settle down now.'

Jimmy told Divina about another emigrant who had returned and confessed that his bride had been a prostitute. 'A prostitute?' exclaimed the mother. 'Oh, thanks be to God! For a minute, I thought you said Protestant.' He had finally embarked on an independent existence with his new wife. But his mother still endeavoured to renew his faith. Her weekly Saint Anthony Guided letters concluded with a Sunday Mass reminder and, one night, a Legion of Mary lady called at her behest to Earl's Court. 'God bless you both in your new life. We'll kneel down now and say a decade of the rosary.'

'We'll do no such thing! We're in pagan England now, where no one says the rosary but the sick are properly looked after and old people get a much more Christian pension than they do in holy Ireland.'

'I'm getting very jealous.' Divina recalled the other persistent legionary who, in the intensity of her Dún Laoghaire reconversion zeal, had failed to notice the ship's gangway going up!

The long-awaited day of his appeal arrived. The sun shone as Divina accompanied him to Elephant and Castle court. 'We'll have a coffee by the Serpentine in half an hour,' he assured her.

'We Shall not be Moved'. The judge proved to be less humorous than Mr Barraclough. He peered down over steely half-spectacles. Divina nudged: 'I don't like the look of him.'

The judge's monotone delivery was swift and stern. 'This case is another clear example of how anti-social elements waste the valuable time of Her Majesty's courts. I am tired of seeing our streets turned into scenes of anarchy. If individuals seek political change, they should do so through the ballot box. And the fact that you are influenced by older people who should know better is no excuse. Those who disregard the law will find that the law will discipline them. You will serve one month in Brixton prison.'

'I'm a peace campaigner, not a criminal!'

'Take him down.' The judge closed his file

A court attendant grabbed his shoulder and escorted him to a windowless basement room. Divina was brought down sobbing: 'You're doing something, while others only talk. The month will go quickly enough and I'll be waiting for you when you come out.'

He was in a state of shock. 'Have a coffee for me every day in the Sou Sol,' he stammered.

'Time up.' The policeman opened the door for Divina.

He was handcuffed to a whisky-reeking Scot and pushed into a prison bus. The giant suddenly scratched his head and nearly wrenched his own arm from its socket. As they drove through crowded streets, schoolchildren pointed at the barred bus. A man kissed a girl outside a flower shop. He wondered where Divina was. People were queuing at bus stops. 'You can 'ave my seat,' a young prisoner laughed through the window.

'Put that stupid briefcase down there.'

'Say "Sir" and speak only when you are spoken to. Take off that watch – and that ring.'

Another prison officer led him to the showers. 'Leave that clobber; you won't need it for some time. Now, in there.'

A few minutes later, the warder ordered him out and handed him an blue serge uniform which ballooned around his shoulders. '6315, another of Bertie's *Beat the Clock* wallies.' The man transferred him to a colleague, who escorted him to the top landing. The door clanged behind him. He was in a stone-floored cell with three others. The only touch of colour was the patch of blue sky visible through the bars of the high half-window. 'Bertrand Who?' The top bunk burglar looked down at him. The bunk heaved: 'You swopped a fine – for a month in nick?' Bertrand was to remain his prison name. He thought his unjust incarceration would inspire sympathy but his fellow-inmates were equally innocent. 'We wus framed,' two tattooed Cockneys protested.

He told them that Brixton reminded him of Flannan's. 'Sounds bleedin' awful, Bertrand. What were you in for?'

Taffy the artist became his best friend. The Welshman had knocked down a policeman while scootering a bicycle under the influence along the embankment. 'The first Paddy who went inside for pacifism and not pugilism! But at least your mother will be proud that you're in Terence MacSwiney's last home, even if it's as a lavatory cleaner.'

He stepped back from the gleaming porcelain and copper pipes and explained that his very orthodox mother might not approve, nor his Garda father.

'Have you got any cream?' Taffy surprised him one afternoon. 'I couldn't get to the shops today.' He pointed to the barred window. 'A fruit lorry crashed going down Brixton Hill and us trusties were roped in to clear the mess. I helped myself to my reward.' The artist produced a punnet of bruised strawberries from under his tunic.

'"She loves you, yeah, yeah, yeah",' the warder mimicked the Beatles hit. 'Who's that ugly tart?' He tapped the butter-glued photograph of Valentina Tereshkova.

'The first woman astronaut and she is now circling the earth far above Brixton.'

The warder scraped the newspaper photo off the wall with the end of his cane. 'A fucking Oirish commie, that's all we need. Now, comrade Paddy, scrub down that wall. And do it well. If it's not spotless when I come back, you'll wash it all over again.'

Nameless, numbered and uniformed; prison was an educational

reminder of man's inhumanity to man. Choky was opened at seven each morning, as a warder gave bread and water to the Greek who had bolted at his mother's funeral. The teenager's bed was moved outside so that he could not lie down. The artificial leg of another prisoner lay outside the adjacent cell. The days and weeks seemed endless. How did the others cope with their longer sentences? He cringed for Wilde and fellow-inmate, Stephen Ward. The Profumo scandal scapegoat would soon kill himself rather than endure the degradation of slopping out.

'Only six more days, I'll be there to meet you,' his wife wrote. 'Tim Sheehan, Benjamin and everyone in the party send their congratulations and regards.'

There were other compensations. A brief letter and a signed photograph from his hero, Russell. And the odd treasure he found in the minute library, including *Homage to Catalonia*, which shed a disturbing light on his new Soviet mentors. He would be asking some questions on his release. He rationed *For Whom the Bell Tolls* so that he read the last page on his final afternoon: 'He could feel his heart beating against the pine needle floor of the forest.' But he was glad to walk into the sunshine the following morning. Free and in his own clothes. The door thundered shut behind him. A fresh breeze brushed his face. How bright and vast the sky seemed. Divina ran forward in a bright summer dress. 'We'll take a bus to Victoria, the tube to Earl's Court and then coffee and breakfast in the Sou Sol, courtesy of manageress Gaby!' They walked down Jebb Avenue. Divina clutched her dress as a green Jaguar accelerated past. The car suddenly stopped and reversed. 'Like a lift, Bertrand?' invited one of the Cockney innocents.

'It beats my last conveyance.' He opened a rear door.

They sank into the leather upholstery and sped up Brixton High Street. As they dismounted at Victoria, his former cellmate advised: 'Give dem bleedin' bombs a rest now and look after your lovely missus. And if you ever need good clobber at a special price, call this number.'

Divina needed looking after. Though his status had soared with the Sou Sol habituees, London Transport informed him that they had terminated his employment. Divina pawned her camera; he signed on the dole. Reading enriched the enforced idleness but

George Orwell and Arthur Koestler raised further political doubts. He helped a Portuguese political exile translate a book into English. Antonio worked in a City bank. 'They're looking for a clerk. I'll arrange an interview for you.'

Six breadline weeks later, he started work with a salary considerably higher than his previous one. As he jostled with the throng of bowler-hatted suits at Monument station, he remembered one old lag's observation: 'No need to be snobbish about it, Pat. Crime is just an alternative means of advancement.'

A City headline stopped him in his tracks: 'Behan Critical.' Two days later the diabetes and drinking finally caught up with his hero. He took his first-ever flight to Dublin.

'Thanks for your letter.' Stephen had shadows under his eyes in the Meath Hospital lobby. Kathleen clutched his arm: 'We knew there was no hope. Sure, we all have to go some time. We'll take you up now to see him.'

The Quare Fella was already in his coffin. It was strange to see him so silent; he half expected him to rise and whoop at the success of his practical joke. 'I don't want to die but I'd love to see my funeral,' Brendan had often jested. Now he remained uncharacteristically immobile and reflective, a lock of dark hair crowning his forehead. A nun stood guard at the end of the coffin. 'He's finally found peace.' An old Russell Street neighbour bent over and kissed his head. 'Brendan, our brightest and best. I'd rather have gone before you.' She wiped the tears with her black shawl, as she looked back from the door. He mislaid his overcoat but he hardly noticed the cold, as he walked through city streets which seemed subdued and empty without the giant who had encouraged him to ask questions. Jimmy was waiting outside Donnybrook church. 'After your Brixton graduation, I knew you'd be over. Lags of the world unite!'

12

He was proud of his party faith but he was to discover the fallibility of certainties and Divina's more pressing priorities. 'We are very happy tonight to welcome back our comrade Brendan. His courage and sacrifice are an encouragement to all of us who are fighting for the cause of socialism and peace.' All eighteen members of the Kensington branch stood and applauded his homecoming. They lauded his newspaper selling and treasuryship skills but they became increasingly concerned about his enthusiasm for the uncomfortably objective Russell. A senior member was shocked by his little library: 'George Orwell? A disgraceful Establishment lackey who libelled our cause. No good party man should read that vile propaganda.'

'Orwell revealed that the Soviets killed many socialists during the Spanish Civil War. Were the Russians there for their own interests, or those of the Spanish people?'

'The party has to maintain discipline; the cause of international socialism is our only and constant objective. If Spanish or any other lives have to be sacrificed, it's all for the better good to come.' His visitor was beginning to sound like his mother; he would have made a good Catholic. Walking him back to Earl's Court, he compounded his crimes by giving money to a tramp outside the station. 'How can there be a revolution if do-gooders like you perform the state's work?'

'Whatever motivates our colleagues, it ain't compassion.' Australian fellow-comrade Benjamin wagged his red beard. 'They climax over formulae, not individuals. Humourless fucking dingos who exploit every cause, while all they do is spout from the safety of west London.'

Orwell's *1984* provided further education, and the real-life experiences of Milovan Djilas, whose *New Class* exposé had returned him to a Yugoslav prison. 'Subjugation and trade-union manipulation hardly seem the way to paradise.' Benjamin cradled his Fosters. 'Something's awry about abstract principles which reduce individuals to ciphers.' His comrades' subservience to the Moscow Vatican and their approval of the imprisonment of Soviet writers finally undermined his wavering faith. 'The persecutors of Galileo and Pasternak are blood brothers; dogma leads to Siberia as well as to the Inquisition.' he opined.

Benjamin sympathised: 'For one breastfed on infallibility, it must be a shock to accept that the only certainty is uncertainty!'

Though his political life had disintegrated, he was at least secure in his home life. 'Divina, you're a miracle-maker. You'd create a banquet out of scraps!'

'Imagine what I could do if we had a real cooker, instead of two burners.' She looked around their room. The wardrobe bulged, books competed for space with the delph and cereals on their table. Divina had had enough of the excitement of Earl's Court. 'Life doesn't revolve around coffee bars and bookshops. Time we moved out and found a real home.' She flopped back on the bed.

'I don't want to go where everyone is the same, I'm not going to die in Ealing.'

'Dying? We're suffocating in this dog kennel.'

After three years, he had come to regard Earl's Court as home. And London the centre of his world. Every day there was Vicky's hard-hitting *Standard* cartoon. At weekends, the *New Statesman* and, each fortnight, *Private Eye*'s latest revelations. *That Was the Week* liberated debate; change was in the air. The Establishment rocked to the Rachman landlordism and the Profumo sex scandal.

'Independence for British Guyana! Rhodesian Leaders Arrive for Talks.' The empire was being dismantled. Kaunda, Banda and Jagan came and went, as the former colonies progressed to independence. His mother and he at last shared common ground: 'The imperialists are on the run. Isn't it great to see the Africans getting their freedom?'

Axel, a Hyde Park orator, was more reserved. 'If this liberation continues, we'll all be out of business!'

'Hey, hey LBJ, How many kids did you kill today?' Though he had abandoned party politics, he still continued his political protesting. One night, he led several hundred anti-American marchers. Windows would have been smashed had not Benjamin and he addressed the rudderless crowd: 'Throw stones and we're just like the bums who are carpet-bombing Cambodia. We'll deliver a letter to the embassy and maximise our protest by behaving like civilised people.' His pulse quickened with the euphoria of mass-action and the righteousness of their cause. They were marching to save civilisation. Benjamin and he descended the embassy steps and the crowd melted into the night. His friend gazed after them: 'Anything as ridiculous as a mob? One minute the fuckers develop enough momentum to demolish barricades; the next, they retreat before a piece of paper.'

'Nice to see an Irishman involved. I have Irish blood myself.' Joan Baez tightened her guitar strings. She sang for him and five others, as they concluded a weeklong Hyde Park fast against the Vietnam War. He never thought he would preach at Speakers' Corner but he was pushed up on to a dais. 'Every little helps. Lyndon might get the message yet,' he told the crowd, before his legs gave way.

'You're not cut out to be a martyr.' Divina supported him.

A Hyde Park regular nudged her: 'Don't tell him but I saw his mates enjoy a big fry in that Edgeware Road café every morning.' Violence increasingly marred the demonstrations; activists sought only confrontation: 'Fuzz, pigs! Down with police violence!' His inspirations were the concern and courage of Martin Luther King, Gandhi and Russell. He curtailed his protest activities until, like the pikes of his mother's heroes, his placard was finally consigned to the attic. His last political act was the most ironic: he rescued an isolated policeman from extremists who had kicked him to the ground. 'I hope you first checked he wasn't the one who sent you to Brixton,' Axel joked the following Sunday.

'Where do you go to, my lovely?' Benjamin's activism also came to a premature end. He had considered going to Africa to fight for the Third World, but Angela didn't share his fervour. He had a job persuading her to allow a political refugee have their spare room. Her attitude mellowed and Benjamin discovered why, when her studio informed him that she now worked only afternoons. The African was a wonderful lover and each morning, when Benjamin left to work for the three of them, Angela invited him into their warm bed. She later revealed to Divina: 'I never knew anything like it! He started on my toes and worked his way up. I was a jelly by the time he reached the vital parts.'

Benjamin raced home to find the sated couple fast asleep. 'I'll fucking liberate you, you parasitic Abo,' he shouted, as he chased their semi-naked lodger down the length of Warwick Road. That was the end of the Aussie's dreams of universal brotherhood and of romance. A fortnight later, he headed alone for Dover in a battered orange camper.

'For the times they are a-changing'. While he had been immersed in Marxism, a real social revolution had gathered momentum. Flower Power superseded Victorian taboos and hypocrisy with more questioning attitudes.

OZ and *IT* soon succeeded the *Daily Worker*; Bob Dylan's wailing mouth organ and Donovan's guitar replaced the Red Army Choir. Dusty Springfield and barefoot Sandie Shaw became favourites. As skirts went up and hair grew down, he embarrassed his parents by returning on holiday with shoulder-length locks. Dan Casey failed to recognise him behind the beard: 'How do you do, sir?'

'Prison?' his mother was shocked to hear of his Brixton holiday. He made sure he first told her about his better job. His father showed him the garden strawberries: 'You've done your bit. Now concentrate on your wife and making a nice home.' He rowed with his parents over their photo-montage of the Pope and John F. Kennedy: 'That's the criminal who started the slaughter in Vietnam.' Divina jumped when his mother banged her teacup. 'He's a good Catholic and family man, and a credit to Ireland. A lot of us could learn from him.'

'The Age of Aquarius'. Music groups hatched one day and perished the next. He thrilled to Marianne Faithfull, Pete Seeger and Joan Baez. With half a million others, he swayed in Hyde Park to the Stones, one of whom died within days of a drug overdose. Divina's guitar-playing friend, Jennifer, progressed from hash to heroin. After being hospitalised, she overdosed on methadone. The puffed-up face he saw in the mortuary did not resemble her at all. 'Hey Jude' played, an electric motor hummed and her coffin glided to the furnace. The curtain clicked, a mourner mumbled: 'The system killed her, man.'

'No Stones number but what a cool send-off.' His equally sky-high friend smoothed his tobacco paper. Both died within three months. He swiftly ceased his own hash experimentation. Drugs had provided a diversion but no answers.

He resumed his reading in a search for some truth to replace his lost faiths. 'Your life is a quest for security,' Jimmy wrote. 'When you find it express me.'

He finally discovered the soul in man, in the distillation of pain and aspiration shouted by Camus, Levi, Kazantzakis and Hemingway: 'A man can be destroyed but not defeated.' Individuals of integrity and commitment to whose example he could well aspire, finally to acknowledge that imperfect man's lot was to seek, not necessarily to find. To better himself, instead of trying to change the world. He now understood Axel, who thundered each Sunday: 'Fascism, communism – all only slogans shouted in the wind. Screw the isms; screw the systems. It's you and me who has to change. We are the torturers; we are the victims. The real revolution starts within!'

The German was equally eloquent with directions. 'Trafalgar Square? Take the next anti-Vietnam War march to the American embassy. Change at Oxford Circus to the Downing Street Animal Rights protest. There you pick up the anti-apartheid demo which will take you direct to the square.'

Kenneth Clark's lectures and art-history classes provided additional nourishment for his thwarted spirituality. 'Great nations write their autobiographies in three manuscripts: the book of their deeds, the book of their words and the book of their art. Not one of these books can be understood unless we read the two others, but of the three the only trustworthy one is the last!'

He bowed before Van Gogh's wild brush strokes, Modigliani's tenderness and the massive grace of Henry Moore. Enduring as the life force which inspired it, art became the only immortality he could comprehend. 'Give me Manet rather than Marx any day,' endorsed his march-fatigued wife. Divina hung her wet towel on the back of the door. 'Wouldn't it be nice to move to a larger flat and not have to leave our room every time we shower?

'A bit longer in the bank and we'll have some more money,' he parried.

'The sooner the better, I can't stand it here much longer.'

She stopped at Whiteley's window: 'Look at that bed. In the flat we don't have even one piece of our own furniture.'

He subsidised their income by opening a weekend Portobello Road bookstall, for which Harry Kernoff optimistically provided signed prints. The market was a mecca for the displaced and the diverting. 'My Boy Lollipop' blasted out from all the music stalls. A Cockney watch-mender scanned Douglas Bader's biography: 'Lucky man, he saw only one war. I saw all three, the Boer, the '14 trenches and that last affair!'

Guernica and Katyn Forest resonated as Spanish Civil War survivors jostled exiled aristocratic Poles. An unexpected Mangan dissolved the grime of a scholarly Irish labourer. From out of the throng floated Cyril Cusack: 'Wherever there are books, you will find an Irishman.' Another substantial shadow fell across the stall as Pike Theatre pioneer Alan Simpson picked up a woodcut of Portobello Harbour: 'I'm working on *Jesus Christ Superstar* now – a long remove from Beckett and Behan in Herbert Lane.'

Lady Epstein replied to his *Kensington Post* books advertisement and donated furniture when she sold her Hyde Park Gate home. Jacob Epstein's double bed proved to be a fruitful one. 'I'm pregnant!' Divina returned from a visit to the doctor.

'You're joking!' He hadn't considered the possibility of a child. The first major achievement of his life. Surprise turned to delight. 'Dinner in South Kensington, put on your best.' He hugged her. Divina's friends called with advice, baby clothes and books on names. Together, they carried home a cot from North End Road market. Over weekly coffee treats in the Sou Sol, they discussed names. 'Laura, if it's a girl, Russell if we have a boy,' Divina suggested, as they walked home one evening. 'Done!' He kissed her on Penywern Road.

He sat for a whole day in the hallway before the phone finally rang. 'Congratulations, you are the father of a lovely daughter,' the nurse told him.

He raced with flowers to Princess Beatrice Hospital. 'She's very small and very red. I can't see who she looks like,' he greeted his tired wife.

'She's cute and healthy and that's the main thing. And she's a lot more energy than I have at the moment.'

'There will be restorative champagne to celebrate your homecoming.' He embraced her before she fell asleep.

Their first burglar? He froze. Someone was breathing in their room. It was their baby daughter freshly arrived from hospital. Divina woke an hour later to find him still spellbound. His mother was equally thrilled: 'Here's five pounds for some baby clothes. I hope the baptism went well.' He savoured the thrill of parenthood, as he wheeled Laura through those once lonely Earl's Court streets. Her mittened fingers played with his face as he searched for change on the 74. The little Hungarian violinist, whose Chagallian frockcoat soared as he raced the Earl's Court buses, stopped to serenade them. 'New life – so beautiful!'

Mary Hopkins sang 'Those Were the Days' as Divina and he held proprietorial hands and helped Laura blow out her first birthday candle at Dinty Moore's coffee bar. Every morning she rattled her cot to Trini Lopez and the Seekers:

Rocking, rolling, riding, out along the bay,
All are bound for Morningtown, many miles away.

'With the three of us, there's hardly room to breathe.' Divina stubbed her toe on the cot. 'We'll have to move now.'

'I'll look around for a bigger flat, promise. I think there's one for rent next door.'

'And continue living in a place we could never call our own? From which we could be thrown at a moment's notice. Anything around here will be much too expensive. We'll have to look farther afield and buy our own place. Be sensible for once.'

While he chased books for his stall Divina started house-hunting. Laura in her arms, she greeted him on the doorstep one evening. 'I think I've found our first home! A lovely maisonette in Fulham.'

'That place is in the sticks; we'd need a compass. There's no life down there. We'd be mad to move.'

'We'd be dafter to stay here and pay rent for the rest of our lives. You'll have to be a bit more responsible about the future; you're a parent now.' She tucked their daughter into her feeding chair.

'It will take me hours to get to work, a bus ride as well as the tube.' He waved the *London Streetfinder.*

'For one extra bus ride, we get two bedrooms, a kitchen, sitting room and our own bathroom.'

Responsibility was a totally new concept. He signed the mortgage and bade a reluctant farewell to Earl's Court and his youthful activism. How would he adapt to the wilds?

13

Fulham's narrow thoroughfares were a shock after the buzz and space of Earl's Court. 'I can read that fellow's newspaper.' He pointed towards the opposite house.

Their first-floor maisonette was on a terraced redbrick street, where life was conducted on two floors instead of six. From every corner could be heard the voices of playing children. Each Sunday brought the alarm call of trumpets and tambourines, as the Salvation Army band paraded with flags, all the local youngsters and the retarded Adrian.

There were no coffee bars or restaurants. Mechanics, minicab drivers and struggling families replaced their former activist acquaintances. Neighbour Jenny's husband stayed out gambling most nights. Rows erupted in the early hours when Samantha's drunken husband returned home. Rebecca wanted to induct them as Jehovah's Witnesses. Tracey called too many times with her six-year old son. 'He's gone again. To the Nag's 'Ead to see his mates, he says. But when he cleans up the Cortina and puts on that bleedin' aftershave, I know he's chasing a bit of spare. I know he's effing seein' someone. I'll kill the bastard. Will you shut up, Shane, how many times have I told you it's bad manners to interrupt when mummy's speaking?'

One night, he held his wife's sweat-soaked hands as Marina was born. He experienced a second childhood himself, as he romped with his daughters and celebrated their freedom from the oppressive ways of his youth.

'You're beautiful girls; you'll save many lives.' Jack Abbott, the proprietor, searched for sweets, while he sought first editions in the Fulham Cross junkshop. One wartime bank holiday, Jack escaped a family birthday party to court a local girl. Minutes later, a parachute mine obliterated his home and his parents, brothers, sisters and visiting cousins.

'Chinese, Japanese, dirty knees and Watneys.' The children

laughed as he rode their little tricycle like a long-legged circus clown, and when he recited Spike Milligan's verse. Each night, they exulted at the triumph of Greek heroes or cried at 'The Happy Prince' and other Wilde stories. As he closed a book, they begged: 'Tell us another.'

'If I could write one story like these, I'd be a very happy prince.' He read an encore. 'I think you'll find the real world more rewarding than the books.' His spouse poured a nightcap.

But on the traditional Trooping of the Colour bank holiday, he recoiled from the brass bands and gleaming uniforms, and the happy crowds with their ice cream, crisps and minerals. 'Domesticity and you are not compatible. But I've just the very thing for the wife to keep you in order.' Jack Abbott reached past the gas masks for a pair of orange boxing gloves.

'It's a long way to Tipperary!' In the depths of his London preoccupations, he occasionally remembered Ireland. As Old Contemptibles splashed past singing 'Tipperary' one Remembrance Sunday, he recalled his mother waving that day to Dev at Shelley's Cross. How heroic visions uplifted man!

The Old Contemptibles might stretch his mother's tolerance but he had long wanted to give his parents a first-hand look at life in London. 'I'll show my mother that the English are not such ogres after all.'

'I thought you didn't believe in miracles.' Divina's laughter shook the umbrella.

'Help an ol' soldier,' requested a Cockney-Irish tramp.

'Wouldn't you like to go back and live in Ireland?' Divina enquired.

'And me after serving in the British Army! I'd probably be shot, like that young fella who went back on leave to Derry the other day. They'll soon start something here too without a doubt. No, I'll see out me days here in the Sally Ann hostel.'

'It's a sad thing when people have to leave their own country. That poor man doesn't belong anywhere now.' Divina closed her purse.

'Emigration should carry a health warning.' He watched the man limp away. 'But I'm more concerned about his remarks that the violence might spread here.'

Divina clutched Marina. 'Bombs here in London? Never, we're not Biafra or the Congo.'

He wrote to his parents. 'Ecumenism is in fashion, high time you saw how the other half lives.'

'We'll show you all the sights.' Divina added.

'We've done all the travelling for this year. But soon, please God, we'll consider it. We could do with a break from village life.'

'Insurance Scam'. Buffetted by brollies and briefcases, he overshot his tube stop as a newspaper headline reminded him of the same village's guru, Darby Kinnane. The butcher's only recorded failure was Con Foley, who saw litigation as the route to riches. 'For the best class of an accident, you've got to lose the memory,' Darby advised. A ladder rung broke as Con was painting O'Meara's shop. Big Jim rushed out and tried to revive him. He slapped the painter's face until he groaned with pain. 'Con, are you all right? Do you recognise me?'

'Oh, No, no!' moaned Con. 'I don't know you at all, Mr O'Meara.'

Darby's most successful supplicant was Jim Phelan, whose crops and livestock had failed disastrously. 'Have you tried the fire?' asked Darby. Neighbours grieved for Jim when his outhouses and old threshing machine went up in flames. But three months later, he drove into solvency with the latest tractor and thresher, the proceeds of a recently acquired insurance policy.

Far from the appetising hum of threshing machines, he emerged at Bank station, in the heart of the insurance empire which had proved no match for Darby Kinnane.

'All the other children have grandparents. Why can't we see ours?'

'Maybe you'll visit us soon. I'll show you all the writers' houses,' he coaxed his mother.

'We'll get over within a year or two. But why don't you all come over here for a break?'

With a bank loan, he bought a second-hand camper van. They drove to Ireland, where he played one final joke on Gordon Birch. His friend was taken aback when two litle girls skipped into his workshop and asked him the answer to a riddle. 'What riddle?' he asked, when he could understand their English accents.

'They were together again last night.' Laura and Marina chanted.

Gordon informed the children why their stamps showed only the Queen's face: 'Because her bottom's too big!'

The saddler looked a little older, as he twanged a farewell tune on the rusting jew's harp. 'Come back when you're bigger, girls, and I'll teach you how to beat your father at draughts.'

The children provided his parents with some pleasant experiences, for a change. They enjoyed late tea the night of Dana's 'All Kinds of Everything' Eurovision success. His mother handed around the cakes. 'It's great to have the house full again.' After his father's retirement, his parents had moved to Wexford. Greying hair had not slowed them; his father subsidised their holidays and motoring outings by working in a solicitor's office. The work stopped as they entertained their London grandchildren with picnics on Vinegar Hill and the headland opposite Wexford's Dufy-flagged boardwalk. 'Just like the storybooks,' the children marvelled at twin-fortressed Ferrycarrig Bridge.

'My litle cuties,' his father called them, as they played on his knee and climbed up for piggybacks. 'You're drunk, I'll call the guards.' He reached for the phone, as Marina staggered around wearing his reading glasses. Their grandmother displayed them to her neighbours and brought them to church. 'She threw water at us.' The children whispered how she had doused them with holy water. 'When are you coming over to see us, granddad?' Laura looked up at her grandfather.

'London is such a long way away.'

'It's the same distance that we came,' Marina interrupted.

'We'll have to go then, I suppose, madam!'

His mother gave them records of the Chieftains and the Dubliners. Traditional music and once-derided ballads were now popular. But the improving EEC-funded roads meant little to him, Ireland was home no longer. His self-imposed exile and political views had distanced him from family and former friends; mortgage and children reinforced the English roots. Wilson and Home had replaced Lemass and Costello. St Stephen's Day was Boxing Day, Sunday car-wash day.

His father suffered a stroke shortly after their holiday. It was a shock to find him in the ward of a run-down brownstone hospital, a shadow of his former active self. Able to recognise visitors but unable to speak apart from painful slurred words, he lay surrounded by peasant gloomies: 'It's only a matter of days.'

But gradually his father began to recover: 'I was due a rest!' Within weeks he was on his feet and his speech returned completely. 'It's great to be gardening again,' he wrote. Nine months later, his mother surprised them. 'Get the red carpet ready. We've booked our first-ever air ticket to London.'

'They could have picked a better time,' he complained to Divina, with whom he had been rowing.

'Maybe now you'll paint the stairway? I've been at you since we moved here.'

'Granddad and grandmam are coming.' Laura and Marina raced off to tell best friends Lynn and Carleen.

When their visitors arrived at the airport, Marina greeted them: 'Céad míle fáilte!'

Next door neighbours Mrs Wren and Mr Larking called. 'You're both very welcome to London.' insisted the street-party organiser, Mrs Wren, who hung out a Union Jack every St George's Day. But despite their twenties-induced xenophobia, his parents chatted easily with his Fulham neighbours. 'People here don't appear to be very different from those brought up in Dublin or Tipperary.' His father put down the *Fulham Chronicle*. Bow-legged Mr Larking brought his father for a spin over Putney bridge in his Robin Reliant: 'My first time in a three-wheeler, a lovely machine.' Mr Larking explained about his legs: 'Dunkirk! I was so small that other Tommies stood on my helmet as we tried to get into a boat. But I'm not complaining. My best mate, Pat Riordan – from your country – fell back into the water when the Jerry planes opened up with machine guns.'

Mrs Wren acquainted them with the realities of the Blitz. 'My father helped pull out the bodies when a bomb fell up the road in Chelsea. But the doodlebugs were the worst. When you heard the droning, you held your breath. If the engine stopped above you, you were a gonner. If it went on, someone else died.'

'Gas masks by the bed. You certainly suffered,' his father sympathised. 'And the bombs were falling every night?'

'You know, I've Irish blood myself.' Mrs Wren surprised them. 'One of my granddads came from Cork. We may speak different, but the English and Irish have a lot in common!'

'You can see the entire world from this machine.' His mother enjoyed the pilgrimage to Hove, where Parnell had died. They visited one of Charles Dickens's homes. 'It seems as if 'twas only yesterday I was reading *David Copperfield* to you. Will you ever forget poor Mr Micawber?' After showing his parents Scotland Yard, he drove them past the Paddington gasometers to canal-fringed Kensal Green cemetery. 'Here's the Chartist leader, Fergus O'Connor, whose funeral was one of the biggest in London. And there are some people from the Cassell's books, the Brunels and Blondin, the tightrope walker.' His mother stopped by a brown marble obelisk. 'Thomas Hood! I don't believe it.

> I remember, I remember,
> The house where I was born.'

The cemetery keeper heard her accent. 'Sure, half of Ireland is buried in the fifty-six acres – including the artist Mulready, from your own County Clare. I'm from Wexford myself but the wife won't let me go back. She's just over there, between the empire builders, still keeping an eye on me!'

'I Dreamt I Dwelt in Marble Halls.' He showed them the grave of Michael William Balfe, the composer of *The Bohemian Girl*. 'And do you remember Lady Wilde, a foot taller than her husband and speaker of six languages? She stood up at Gavan Duffy's treason trial: "I, and I alone, am the culprit, if culprit there be!" She was buried there in that pauper's plot with a hundred others. Wasn't it a shame that after all her work for Ireland, no one cared about Speranza of *The Nation*?'

'When did you come to England?' `accused his mother as she prepared to leave through the Doric-arched gateway.

'Just after the war, missus. No jobs at home but loads here in the building. A hard oul' station but then I got this position and I married. We reared a family of three; the youngest's now a doctor. If I'd stayed in Ireland, my children would have had no chance.'

'Well, you're great to have achieved so much.' It was the first time he had heard his mother show understanding of an emigrant.

She enthused about London's variety. 'Dublin's beautiful but there are so many interesting places here. Next time, maybe you'll show us George Bernard's place in Ayot St Lawrence?'

His parents were delighted with Divina's housekeeping. Her practicality was at odds with his less productive lifestyle. He increasingly worried about their future. 'You can recite James Joyce but you can't fix the tap or replace that broken pane.'

Mrs Wren and Mr Larking saw them all off to the airport. 'Slán libh!' waved Mr Larking, who had been coached by Laura.

'We hadn't enjoyed ourselves so much for a long time,' his mother wrote. 'Give our regards to your nice neighbours. Tell them we'll show them around Wexford, if they ever come over. We'll be back, please God.'

His mother surprised him again, after reading of his attendance at Bertrand Russell's funeral. 'He was a far-seeing man, I suppose, and that was a good thing to do.' He had been shocked by the sudden death of his ninety-seventy-year old spiritual father. For him, the philosopher was a twentieth century colossus, the fearless conscience of his time. The passionate sceptic who had never lost the faith, his Parnell. Russell chuckled at their last Conway Hall meeting: 'The Irish are noted for keeping the faith!'

'Britain's Voltaire,' mourned *The Times*. With the family's permission, he was a pall-bearer at the Colwyn Bay funeral. The Nobel prizewinner's coffin rested on his shoulder as lightly as the flurrying February snow. 'I have lived in pursuit of a vision. To see in imagination the society where individuals grow freely, and where hate and greed and envy die because there is nothing to nourish them. These things I believe and the world, for all its horrors, has left me unshaken.'

'He discarded a lot of wives,' Jimmy disparaged.

Irish realities lagged behind Russell's idealism. The Guildford and Birmingham pub bombings plunged him into despair and friction with his neighbours. Mrs Wren rushed into the street: 'Bleedin' cowards who bomb the innocent and run. But we survived Hitler and we'll survive these bastards.'

He could understand her anger. Her father had been wounded protecting England, and Ireland, from similar totalitarians. Jack

Abbott closed the shop one evening: 'Keep away from the bars. We wouldn't want a Paddy killed by an Irish bomb.'

'Cancer pioneer Doctor Fairly blown up.' The carnage continued. Republicans slaughtered bandsmen in Hyde Park and Regent's Park, and a Tube train guard in the East End. They murdered Colditz hero, Airey Neave, a bomb disposal expert in Notting Hill Gate, and an unarmed policeman at Baron's Court, a mile from Fulham.

'Mammy, let me go to the museum with Lynn and Carleen.' Laura packed her toys before bed.

'No! You know it's dangerous to go where there are big crowds. There might be bombs.'

He listened as he washed the dishes. For the first time in his life, he was ashamed to be Irish. Laura put the box away. 'I don't think granddad and grandmum will come back now.'

Her grandmother wrote: 'The weather here is great. I hope you are all very well. We won't be doing any travelling for the time being. We're not getting younger.'

As neighbours recalled their fear of invasion, he remembered his own perusal of the war's progress through those *Irish Press* maps. While only a thousand miles away, Hitler's political opponents died on meathooks and hapless Jews, including Joyce's friend Paul Leon, were liquidated.

'More than all the population of Ireland was gassed to death by the Nazis, yet holy Ireland offered refuge to none,' he complained to visiting Jimmy.

'Trains to Belsen, night ships to Holyhead; we were far too busy getting rid of our own lot to be able to offer asylum to anyone.' Jimmy treated him to *The Irish Times*. 'But we did accommodate some people after the war, Oswald Mosley and the war-criminal Menton!'

The lives of many Irish emigrants had disintegrated in loneliness and booze. Ashamed to return to the country which disowned them, despised 'Paddies' pulverised ballads outside shuttered night-time pubs. Eternal aliens, veterans of the ships of shame that lurched though nights with slamming doors, rolling bottles and the sound of retching, while holy Ireland slept.

'I'll take you home again, Kathleen'. The coffin of a repatriated emigrant pierced the spray as he sailed to Dublin. Kathleen Reilly, 1913-1971, lay on the night-mail deck, sodden mail bags her sole bouquets. A fellow-passenger turned up his collar: 'Like Kathleen and the million who fled or died in two world wars, we are the invisibles. The country survived on our earnings but never acknowledged us. God Save Ireland? We should be singing God Save England, which solved all our unemployment problems.'

His neighbour, Charlie, shocked him one morning: 'Tommy passed away last night.' The brothers had often spoken about returning to Wicklow and constantly played 'The Green, Green Grass of Home'.

The chippie revealed: 'I've been called in myself. A lump on my rear; it feels like a hip flask!' Three months later, he joined his brother in the rusting vegetation of Acton cemetery. On a Fulham Broadway bench, a wizened compatriot read the *Sporting Times*. 'Ireland – what's it like now?' The man pushed back his cap. 'Not that I care. I left the fucking place forty year ago. All priests and heroes, I'd rather die alone than live among such a shower of hypocrites.'

'Jasus! There's no need to be gloomy about it.' Newsagent Jim Walsh untied the bundle of *Evening Standard*s. 'Didn't lots of us get a good living here and a lifestyle people only dream about at home? I know girls who blossomed here, while their sisters died childless spinsters. Look at Murphy's Builders lorries flying up and down Munster Road. And the guy who owns this is a millionaire!' He waved a copy of the *Irish Post*.

After a misunderstanding with Divina, he went to the Boxing Day motor races at Brands Hatch. First home in the main Formula Ford event was Irishman David McClelland. 'Where exactly are you from?' he asked the race-winner.

'Toomevara.'

Wild hurling cries rent the Kent air as he was reunited with the son of the peripatetic New Zealander whose Rolls Royce he had once admired in their little village. He remembered his own racing dreams, when David invited: 'Come with us one day when we're testing at Silverstone.'

'More bloody books. That money would buy new anoraks for

the girls.' Divina looked up from her ironing when he returned from an auction.

Someone rang the doorbell. Laura ran back up the stairs: 'He's Irish!'

It was Billy Fogarty, a visitor from a previous life. The Tate Gallery patron didn't endear himself to Divina when he observed: 'Jasus, you've become very domesticated since you left Dublin.'

They adjourned to The Cottage. 'I'm now more interested in travelling than women or politics,' Billy expanded. 'The ladies only want to tie you down, and organisations and I never agreed. All a humourless, unimaginative and puritanical lot. Ireland was restrictive but London's dark and unreal.'

'Steady with the emotions, old chap!'

> …for my purpose holds
> To sail beyond the sunset, and the baths
> Of all the western stars…

Billy was off to America. 'San Francisco first, to see where Jack London skippered his own oyster boat at the age of sixteen. There was some man! I like everything he wrote – except *John Barleycorn*, sure that would put you off the booze. Now, lend me a tenner and you won't see me for some time.'

He thought of Ireland and their election adventures, as he saw the refined hobo to the station. How tame his own life had now become. 'Farewell, Carruthers,' Billy saluted, before speeding to his dreams down Liverpool Street's inviting rail tracks.

14

'Happy birthday, love. And may all your dreams come true!' His most memorable birthday present was his first hardcover edition of *Ulysses*, given to him by Divina. Joyous were those early marriage days. Life was so full; there were no fears of disharmony or divorce. All one had to do was to wish, educate oneself or go on a march to realise visions and make the world a happier place. The bold bow on the green Bodley Head spine provided a stirring replacement for Peter's keys, an encouraging *imprimatur* for all his strivings.

The loss of his political faith unfortunately made him over-dependant on his wife. His appalling ignorance of the ways of women, and of everyday compromise, did not help when misunderstandings arose. Their rowing increased. He returned from work one evening to find Sandra sipping wine with his wife. 'I'm sorry, your dinner's late.' Divina stood up.

The August heatwave had got to him. 'You're here so often, you might as well move in.' He startled their visitor.

'I'm sorry. I'm going now.' Sandra grabbed her handbag.

Divina raced back up the stairs. 'You lout, where are your manners? I never behaved like this when you brought back your drunken friends.'

'I had to stand in the stifling tube from Monument to Earl's Court; my shirt is soaking. I'm tired and hungry, I need my dinner.'

'I work too and, unlike many husbands, your dinner's on the table most evenings. But there's never a word of thanks now. You take it all for granted.' She banged the oven door.

'I know you women like chatting but why do you have to see so much of that boring one?'

'Women talk about women's things that most men don't understand. Why don't you go to a football match like her husband, instead of watching those motor races? Or chat to some of the men in the pub, instead of tearing around the junk shops and dragging home fresh rubbish every day?'

'That's all that you and Sandra and the pub men ever discuss, rubbish! There's more to life than children's aches, the latest fashions and football transfers.' He flung his *Times* on the table.

'That's your problem. All you know of life is what you read in your paper and books; you live in a black and white world.'

'Marriage is not an idea; it's something to be worked at. Maybe, one day you will come down to earth. But maybe it will be too late. If you don't want to live a responsible life, I think you should find the courage to consider some alternative. I don't want to expose the girls to any more rows.'

But he had a long way to go to understand that love was a flower which had to be tended. 'When we're both calmer, we'll talk about it.' He started to eat. 'I often thought that we rushed into marriage. We should have lived together a bit longer first.'

'Some people would say that now we're married, we should stick at it.'

As the children progressed to C. S. Lewis, the marriage grew progressively weaker. Carefully papered-over cracks became chasms of resentment and recrimination. The best chosen words added fuel to the flames. Fear and silence replaced spontaneity; communications irretrievably broke down. Even the bowls of steaming tapioca ceased to fly across the dining room.

'You'll never be any good; you'll wind up a corner-boy.' From his childhood, he recalled the power of women to subjugate. He feared it could happen again. While his adaptable wife mixed easily with their neighbours, he grew increasingly apprehensive of a terminal decline into suburban uniformity. Cars, *Coronation Street* and Saturday's football pools.

'Closed doors, closed minds, closed legs, closed everything,' said local teacher, Odette, who invited him in for a drink one afternoon. 'Prison for banning bombs, that's amazing. And you knew Brendan Behan?'

A couple of glasses of vino led to Odette's confession that she was sometimes lonely. A consolatory caress was followed by more passionate embraces. Smitten with guilt, he bought flowers next day for Divina. 'You've seen another woman!' When all they did was fight, it was time to go. The children would suffer – but wouldn't they suffer more if they remained together? Victor Waddington helped dispose of their treasured Paul Henry, a Portobello market find, which subsidised the first painful separation.

An optimistic reconciliation was followed by a more permanent separation from the woman who had done more for him than any other person in his adult life. How was he going to manage without her? Those book inscription dreams were resolutely defying achievement. One had flown; the travel and motor racing would remain just wishful thinking. And his job was taking him nowhere.

'My feet are in Moorgate and my heart under my feet.' Recoiling from the meaningless trial balances, his feet grew heavier as they dragged him each morning to the underground. Integrity and individuality were valued at one hundred and fifty pounds per annum, as emasculated clerks shafted each other in pursuit of a coveted signature. 'Jasus! There's more to life than Wimbledon tennis, house prices and Morecambe and Wise,' he expostulated at a colleague's engagement party. His workmates spoke in numbers as they recounted their weekend motoring adventures. 'The A40 and the A420 to the White Horse? No way! We took the M4, the A338, the A417 and the B123.'

'You all sound like the MI5!'

'No such road, Pat,' a messenger informed him.

Birthday cards and cakes arrived with cheerless punctuality. Ponderous in pin stripes at the age of twenty-six, the assistant accountant leaned back against the Schooner counter: 'We've booked for Marbella – for the next two years! You've got to plan ahead these days. James Hunt has a place there now, you know.'

He shuddered to think that this might soon be him. Dutifully renewing his annual season ticket and knowing exactly where he was going to be every August for the rest of his life, his mind and limbs atrophied a long way from Silverstone and the Taj Mahal. After one too many, he rashly nudged his colleague: 'Have you planned the funeral yet?' An urban Laplander, he rarely saw daylight in the winter months, descending into the bowels of the earth at eight each morning and emerging again in the dark at six. 'Is this how we're to spend the rest of our lives, pale troglodytes staggering into retirement with Tellson's blue mould on us?' he asked bank-mate Archie, as round-the-world voyager Francis Chichester tied up at Tower Bridge – a sixty-year old who had realised his dreams.

Playwright Tom Gallagher unlocked his bike in Sloane Square. 'Don't sell your life to a mortgage.'

The absences grew longer. And the walks in Brompton cemetery, where he despaired with the ghosts of the Pankhursts, and the candles flickered ghostily on November nights for the forgotten victims of his last faith, the displaced Poles and White Russians. But inspiration beckoned from the snow-covered graves of Richard Tauber, suffragette leader Emmeline Pankhurst, record-breaker Percy Lambert and restless William Reid: *He died on the trail facing the sun.*

His mind concentrated, another fearful separation ensued. 'Reggie Perrin's off,' he overheard the senior clerk say. Archie accompanied him to London Bridge for the retirement ceremony. In front of uncomprehending commuters, he flung his watch high in the air and watched its flashing descent until it disappeared under the Thames swell. 'Just like Con Flaherty's election pennies,' he informed the Magritte-attired tide, which plodded with Balaclavan fortitude towards the 5.45 for Sydenham, the 6.15 for Orpington.

He walked the streets to alleviate the pain, fear and guilt. Over the years, he had developed a special affection for the city which had welcomed so many political and religious refugees. From seething Fleet Street, he took an archway into the labyrinth of the Temple, to retrace the footsteps of his favourite essayist, Charles Lamb: 'Cheerful Crown Office Row (place of my kindly engendure).'

Time had stopped in the medieval enclosure of fountains, sundials and lawyers' chambers. In the gently encroaching evening, a Robert Louis Stevenson lamplighter climbed his ladder to switch on the gaslights. The ghosts of former residents John Evelyn, Samuel Johnson and Goldsmith brushed past, a bewildered Yeats searched every pocket for his Fountain Court keys. The Sandeman shadow of Edward Martyn crossed cobbled Brick Court to meet with fellow Irish Literary Revival conspirator, George Moore. Unintimidated by alien soil, hadn't the Galway man once said the rosary in the window of the Ascendancy Kildare Street Club?

'More places for you to see. As well as Hugh Lane's and Wilde's Chelsea homes, I discovered George Moore's house today,' he informed his mother. 'Next weekend, I'm on an O'Casey pilgrimage. A bookshop owner told me that London is Ireland's literary capital!'

'You can feel the breath of Ann Boleyn.' Amateur archaeologist Spike Milligan rested his trowel on the dripping Thames-side walls of newly excavated Baynards Castle.

From Waterloo Bridge, he savoured St Paul's triumph over Mammon's oblongs. And its delicate necklace of lesser Wren churches, some now sonnets of beauty and war destruction. He remembered English teacher Rodney Bent as he worshipped from Westminster Bridge:

> Dull would he be of soul who could pass by
> A sight so touching in its majesty.

The pungent scent of spices clung to demolished warehouses in the laneways of Garlickhythe; he could have been off Zanzibar or Java Head. He unearthed treasures in the weekend Portobello and East End markets. A lithograph signed by Max Jacob, friend of Picasso and Modigliani. *The London Chronicle* for December 20, 1764: 'Yefterday was publifhed *The Traveller*, a Poem by Oliver Goldsmith, M.B.' Diversity was London's greatest attraction. From being overwhelmed by the physical enormity, he had finally grown to appreciate its vaster contribution to art, literature and history. That painful introduction had been but an appropriate probationary test.

He'd forgotten what it was like to be lonely. No one to talk to, no one who cared. Everything seemed hollow and futile. Divorce was in the air. Would it be better to be fighting than to be lonely? Should he make another attempt at reconciliation? He penetrated those once intimidating pubs to find that the Lion of Leeson Street had beaten him to Notting Hill's oak-panelled Windsor Castle. 'We can discuss anything – except art.' Nevill Johnson brushed his silvery mane. 'Five hours a day painting at seventy-plus is art enough for me.' Nevill revealed that Fay Taylor had brought him to the Shelbourne Park races he himself had seen as a teenager. 'We took an instant shine to each other in Nesbitts pub. She'd a remarkable body; how she fitted into that machine I'll never know. She invited me to try the car, but forgot to demonstrate the damn "off"-switch. I circulated Shelbourne Park until the petrol ran out!' The artist introduced him to Charlie Martin, who had raced in the

Cork Grand Prix and gone through several women and fortunes. He shook the hand that had confounded the Nazis and steered a little English ERA to success on Berlin's banked Avus track. 'I'll never forget the Cork practice morning, I came around a corner to find a herd of cows across my bows – the only time a full-blooded Grand Prix Alfa had been stopped in its tracks! There's nothing like the driving.' The veteran's eyes lit up. 'The speed, the wind in your hair, the jousting. I'd do it all over again, if I could.'

He told Charlie of his own driving ambitions. 'What's stopping you? If I was your age...'

Desmond MacNamara revealed the tribulations of sculpting Brendan Behan. 'One of my more difficult undertakings. Due to his penchant for late nights, whenever Brendan sat he invariably fell asleep. I got around this by propping up his head with volumes of an old encyclopaedia and a telephone directory. He was such a sound sleeper that even when I shaved him in order to see the form of his face, he never woke up!' The Windsor's clientele included City brokers, who dragged in their problems like leg irons. Clive revealed after drinks: 'If I'm reincarnated, old chap, I'll come back as an Irishman. You buggers know how to live. Like the Bard over there, he can sniff a benefactor long before he reaches the threshold!'

The Bard of Kensington was Burma veteran Michael Mannion, whom Dame Edith Evans commanded to be a poet after he had recited Yeats while trying to sell her an encyclopaedia. With a rhyme for every occasion, Michael explained: 'Transitory molecules, I make my friends feel the men they might have been.'

When tipsy, his thinning white hair would part as he waltzed a surprised lady across the sloping floor to the accompaniment of his Kingsley party piece:

> Then hey for boot and horse, lad,
> And round the world away:
> Young blood must have its course, lad,
> And every dog his day.

One flying visitor who didn't fill the Bard's glass was Jimmy. 'Why do you buy him drink – sure he's better off than you and more smartly attired, even if it's from Oxfam?'

'He gives us a bit of art, a chance to aspire to something more sublime than the exterior mayhem.'

'Bard my arse – he's a conman. Anyhow, what's the latest faith now?'

'At least the Bard lived a life of "doing soon"; you never tried anything.'

'Well, you've very smart since you took the mailboat,' Jimmy snorted. 'Bloody easy for the kept Bard, I've to work for my keep. You've opportunities here but, as you well know, Houdiniism is only possible at home. Suppose I married that Yank I met last year and she tired of Ireland, where would I be then? Work and drink are a damn sight more reliable than any woman. Why take chances? You're not such a great advertisement yourself for the romance you were always prattling on about. I bet you don't believe in that chestnut any more.'

'The Bard says that if you don't dream, you'll become a Nazi or a sleaze columnist.'

'If you don't aspire, you don't fall! Grow up and lower your expectations, like the rest of us.'

Having fallen so much on his own face, he was hardly one to lecture. 'Life's a chance from beginning to end; if you're not in the thick of it, you're not living. My mother's eternity is real to her because of her faith. Better believe in romance or you'll never experience it! Henry Miller says life is in our heads. I've had my blue period, now I must do some living for a change.'

'In your head? After all your somersaults, I think yours is in your arse. Speaking of which, mine is sore from this thirsty sermon.'

Supporting the opposite counter, the Bard sensed the move. 'That fucker should have been a seismologist,' Jimmy spluttered, as the poet bore down on them. A refined practitioner of the merry outlook, the Bard launched into Yeats: '"Pour wine and dance if manhood still has pride." Now, who's this handsome young stranger?'

The post brought notice of the divorce proceedings. His horror of courts was equalled by his fear of the great unknown after marriage. And how could he listen while his failures publicly re-emerged from numbered files? Aware of his aversion to the law, his wife offered: 'I will deal with all the court work, if you like.'

160

While he pondered his future, he sought new companions outside the bar. 'Try this.' A drinking mate showed him *Time Out*.

'Indian men only talk about money,' bubbled Lambrusco-lover Nanu, who declined Mombasa vacation offers and unveiled her sari for him. Jasmin from Richmond lit joss-sticks and played mystical music before entertaining him under the image of a benevolent maharishi. A wire-melting exchange with a Leicester lady resulted in a passionate halfway rendezvous at the M1's Junction Thirteen. Lunch on the *Brighton Belle* was the pleasant aperitif to an educational weekend with a Cambridge graduate, who introduced him to Donna Summer and a new use for an Irish cream liqueur. But making love, not war, had its hazards. John Lennon's 'Imagine' soothed as he lay in Bayswater with archaeology student Rebecca – before her elder sister ran in. 'What are you two doing? You are corrupting my innocent sister, you bastard.'

'We're fond of each other. Give me time to explain.' The sister wasn't into explanations. A laser-directed electric iron expedited his premature departure.

'You're sure you haven't got a jealous sister?' he asked a startlingly mauve-haired lady he met a few weeks later. On the wrong side of thirty and pleasantly filling out, she smiled: 'My dog's my only pal – but I could be open to offers.' They hastened to her Islington maisonette. He had learned a lot since his London arrival. 'You're a wonderful lover. Now, let me do something really nice for you.'

'No need to rush,' he feigned. At a crucial moment, the animal barked. 'The dog's jealous.' His anticipation grew. A key turned in the downstairs door. 'My God! He said he wouldn't be back before three.'

She thrust him into the hitherto alluring mirrored wardrobe, grabbed her nightdress and raced down the stairs. The cataleptic's life passed before him, and repassed. He recalled both the Passionists and O'Toole-King's prescient words. Like Dangerfield, he tried telepathy: 'There is no one hiding in this wardrobe.'

He moved to the door but could hear only muffled sounds from below. No raised voices; there was hope of a sort. He looked out the window – a long drop to the concrete and his blue van. A door opened. He heard hastily ascending footsteps. 'March to the Scaffold.' The bloody woman had confessed everything. Luckily, it was her, alone. 'Go! Go! He's taken the dog around the block. Go now!'

His shirttail flapped as he sprinted to the van. As he sped around the corner, he passed a Charles Addams cartoon. A Lilliputian dog and a handler whose physique would have made heavyweight champion Sonny Liston quiver. Missing the bank salary, but not the bank, he survived with a series of part-time jobs. Neighbour Carlos sold him a blue Cortina. 'Easy money, partner me as a minicab driver.'

Cat Stevens asked him to lower the rear window as he took the piss out of King's Road trendies. 'Are you David Bowie?' he asked every blonded youth. 'Ciao darling,' whispered a film actress to her husband, before directing her chauffeur to her lover's Hampstead pad: 'Can't you go any faster?' He ferried a shocked woman from Fulham hospital to her Ealing semi-detached. 'He made the breakfast at eight. Now he's dead. What will I do with this?' She handed him her husband's overcoat. He dropped four tattooed compatriots in Kilburn High Road. 'We forgot our wallets. What are you going to do about it?'

One tired morning, he assaulted the Cenotaph steps under the eyes of a policeman. 'London's widest thoroughfare, how could you hit such a prominent monument?' Soon afterwards, an articulated lorry challenged him for the same piece of Trafalgar Square, leaving little to salvage from the Cortina.

His next job was in a British Airways lost property office. Anything not already lost was purloined by the staff. The smell of polish competed with cologne as the braided boss shined his shoes: 'Why worry? Everything's insured.' His most rewarding work proved to be entirely his own. A series of diffidently written features which capitalised on his encyclopaedic London knowledge. His mother wrote: 'We heard 'Yeats's London' being discussed on the morning media review. Well done – but why didn't you say more about Maud Gonne?' The *Irish Press* took some more stories. He wondered if he could turn the writing into a living. Another fantasy?

Divina contacted him again. 'The court has agreed to the divorce, unless there is any objection by either of us within the next month.' Costa's taverna cat observed them as he shared a bottle of

Aphrodite with Nevill Johnson. 'Our last opportunity, I still have a choice. None of the women I've met could measure up to Divina. 'Twould be wonderful to start off, as we did so happily before.'

'But what if you commenced as you had finished? You could hardly go through all that again? And neither should your wife or children, I think you've all had enough. You must now find the resolution to press on and do something worthwhile with your life.'

He let events develop their own momentum. On the embankment, he met a pensioner who had escaped through a nursing-home window for a final look at his native city. 'Now I'll go back and die happy.' The man measured out his tablets opposite Scott's *Discovery*. 'And don't forget what I told you: life shrinks or expands, according to one's courage!'

A pneumonia hospitalisation further underlined that dreams were realised now, or never. David McClelland offered him a test drive of his Formula Ford car. When he slid down inside the ground-hugging machine, he entered an exciting world from which the outside was totally excluded. David tightened the belts. 'Leave me space to breathe!'

'Gear lever....right.' David gestured above the engine noise.

With only basic instruments and a small black steering wheel, the car's functionality focused his attention. You drove practically lying down, it was impossible to see around the corners. Each rise seemed an Everest. The five-point harness anchored him to the machine. He could anticipate any deviation. The car responded to every control. The speed stimulated senses he hadn't known existed. He used his share of the house proceeds to buy a secondhand Hawke. The Circuit of Ireland dream had had a long gestation.

'You're not a child any more. That nonsense is for rich people. You'll be a laughing stock,' his mother protested.

How fortunate to have escaped her. If she'd had her way he would still be a fiver-a-week pen pusher. Jimmy added his encouragement. 'You could find a cheaper way to suicide.' Vern Schuppan gave him his Le Mans overalls. 'Us Old Brixtonians must stick together.' Great Train Robber and fellow-racer Roy James recommended a mechanic with impeccable form. An accomplished silversmith and driver before his imprisonment, the diminutive Fulhamite commented: 'Nicking used banknotes was the crime of the century. But when I was a lad, I was conscripted to defend rubber robbers in Malaya. Blighty's a rum place.'

Soon, every weekend was a bright one, as he and Trevor hit the motorway to the accompaniment of 'Country Roads' and 'Seasons in the Sun'. Trevor handed him his helmet, which matched the red car: 'Ignore the rest of the grid. Just concentrate on your own start.'

He would never forget his first race at Cadwell Park. The heavy helmet restricted peripheral vision. His ears tingled with the roar of the other cars, only the instruments' flickering confirmed that his engine also was running. He checked his mirrors. Demonised by helmets, two pairs of eyes bored into his. When the starter held up a Union Jack, he thought of his mother. The revs rose to a climax. The sound waves multiplied. The ground shook. After a lifetime, the flag fell.

He was enveloped in the smell of engine oil and the blast of exhaust heat. Every instinct warned him to flee. But there was nowhere to run. Only forward with the jockeying pack. A kaleidoscope of faces, flags and hoardings accelerated past. How are all these lunatics going to get around the first lefthander? Brakes locked, tyres screamed, cars juddered. Two cars touched, a helmet turned, a fist went up. Everyone immediately leaned right and swept around the long corner which led to the highest part of the course. The better cars and drivers pulled away on the ascent. He willed the Hawke to go faster but it was plainly no match for the leaders. By the time he negotiated the one hundred-and-eighty degree Druids bend, they were halfway down to the swerving Gooseneck.

Against all his instincts, he kept his foot down on the descent. He slid to the edge of the ill-defined left-hander; he would have to be more careful next time. A two hundred yard sprint to the blind left turn. He stood on the brakes. But too soon, for the car he followed gained many lengths. Next time, brake later. Around the corner was the acute right-hander into the stomach-churning mountain hump. 'You'll never make it over the hill,' champion Tim Flynn had joked on their previous evening's reconnoitre. But the revs rose, as his wheels left the ground on the acceleration for the succeeding series of s-bends. Mind that Armco! His arms were crossed to their extremes as he took the hairpin which led down to the last right-hander before the start. On his left was the barn, its doors reputedly left open so that overshooting cars could pass through. He could see the leaders streaking away. He accelerated before he wanted to, defying his sight of the lake through the left-hand hedge.

The racing surpassed all his expectations. Every sense went into overdrive. His feet danced a constant tattoo on the closely-packed pedals. Accelerator to brake and clutch. Back to accelerator again. He was thrilled by the challenge of impossibly late braking. The scrotum-tightening cornering. The surge of exit power. But not applied too suddenly, or the car would flick sideways or backwards into the Armco. On the third lap, Trevor held out his pit-board: P10 – he wasn't last! His confidence grew. He started to brake later and accelerate earlier. He gradually gained on the car ahead. A white machine – the veteran, Gordon Rae. He tried to take him on the corner before the startline. But he went in too quickly and Gordon drew away on the exit. Clown! First time out and he'd broken the cardinal rule, slow in, fast out.

He closed again around the long left and right bends. This time he stayed with his quarry up the ascent to Druids. A potential winner, Gordon must have an engine problem. He hoped he wasn't dropping oil, the track would be a skating rink. He feinted left and went to the inside, but Gordon was much too experienced for that. Half-way down to the Gooseneck, his rival's car hiccupped. He accelerated past and felt like Fangio. But not as fast as the leaders who suddenly flashed into his mirrors. Blue flags waved. Would they catch him before the lefthander? Yes? No? He had just enough space to turn left and right, before they swept past at the Mountain. Tim Flynn, at a scarcely credible rate, his helmet strap flapping wildly; Peter Wimhurst on his tail, head down, steering wheel tightly clenched. Their slipstream rocked his car. Whose was the third machine? Too late, he saw Gordon Rae wave from the cockpit.

Once he re-passed Gordon, he set his sights on the next car. Yellow – fellow-newcomer Mark Goddard. But Mark was no slouch. He attacked the mountain so violently each time that all four wheels flew in the air. For two laps, he harried the yellow car. He would close in the slower corners, but Mark would pull away on the faster ones. Next time, he would take him. But around each corner, he could only see his rival's exiting tail. He began to think Mark had just half a car.

On the descent from the Gooseneck, the yellow car suddenly swerved off line. He had him now! He charged past but, before he knew what was happening, he was spinning wildly. He had missed what Mark had seen, Gordon Rae's oil. Like a lawnmower, the wheels threw up the grass before he finally regained direction and the track.

But he was to have the last laugh. Two laps later, he was confronted by a mass of flying debris around the blind lefthander. A car lay upside down in the Mountain ditch. Like a stranded turtle, its wheels still spun among the smoke and dust. Underneath, a flipper appeared, Mark's arm, while flowing petrol darkened the grass around him. Right above Mark was a spectator – a lighted cigarette in his mouth. A good job they had only small tanks.

A lap to go. P7, Trevor jumped up and down. Around the sweeping right-hander for the last time, he accelerated up to Druids. His car mightn't have been the fastest, but it hadn't missed a beat. 'Good old Hawke.' He patted the dash. What's that up at Druids? Another accident? No, a breakdown, the driver was climbing out. The leader, Tim Flynn. He would collect his first championship points; he was sixth!

'Motor racing is dangerous!' programmes warned spectators. For drivers also. A sticking throttle impelled him into the Lydden barrier in his next race. The Islington wardrobe was safer, he reflected, as he flew through the air. The inverted car slammed the top of the bank. Bodywork splintered. Peripherals flew like shrapnel. His head scraped the earth, the car toppled over again. Silence returned. The horizon readjusted itself. He had cartwheeled over the ten-foot banking. Marshals were shocked to find the on-course dust cloud empty: 'You vanished like a leprechaun!'

He repaired his car in time to fulfill a long-held ambition. He returned to Phoenix Park where, in the white heat of a cycle event, he had once fantasised about racing on four wheels. Tears fell inside his helmet, as he started his first exploratory lap in the wheelmarks of Prince Bira and Rudolf Caracciola. 'A man of many parts.' Joe Christle towered over the anoraks in his dark suit. He enabled other Irish enthusiasts to realise their motor-sport dreams by co-launching an inexpensive class. 'Delighted to help, I started in Formula Vee myself.' World Champion Emerson Fittipaldi gave him a trophy for the inaugural event. He knew he was home when a startline scribe enquired: 'What's in it for you?'

Thanks to superior wet tyres, he scored his first and only race win at rainy Mondello Park. His bloody hand from a recalcitrant gearchange went unnoticed; was there anything to match the buzz of success? Mondello was only miles from where he had once watched Powys-Lybbe, cap back to front, ricochet across the Curragh in his scarlet Monza Alfa. Two schoolboys approached: 'Will you sign our programmes?'

The decree nisi arrived. That was what he wanted, wasn't it? There was no going back. An old life was over, a new life was about to begin. His racing involvement proved educational. He knew what questions to ask the professionals who tested gravity's limits; he knew that races were won by repetitive testing on bleak circuits, far from flags and glamour. A *Fulham Chronicle* feature led to a column with the *Irish Post*. Sports editors invited him to lunch. After three eventful seasons, he curtailed his racing and concentrated on his new life as a Grand Prix correspondent.

'I've just interviewed Stirling Moss, who scored his first big win in Ireland,' he informed his mother. 'And Phoenix Park veteran Sammy Davis, who saw the Gordon Bennett race that you often mentioned. I am planning a book on Ireland's unique racing history!'

'I always told you that you could write. But couldn't you have found some better paper than that rag, whose lies nearly destroyed poor Parnell?' his mother protested after a *Times* feature.

One weekend azure Monaco, the next wind-swept Zandvoort. Then south again to forested Nurburgring or the Spanish dust-bowl of Jarama. He remembered those Circuit of Ireland competitors disappearing over the hills. Was there anything to match the accents, colour and drama of the mobile circus, the comforting feeling of a shared passion? And he was able to do the odd good turn. When future European Champion Mike Thackwell was running short of money, he persuaded World Champion Alan Jones to bail out his fellow-Antipodean. He introduced Irish drivers to Grand Prix constructors and lent the balance of his house money to one in particular need. His bank balance would have been better served had he not declined an offer from the worldly-wise Eddie Jordan. Being on the inside was intoxicating; he gained insights into drivers' characters. But even his best stories did not please everyone. '*Camper vans to Concorde*, do you want the fucking taxman on my door?' Alan Jones brandished his *Observer* story.

Ayrton Senna was a model of affability outside the cockpit. But while John Watson relaxed with John Le Carré, Ayrton pored over rivals' lap times: 'I must know everything about every driver and every car, on every corner and every circuit. Racing is about winning and winning is about knowledge.' Even that proved insufficient; the Brazilian obsessive went on to perfect the art of deliberately shunting his rivals. Given up for dead after his Nurburgring crash, Niki Lauda raised a burned eyelid: 'I knew that if I concentrated, I could control my body. I forced myself to stay awake.' Patrick Depailler lit a Gauloise and pedalled his bicycle backwards after a Brands Hatch accident. 'Danger? That's why I race!' Two weeks later, he perished at Hockenheim.

In a Monaco downpour, pint-sized Gilles Villeneuve fought for fourth place as others did for first. He broadsided his muddied Ferrari, more like a boat than a car, out of San Devote at full throttle, his arms a blur of beige beneath the spray as he controlled the slides and skated uphill past Rosie's Bar. Even veteran Innes Ireland waved his programme: 'A real racer.' And he raced Villeneuve himself! One Belgian Grand Prix practice morning, his camper outran the driver's 911 around Zolder's narrow back roads, alternatively blocking then teasing him with oncoming traffic, until the Ferrari man finally blasted past with a conspiratorial wave. 'My first vehicle was a VW van – and I drove it the same way!' The Canadian swung the camper's door in the paddock that evening.

What a charmed life he had enjoyed, meeting such enthusiasts as Villeneuve, Mike Hailwood and Innes Ireland. It was a long way from the pot-holed roads of Toomevara to the yacht-lined quays of Monte Carlo. His parents listened to his Irish radio reports. 'Your father says you're as good as Micheál O'Hehir any day.'

> How often have I led thy sportive choir,
> With tuneless pipe, beside the murmuring Loire.

Between Grand Prix races, he indulged his love of travelling. He munched baguettes opposite anchored Notre Dame, exactly where Jongkind and Paul Hogarth had stood their easels. Barges throbbed past with laden washing lines and a Renault on each deck. In Père Lachaise cemetery, he paid homage to Piaf, Abelard and Heloise, and remembered that double bed at Epstein's tomb of Oscar Wilde. Brendan Behan had also knelt here. When asked what he had prayed for, he replied: 'Spondulicks!'

He marvelled at the clay's metamorphosis to orange, as he hit the route Jean Moulin to Provence's cocktail of sunflowers, vineyards, wild lavender and rosemary. His student protest past caught up with him after a Saône river picnic, when he gave francs and food to a stubbled *clochard*. The sunbaked traveller smothered him in a wine and garlic embrace, before raking his hand across his throat: 'Algiers my home, before nationalists burn my house.'

Money, politics and computers were impelling Formula One down an inglorious cul-de-sac. Television revenue became the priority. Entrepeneurial smoothies blossomed; sportsmanship wilted. Drivers turned to PR-speak; most scribes recognised only the winners; a literate exception turned out to be a CIA man. Veteran Innes Ireland pointed: 'In my day, only mechanics on the grid. Now, all marketing buggers like Mr Fix-It over there, who can go in a door behind you and come out ahead. Boxing's more respectable.' He photographed René Arnoux being arrested in Canada, following an incident with a policeman. His team-mate had been injured the previous day, so no Renault contested final practice. 'What will I tell them back home?' Gerrard Larousse surveyed his parked cars. 'One driver in hospital, the other taken by the *flics*!' The team manager returned from meeting the authorities. 'René will be allowed to race tomorrow, provided there is no publicity.'

Single-handedly, he could ensure Renault's racing exposure in the multi-million dollar North American market! 'I'll sit on the photos.'

An agency man pressured him. 'Three hundred bucks for those pics, no problem.'

Fellow-journalists laughed at him for declining the windfall. To the accompaniment of supercharged Grieg in a lofty restaurant, a colleague advised: 'Words such as good and bad have no meaning in this game. In Formula One, there are only winners and losers. You're on top now, milk it for all it's worth.' Born far from dreams in country boreens or Scandinavian spaces, how his colleagues would have relished his many confidences: the champion who'd failed his driving test; the one who raced with an Irish licence after a UK road conviction; another who had shared out his girlfriend to secure a drive.

It was time for a change of direction. Back on his own two feet, the only way to live. Some ambitions achieved, now was the time to travel further afield before he grew any older or disillusioned. Far away from corruption and the spectral cold and damp of northern Europe. 'A capital idea! I'd go with you but, at ninety-four, while the engine is willing the chassis is weak!' Racing veteran Sammy Davis cupped his favourite Irish liqueur.

His media contacts enabled magazine commissions to subsidise the land voyage eastwards. Rajasthan and the Taj Mahal of his childhood encyclopaedia would finally become a reality – with Ephesus, Byzantium and Petra en route for good measure. 'The van's first owner drove it to India, it will know the way by itself,' he informed Jimmy.'

'Jasus, will you ever be satisfied at anything? You couldn't even kill yourself at the racing. You had a nice wife and you left her. What are you trying to prove?'

His new course materialised sooner than he had expected. He found it was less easy to disentangle himself from another woman than it had been from Divina. He had a shock communication from the land of permanent dreams.

15

'Your father is sick. It's nothing serious, no need to worry. I hope you are all fine.'

He knew his mother's shorthand too well to dally. He found his father in the Meath Hospital with a kidney problem. 'James Clarence Mangan may have been content here, I'd rather be home listening to *Letter from America*.' His mother furled her *Irish Press*. 'What are you doing here? We can look after ourselves, as we have since you all left.'

The ten active post-stroke years were over. Confined to a wheelchair, the Sergeant and his wife entered a nursing home, closer to both care and the chapel.

'You'll never know the sorrow of breaking up the house.' His mother fiddled with the Teasmade. 'We could only bring our clothes and a few objects. Everything else had to go but sure the pictures and the odds and ends meant nothing to anyone but ourselves.'

The pictures were dumped, together with his father's yellowing press cuttings, planes, chisels and saws. He was with his father for the last forty-eight hours of his life. He could only whisper. 'Thanks for coming over. A drive is out of the question today! Will you keep an eye on Siobhán for me?' He died on an early August morning, with the self-effacing dignity which had marked his conscientious life. His mother was inconsolable. She sobbed and prayed in a corner of their room. 'Fifty years we were together. He was all I had left when you had gone. How can I live without him?'

He had never seen his mother so vulnerable. Too late, he admired her courage in facing a new life in a strange place, in coming to terms with the end of her wedding-day dream of her own speckled store, a place on which to stamp her personality. No more homemade bread, no more parlour to polish. Just a room in a nursing home.

He was appalled at his irresponsibility in not thinking sooner of his parents. They had suffered while he had been indulging himself in London. He should have been there to help. But how could he restore some normality to his mother's life, particularly as they never agreed on anything? Was it arrogance to think that he could help, he who couldn't even keep a marriage together? What would he do for a living if he returned to Ireland?

Jimmy's derision dissipated the telephone static: 'Return? Jasus, you couldn't wait to leave the bloody place. The pair of you never got on before and you have less in common now. Do you want to add another disaster to your long list?'

'She's my mother, it's the very least I can do. The travelling will have to wait.'

'Quixote's final tilt.'

He indulged in some speedy house-clearing himself, breaking up what he had thought would be his permanent London flat. The Bard called for the poetry books. 'It's like an archaeological dig!' He unpeeled the layers of a quarter of a century, his last scapular, that battered placard, motorsport memorabilia. And the first letter his mother had addressed to him in London. 'Remember that you can always call on us for anything you want. If you aren't happy there, come home and we'll start you at something.'

Leaving his adopted home was almost as traumatic as his sixties emigration. Walking out on civilised friends, never again to banter with chef Mitsios in Costa's. From Kensington's laburnum-bright streets, his Windsor Castle friends came to see him off. 'Give my regards to dear Tom in Stephen's Green.' Leslie Kettle questioned everything except his uncle's courage. Bill Sweeney offered the *Treasury of Irish Literature* a good home. Nevill Johnson presented a drawing for his next accommodation. 'On the road again, I envy you.' Charlie Martin tapped the ground with his stick.

'We'll pop over and see you, old boy. To Violette Szabo and Noor Inayat Khan!' He drank a final toast with Charlie and Lysander pilot Robert, who had also landed agents in occupied France. The understated English had some courage.

'Pomp and Circumstance' appropriately played him on his laden way to Holyhead. The North Circular A406, the M1, the M6, the A5 – he recalled his former bankmates. He felt a debt of gratitude to the country which had enabled him to grow and to fulfill so many hopes.

Yet, he also felt a surging admiration for his mother's courage in coping with the harsh reality of deprived Ireland. And for his father's dutiful plodding of those dull streets for thankless decades. Former neighbour Pat Cunningham had reminded: 'Our parents and their contemporaries were of a heroic mould. They picked up the pieces after the mayhem of the Independence and Civil Wars.' Helping his mother at this late stage was the least he could do. The miles and England disappeared beneath his wheels.

He paced the ferry's deck. How would he get on with his mother? Establishing a working relationship would be tricky, maybe impossible as Jimmy insisted. What would it be like to live in Ireland after such a long absence? Where would he find work? Where would he live?

'Conceived by God, sculpted by Praxiteles,' said James Stephens of Dublin's hills. How he had clung to their last impressions on tearful departures, as they faded between sky and sea and all the concentration in the world would not restore them. But now his heart exulted as the first inky outlines of the Featherbeds assumed their reassuring shapes. He could almost smell the heather and hear the hovering curlew above the Sally Gap he'd climbed on cycle training evenings, inspired by Shay Elliott and the handlebars photo of Charlie Gaul, the 'Angel of the Mountains'.

Swooping gulls and gorse-hued heights flashed a sunlit morning greetings. 'Isn't a ship the only way to enter Dublin?' a railside companion celebrated.

The Kish lighthouse approached, and the twin sentinels of Bray and Howth Heads. Behind the Bailey light lay the haunted house with the rattling windows of Balscaddoon's most famous resident, Sebastian Balfe Dangerfield, the wild and unforgettable Ginger Man. And over there was the Sandycove tower, where his Bodley Head bible commenced: 'Stately, plump Buck Mulligan came down from the stairhead.' They breasted the lighthouse he'd climbed years before and Sandymount strand, across which ashplant-swinging Stephen Dedalus had crunched. And beside it the place of which the real Buck Mulligan had written: 'I will live in Ringsend, With a red-headed whore.'

Dublin. Lively, human, dirty, peerless Dublin!

Apart from Athens, had any other city been as fruitful as that sociable birthplace of Swift, Sheridan, Congreve, Farquhar, Mangan, Moore, Wilde, Boucicault, Yeats, Shaw, Synge, Stephens, Stoker, Le Fanu, Joyce, O'Casey, Beckett, Behan, James Plunkett, Austin Clarke, Elizabeth Bowen and genial Maeve Binchy? And that practising Christian, Doctor Barnardo.

And whose streets had been enlivened by the eccentricity of Goldsmith and Maturin, and the wit and scurrility of Gogarty, Ben Kiely, Flann O'Brien, J. P. Donleavy, and the booming 'Chatham Roar', Sean O'Sullivan. And consecrated by the spirituality of Æ and Patrick Kavanagh. Mighty, saintly Kavanagh who saw heaven in rude stones and clods of earth.

Energised equally by native pride, time-gilded memories and summer expectancy, he watched spires, rooftops and the lofty gasometer fall into once-familiar place. Further down, the green-domed Custom House floated on the water. Gandon, Ireland's Christopher Wren. Tchaikovsky church bells rang across the greeny Liffey. Like Ulysses, the years fell off his shoulders; he was mistily overcome by the long-forgotten feeling of being home.

And, an echo from a different time, a musical litany sprang to his lips of his village's leafy townlands: Coole, Clash, Ollatrim, Aghnameadle, Latteragh, Loughisle, Monanore, Shanbally, Garanafana, Grenanstown. How pleasant the prospect of being able to cycle them soon again.

Joy turned to alarm as he realised he hardly knew anyone in the city that had changed so much. He no longer recognised car registration numbers. 'Emigration exacts a dual tribute; it's like entering a new country.' He shook Mary King's hand across Parsons unvarnished counter.

Like Sylvia Beach and Adrienne Monnier among the invaders, underawed Mary and measured May O'Flaherty still tended their beacon of culture on Baggot Street bridge. The Oriel and Taylor Galleries and Greene's bookshop likewise illuminated, but every creak of Parsons floor was a haunting evocation of a firmly departed past. 'Brendan, Patrick, Myles, Harry Kernoff and Sean O'Sullivan are gone. You can hear the quiet; the place will never be the same again.' Mary King looked out the door. 'What a pity they didn't survive to see themselves on the school curriculum!'

'I wish I could meet you at the Met tomorrow.' Artist Noel Lewis gave his beard a disbelieving tug. 'But it's history now – with the Theatre Royal, the Royal Hibernian, the Irish House, the Turkish Baths, Molesworth Street school and half of Georgian Dublin. If it wasn't for the likes of David Norris, the rest would also be long gone. The quayside bookshops? All video stores.'

They walked down Baggot Steet. No more mouth organ or harp players. 'Change for the hostel.' A spectral addict's arm reached out from a doorway.

'Phil Ryan's? It's under that banking glass oblong – wait till you see the concrete one in Dame Street. Only a few bedraggled curtains hold out against the office invasion of Upper Mount Street, Lower Mount Street's a de Chirico wasteland of semi-state glasshouses. The city fathers and speculators have wreaked more havoc than all of *Helga's* shells!'

'Shall I tip the driver?' Oliver St John Gogarty asked the gunmen who kidnapped him from his Ely Place *salon*. His humour would have quailed at the angular mass that had replaced his balconied home. The Bailey, outside which Pádraic Ó Conaire tethered his ass, had become a muzak bar; now the braying was inside. Ancient High Street had sacrificed its homely shops to a dual carriageway. Once gracious O'Connell and Grafton Streets had degenerated into one giant hamburger arcade. 'McVomit Way.' He kicked a discarded carton towards Noel. But politics seemed to have changed for the better. God's Anointed of Fianna Fáil no longer monopolised power. Once conservative Fine Gael bubbled with progressive ideas; Labour and Independents were on the march. Shane Ross loud-hailed Leeson Street students from his sleek Scimitar. 'We'll give the car our Number One.' They raised their Hartigan's pints.

Unlike Gallagher, now happily married with five handsome children and two houses, Jimmy had never let wifely or property aspirations distract him from liquid appreciation. Firmly anchored in pinstripes at his Old Stand berth, his lenses had thickened, his quizzical expression was more deeply etched and strands of grey flecked his once dark hair. 'I've booked a grandstand seat.'

'For what?'

'World War Three, of course. You and your mother. Jasus, you're a gas man! Like the *Marie Celeste,* going around in circles. Saving the world, fleeing the Church. I always knew you'd be back with your tail between your legs. Will you come down to earth! You can't live in that van. What are you going to do for a crust?'

It was no Baron Hanley homecoming. The motorsport compatriot he had helped airily declined to repay him. All he possessed was four hundred pounds, his camper van and a credit card. How indeed would he survive? But how minor these problems were compared to his mother's desolation! How she had been diminished since she lorded over their village home and ruled his every move. Approaching eighty, her once dark hair had turned completely grey; she was but half a person without her husband. True to form she reiterated: 'The nuns are taking good care of me. I don't know why you are coming back here at all. I'll be all right as long as you write to me now and then.' He knew then that she needed him.

Despite his antipathy to gossip and other restrictions of rural living, he considered renting a Toomevara house. His mother would be back where she knew so many people; the distractions of cooking and housekeeping would keep her occupied. 'With Dublin only two hours away, I can work as if I were living in the city.'

'Is it daft you are, God bless the mark? Sure, that place is riddled with damp, it's been lying vacant for years. Is it trying to finish me off altogether you are? You should go back to England now, and leave me alone. You'll never get any work here. I'll be all right in the nursing home.' Their lifestyles and opinions had grown so diametrically opposed that there was very little on which they could agree. This was probably the damp to which she alluded. There was no underestimating the challenge. But if she was arguing, she was living.

'A nominal rent for my Dromineer bungalow,' his former schoolmate Micky Gilmartin told him. 'Seamus Cleary? Poor Seamus died twenty years ago after falling into a diabetic coma.'

His mother did not settle easily into her single room. He saw her several times each week.

'I'll never get used to living alone.

'It's like a hotel here, with the attention you get!

'I suppose it's safer than living outside, with all the break-ins and the attacks on old people.'

His life's dramatic change and new responsibility demanded unaccustomed resolve, Camus' *The Myth of Sisiphus* was appropriate reading. He pounded Dromineer's byways for miles, oblivious to space and time. The winter gloom wrapped itself around his heart. Icy spray lashed the grey pier and drowned the cries of the water-tossed birds; bare trees stood etched against the brief winter sun. But each night, the frozen Ruysdael sedge and white fields glitttered in the light of a million stars. He skidded the van to his heart's content across the icy roads. The melancholy of Whitehall began to seem a distant aberration. He sold a few features but his money soon went. He would have to be nearer to the newspapers. 'Greetings to Brendan!' He gritted his teeth, and parted with his signed photographs of Rudolf Caracciola, Mike Hawthorn and other racing idols.

After three months, his mother was a little more secure. He moved to Dublin and white-emulsioned a third-floor Pembroke Street room in what, despite office encroachment, he still fondly regarded as Dublin's Latin Quarter. Their paint-flecked books yellowed on the window-sill, as he nightly heard the ghostly footsteps of Behan, Donleavy, Des MacNamara and McDaids companions hastening with laden paper bags to the nearby Catacombs. But he often awoke to the gulls' unnerving dawn shrieks – the only person on the planet – and questioned on his floor mattress the sanity of leaving his comfortable London routine. What story he could he invent to put food on today's table or a slow noggin at Nesbitts? Could he chance an extra helping of porridge this morning?

'Chaplin in *The Gold Rush*.' Jimmy found him contemplating stringy synthetic meat and tinned semolina. The wind whistled through the door which he left open, fearing to miss an editorial commission on the distant first-floor payphone. He pounded out features and interviews. After each rent payment, he sprinted to a newspaper office for a covering disbursement.

'The cheque must have got lost in the post,' shrugged the annual editor to whom he had supplied premium features. 'We'll have that for you next month,' a motoring publisher feinted playfully.

They didn't wear plastic bags inside leaking shoes. He thought of London, where he was always paid on time. Would he chance another story in hope, or sacrifice a scarce outlet?

Joe Christle's frame filled the doorway. 'A garret, a broken window, a clattering typewriter – *La Bohème* is alive and well.' After his numerous prosecutions, Joe was now a law lecturer. 'Now that you're back home, maybe you'll finally concentrate on building a career for yourself? You've led a butterfly life, cycling, motor racing, politics, reporting for top papers – but you never stuck at anything long enough to make a success out of it.'

He envied Joe, for whom diffidence and self-doubt were alien concepts. 'Focused like Adolf and Uncle Joe?' He proffered a tea in his sole mug. 'The world's a big place, I want to experience as much as I can. I refuse to grow old in some cul-de-sac of either place or faith, no matter how well rewarded. He changed the subject.'Tell me, was it your Athy haul that finally divorced Nelson from his pillar and Sackville Street symmetry?'

'I thought you didn't live in the past,' deflected the diplomatic one, who had breathed fresh life into Irish cycling but whose disciples had also allegedly destroyed Dublin's most outstanding monument and sole equestrian sculpture.

Making friends took time. In Scruffy Murphy's, a tweedy figure waved across the crowd. Mistaken identity. 'Shure 'tis neither of us. But allelulah, we're here anyhow. What are you having?' Architect Peter Stevens dragged him to the counter. 'I know a guy in the PR business who needs some help.'

The ensuing lucrative spell in public relations boosted his property aspirations. It also reinforced the suspicion that life was more about perceptions than reality. 'Highlight my name.' A pink-collared executive's ambitions were more personal than corporate. A motoring correspondent relieved a waiter of another glass: 'Would you ever leave that test car to the airport. I can pick it up on my return from the Florida launch.'

'Lovely to see you again, minister.' Suave practitioners flattered those who could be of use to them. Bright sunshine dissipated the wallchart spotlights at one morning pep-talk. A timely reminder that life was about more than making money. A canal wild flower nodded approval; he resumed his writing.

An argument with his mother after gunmen murdered a schoolbus driver in front of children underlined how far they had to go. 'Republican terrorism and protection racketeering makes the Black and Tans look like choirboys. What about that young British soldier who strayed over the border and was shot in cold blood?'

'He had no right to be there.'

'A fine excuse for murder.'

An eighteen-year old from Fulham was blown up by a bomb. 'Nobody slaughtered as many fine youngsters as the British did in this country, including men I knew. Don't you remember poor Kevin Barry?'

'Barry and his group killed three other teenagers, but you never informed me of that. Neither was I ever told that two respected RIC men were gunned down outside Toomevara chapel after a St Patrick's Day devotions. Irish history's just thuggery and lies. What about the Belfast mother of ten shot for the Christian act of helping a dying soldier and whose body hasn't been found yet? The so-called republicans have murdered two Gardai and an Irish soldier in the past year. They're barbarians, not patriots.'

His mother's lips quivered. She laid down her *Irish Press* and picked up her rosary beads. 'God help me, I'm getting too old for all this fighting.'

On his way back to Dublin, he felt ashamed for arguing with her. She had few securities left. Her husband dead, her political party now a sleazy mafia, her favourite newspaper facing bankruptcy. He remembered how the British had fuelled the anarchy by gunning down unarmed Derry marchers and how the Tan terror had blighted her youth. His mother deserved more respect. But so did human life. So did all those unfortunates who were being slaughtered daily. Hadn't she also a responsibility to look beyond tribalism as he had but was the comfort of his abstractions worth the reality of the hurt to her?

Jimmy wagged a greying eyebrow. 'Why couldn't you keep your bloody mouth shut and just discuss the weather? I told you you'd never get on.'

Freelancing was both eventful and educational. Resplendent in three-piece tweeds, J. P. Donleavy squired him around multi-bathroomed Levington Hall: 'Contrary to accepted opinion,

Brendan Behan was immensely competitive and serious about his work. He was also a perceptive critic and the first to read *The Ginger Man* manuscript, which he decorated with corrections and encouragement: "Mike, this book will sweep the world!"' But eighties Ireland was more interested in scandal than literary criticism. 'Get us the low-down on Brendan's son and we'll run your interview with his widow, Beatrice,' insisted a Sunday editor. Another precious source of income gone.

After ventilating the destruction of Paddy Kavanagh's favourite canalside seat, he maintained a vigilant eye on other literary outposts. 'Your *Irish Press* features finally convinced Haughey to save Shaw's house,' Norah Lever thanked him.

'Only Joyce's example kept us going in the dark days.' *Envoy* founder John Ryan displayed his battered copy of *Ulysses*. He braved the dust clouds to pen progress reports on the emerging Joyce Cultural Centre. 'Another million and we're there.' Administrator Ken Monaghan had inherited his uncle's purposefulness. Hearing of the threatened removal of artefacts from the Joyce Tower, he blitzed donors and interested locals. 'Over my dead body.' Artist Paddy Collins waved his scalpel. 'In Sandycove, our benefactions will remain,' intoned Cyril Cusack. After his *Sunday Press* exposé, they did.

In the lean winter months, he sought the heat and light of the National Library and finally concluded his motorsport book. Enthusiastic reviews rewarded the four years' plodding and all the tea in plastic cups. 'My neighbours saw your photo with Lord Mayor Briscoe. You forged a new trail,' his mother wrote in a card.

He was stimulated, meeting so many strivers and achievers. Unlike his pessimistic mother, how positively the life force surged through their vitals! Kathleen Behan's eyes sparkled under her newly clipped grey hair, as she sipped her second Baby Power. 'Sure, what use is life if you can't enjoy an oul' song and a dance? I reared a family I'm proud of and they all lived life to the full.' She leaned forward in her new polka-dot blouse: 'Did I tell you Brendan's definition of the perfectly balanced Irishman?' Her spectacles danced, her lean face creased: 'One with a chip on each shoulder! Poor Brendan was always a generous boy. Many a sunny day he hired a taxi and brought the da and myself up the hills. We picnicked where we had cut turf during the war and then headed down to Johnny Fox's. I knew Michael Collins, Maud Gonne and Willie Yeats – my brother Peadar wrote the national anthem. They're all gone now but isn't that life? Everything comes and goes; you must enjoy it while it's here. Now, would you like to hear another little song?' Like her son at that cinema queue, she was off before he could reply:

> And we'll drink to the days of old Ireland,
> The days that we all did desire.
>
> So, then, Mary dear, be of good cheer
> And throw an oul' sod on the fire.

'I believe she drinks a lot.' his mother observed. 'That stuff will kill her.'

'She's ninety-three this year!'

The hard-earned cheques proved resolutely insufficient to fulfill his house dreams. 'How much are you short?' Mike Thackwell raced to the rescue. Complete with bootscraper and the luxury of an off-floor bed, his new Portobello cottage leaned happily against the Grand Canal, on whose Parnassian banks George Moore and Joyce had discussed their theories of art and Patrick Kavanagh had been reborn. 'And whose sturdy trees were more sinned against than sinning,' said Owen Walsh, recalling his first tryst with actress Blanaid Salkeld.

Artists sprouted like the same trees along the restful waterway. Billy Noyek and his fresh red rose, Liam C. Martin, a sherpa with his folding stool and paintbox and the unlikely Chinese impressionist, Sunny Apinchapon. Keen eyes darting from horizon to easel, Pete Hogan recorded adjacent Georgian elegance, Bob Ó Cathail the noisy bin-men. 'Life without style is death.' D-Day survivor Kevin Monahan strutted his latest exotic tie. But even Kevin was outshone by rainbow-attired and opinionated Frances Bunch Moran, as she immortalised the canal's luminosity and falling leaves: 'Everyone tells me what a draughtsman Harry Kernoff was. Sure the man couldn't draw a straight line.'

'More good news: the *Irish Press* has agreed to a weekly art column,' he told his mother.

'Be careful of that art crowd, they're a strange lot.'

She wasn't far wrong. 'Where the hell's that man?' proprietor Tom Caldwell sought John Kingerlee before a Fitzwilliam Street exhibition opening. He found the convert in the patio corner facing Mecca. 'First time I've seen an artist horizontal through prayer.' A group of London visitors leaned across James McKenna and himself to admire the Davy Byrnes murals. The sculptor erupted: 'I hate the fucking English. I had to work as a milkman there to survive – and you shat on me, you artless humourless bastards.'

'Never darken this establishment again, you bowsies.' He was thrown out of a pub for the first time in his life. 'He is not welcome at Goggin's door,' mocked street poet, Christopher Daybell, heading home with an armful of equally rejected masterpieces.

The scale of social change matched the topographical transformation. Casual clothes brightened speeded-up streets; few women wore skirts. The aroma of coffee and pitta bread replaced the fifties reek of bacon and egg. There was no ostentatious grace before meals; no one whispered any more, cap-doffing and guilt had flown with censorship. No more Maria Gorettis in the backs of chapels; one bookshop even boasted a section on relationships, *Caidreamh*, through the medium of Gaelic! 'A cleric is now as rare as a policeman or the 47A.' Jimmy surveyed O'Connell Street, once monopolised by earnest young priests and dark-habited nuns.

'Red or green, sir – or would you like strawberry-flavoured?' Condoms were no longer illegal. Women had come out of purdah. 'So many unmarried mothers parade their progeny on cycle-carriers that one wonders if they come from a hire-shop.' Jimmy surveyed the office of the Cherish, the single-parent association. When you left, enjoyment was a sin. Now, it's compulsory. But all a bit late for my generation. With four eyes and detachable teeth, most of my colleagues atrophied on their high stools without having ever had a woman, Murphy's and masturbation were our only release. Will you join me at the Merriman Festival; it might be my last chance?' Surrealism on the edge of the Burren and Atlantic Europe. The sea-setting sun glinted off a procession of slow-moving cars, as they streamed back from a Fanore afternoon dance to an even wilder

Merriman soirée in Lahinch. 'God bless organiser Con Howard and all his enthusiasms.' Jimmy conducted an imaginary orchestra.

Daytime Leeson Street slumbered in Georgian respectability. By night, it throbbed to the siren call of clubs where one could drink and disco to unconsciousness, before staggering into daylight from the equally improbable Manhattan. He embraced the society of senior swingers in Joys, who were desperately making up for lost time like himself. 'I Wanna Go Where Love Is'.

'Okey dokey, doesn't every senile sybarite.' Peter Stevens brandished another bottle.

With an audience of voyeuristic seals, he gambolled on a Blasket strand with a beached nurse. A bottle of Chianti chilled in a Wicklow stream while he communed with a separated teacher. 'Let's wait until a train is coming.' Unshy Rachel draped herself across a slab of glistening granite as the waves surged on Kilcoole strand.

'You suffer from an over-exposure to Wordsworth.' Jimmy tested the counter of the new Duke. 'If this leaks out, CIE will be packing safari specials.'

Aware of Dublin's slide to decadence, his mother frequently hid religious medals in his jacket pocket. 'Call me some time,' a nocturnal goddess invited in Buck Whaleys. As he fumbled for a pen, a Miraculous Medal clattered to the counter between the glasses of Chateau Leeson Street.

'They never should have done away with that ould Latin,' his mother sighed, before realising that she was speaking to someone who had not been near a church for years.

She fought a rearguard action in the teeth of the mushrooming political and church scandals. 'Disgusting the way journalists abuse their power, always inventing a new exposé. Trying to drag down Charlie Haughey, while he's doing his best to keep the country going. Phone tapping isn't good enough, I'd lock them all up.' He could tell her the harsh realities or leave her faith intact. She chuckled when he agreed: 'A great idea, and a lot more work for me.' They met Father Quinlan in the nursing-home corridor: 'Isn't it disgraceful the way those muckrakers are trying to destroy the reputation of poor clergy like Father Cleary and Bishop Casey? What do you expect when people abandon God?' He accompanied his mother around the grounds. 'Where's it all going to end?' She shook her head. He made her laugh when he quoted Brendan Behan: 'Those speculative byways would put years on you. When Gertrude Stein was dying, she asked: "What's the answer?" Then she sat up: "But, what is the question?"'

His mother shared his regard for the playwright whose short stories first appeared in her favourite paper. 'Poor Brendan was a dacent craythur, God rest him.' She leaned against the bridge. 'But the British destroyed him with all that drink and flattery; he should have stayed in Ireland.'

> And we sigh for dear old England,
> And the Captains and the Kings.

He realised then that his own emigration had been worthwhile after all. 'The British completed his education – and mine. Even our respective incarcerations proved financially beneficial! Are you settling down now?' he enquired.

'I suppose I'm used to having you around, if that's what you mean! I was very worried when you came back, that you wouldn't be able to get any work. But you've done well, with your house and your name in so many papers.'

As he chased commissions at an age when most were considering retirement, she still hoped that he would settle down to a good nine-to-five job. 'Any chance of a regular opening with the *Irish Press?*'

Jimmy visited his mother. Their conservative outlooks ensured it was an agreeable meeting. 'That Jimmy is a very sensible man; he stuck to his CIE job. He always looks so smart in his collar and tie. Why can't you be like him?' He hoped his friend hadn't discussed their artistic adventures. He had recently enlivened his social life by bringing him to exhibition openings. 'You meet a better class of person here.' Jimmy surveyed his Leinster Gallery goblet, though he ungratefully declined to return to one gallery: 'I'm not going to die from their Bulgarian plonk.' Since considering early retirement, Jimmy had become more argumentative. 'The most stupid man I ever met – all the time you wasted before you finally found that the world wasn't black and white.' He prodded with his catalogue at a recent exhibition. 'Speaking of which, the colonial liberators for whom you marched have corrupted everything they touched. And their dispossessed are arriving by the boatload, shitting babies at the taxpayers' expense. BeJasus, you joined every do-good organisation, foisting your inadequacies on the deprived masses, and where did it get you? Time inside, loss of work, sore hooves from all those marches, abuse for your silly papers. And no one ever gave a monkey's. The world doesn't give a fuck about us, so why should we care about it? I told you that years ago. And you never really escaped the religion. You can't even visit the supermarket without making a moral judgement. Now, after all your mighty ideas, you're just like the rest of us. A pint, a woman and eyes going square from the telly.'

'Wisest is he who knows he does not know.'

'Bloody typical! Berating the Christ believers but scurrying behind Socrates' pyjamas with all the other misfits and smart alecs. And admiring every bloody philosopher and shithead who manages to string a few words together. Sure those fuckers are only farting around in the dark like the rest of us.'

Though he wasn't much concerned these days about changing society, improving himself remained an ongoing challenge. An effort to understand his friend's passivity might be an exercise in self-enlightenment: 'You've always given me food for thought.'

'Never mind the food, pass me some art,' Jimmy hiccupped

'Bishop a dad!' The papers broadcast that both Bishop Casey and Father Michael Cleary had fathered children.

'Your fellow-scribes are very brave now, hunting in packs and faking interviews, like O'Reilly's rags. But they were spineless bastards in the fifties when they were most needed, all apart from *The Irish Times*.' Jimmy waved his favourite newspaper. 'And not one of them credits Casey for his work with London's Irish homeless.' Jimmy knew like him that priests were also victims.

For his mother, the revelations were a body blow. 'Gutter press, they should be banned.' She called on her next-door neighbour. Nancy always agreed with her: 'God help us, nothing's sacred any more, Mrs Lynch.'

'I hope they'll sue and put an end once and for all to these libels. I'll gladly make a contribution.' His mother shook her handbag.

But her money remained safe; her spiritual guardians did not sue. She was forced to accept the reality of their failures. 'None of us is perfect.' She fingered her beads. The political and clerical disillusionment hastened her retreat from the outside world. 'Go into our little chapel any time of the day and your mother's nearly always there. She'll beat us all to heaven!' the Reverend Mother said as she saw him off one day. 'Your support's a great encouragement, but she will need you even more from now on. She's not getting any younger, you know.'

16

'You'll be tired out with all that driving.' While she pretended that he had interrupted her *Irish Press* reading, his mother's coat was always lying ready on the bed. She came alive on the fortnightly trips back to Toomevara where his father was buried. 'Wouldn't you miss the swerves and the cambers and dips, and the primroses under the stonewalls?' She surveyed the straight approach to Shelley's Cross. 'The roads were more human before; now they're racetracks. Billy Delaney's poor son was killed here last year. You won't see Billy and the cows any more; the farmers all have milking machines. Robinson's beech walk was cut down, the riverside lilac went in a Tidy Towns beautification. But weren't they awful amadáns, concreting over our lovely flower garden for a carport?'

The roof of Gordon Birch's workshop had fallen in. Mrs Birch gave him the jew's harp. 'Gordon would be happy for you to have this. I'm afraid Jack Hackett, Mrs Regan, Dick Casey, the Oracle and the Looby sisters are all gone too.'

The village seemed smaller; the chapel's high wall and trees had been removed. His mother surveyed the new gates: 'Like a Yank with one of those awful crew-cuts, the mystery's gone. And the candles are all electric.' It seemed that nothing had changed, as they sat around Looby's Aga cooker with a niece of the aunts and the river chattered outside the window. But Bert Patterson's banjo would dazzle no more village audiences. Shrubs and a Blessed Virgin statue would likewise deter any travellers tempted by the square's inviting space. No room here for a Christmas carpenter and his pregnant wife.

'Look at that screen, Mrs Lynch.' Dan Casey displayed the new security camera beside the canopied petrol pumps.

'Lord bless us and save us. I can see the entire village!'

A television set had replaced Dick Casey's wireless. Masts proclaimed the medium's supremacy from chimneys whose Paul Henry smoke had once advertised the wind direction. A loftier

Mondrian lattice relayed its message from heights previously lit by a papal cross. His mother clutched Jim Shanahan's arm: 'It's like a new religion; it's destroyed the open door, the curdeeking and the card games. And everyone speaks the same now. You don't hear accents any more.'

'The box has brought more changes in thirty years than we had in the previous three hundred.' Jim stood with his back to the set on which he never missed a race meeting. 'We're now watching the same programmes as those beyond in London or New York. All the old stories are being buried with each senior citizen.'

'Despite Ned O'Donoghue's hopeful words, Jim, I think the electric darkened more than it illuminated!'

'Do you remember the pre-electric summer day, when a Yank bought a lemonade from Darby Kinnane?' Jim switched off the kettle. '"Could I have some ice, please?" says your man. "Yerra, where in the name of Jaysus do you think you'll find ice in the middle of July?" Darby answered.' His mother stirred her cup. 'Weren't we lucky to live in a time when there was wonder and characters? When the farmers worked, instead of listening to pop music in their tractors and being handed Common Market money *not* to grow things. What's the world coming to?

'Will you ever forget the Timekeeper? All the pens and he could neither read nor add up. Do you remember the day he made that table for Boss O'Meara and then couldn't get it out the door? And Johnny Kennedy's horse trap shaft? "I'll make sure of the measurements first." He placed a length of timber on the good shaft and then sawed through both pieces of wood.

'And the Oracle, listening to the Irish commentary on Casey's wireless, and telling everyone what a great player Puck Saor must be. He didn't know that *poc saor* meant a free!'

'The best characters and the best days, Mrs Lynch. And, thanks to the Sergeant, we could always leave the door open. Do you remember Johnnie and Peggy Reilly coming down the aisle after getting married? Johnnie turned to Peggy and said "We're one now, Peggy." "– An' I'm the one!" she replied. Poor Johnnie went last year.'

'You know, we're not getting any younger ourselves,' his mother sighed.

'Go away out of that; there's lashings of life left in us. The ould dogs for the hard road!'

Dusk often overtook them before Nora Shanahan's apple tart set his mother up for the return journey to the home. She gradually resumed her reading and radio play listening. Only Homer's *Odyssey* and a few odd volumes had survived the move to the nursing home. 'I miss the books.' She looked around the room one afternoon. He began rebuilding her library with an illustrated biography of her hero, Éamon de Valera. She turned the pages: 'As I was saying before I was interrupted!' A book on the Emergency stirred further memories. 'The LDF parades and rationing. Will you ever forget your father trying to put out poor Johnny Armstrong's fire with the stirrup pump?'

They celebrated with tea and cakes in the Tower hotel when his London enquiries produced *Saint Elmo*, a long-sought nineteenth-century romance. Mannix Flynn's *Nothing to Say* resulted in regular donations to Father McVerry's hostel for homeless delinquents. Peadar O'Donnell inscribed copies of *Islanders* and *The Big Windows*: 'We both shared the exciting times, Mrs Lynch.' They corresponded each week but one Thursday there was no letter. That afternoon, the Reverend Mother phoned. 'Your mother asked me to call. She's in bed with a cold and can't write. The doctor's advised her to take it easy for a while.' Doctor? His mother had been ill and he hadn't known about it. He was shocked to realise that, as helpless as she had been when he returned, she was even frailer now. He sped to Roscrea.

'You're an awful child.' She sat up in bed to take her antibiotics. 'Traipsing across the country for nothing. Sure I'm only a bit under the weather. I'll be up and about in a few days.'

'You wouldn't be taking those things if you were that well.' He took the glass from her. 'I'll have to keep a closer eye on you from now on, to make sure you don't overdo it.'

'No more discos!' She lay back in the bed.

'Don't be taken in; she's delighted to see you.' The Reverend Mother interrupted her bookkeeping. 'You've got to accept her ageing. You don't see many eighty-five-year old machines functioning as well as she does.'

His mother provided another surprise. He had brought her a book on Clare social history. 'When I'm better, I'll reveal a secret to you. Some real history. I should have told you long ago, perhaps, and then you would have understood many things better. You should go now; I need my beauty sleep.'

'Maybe you're the son of a bishop?' Jimmy reacted to news of his mother's confidence.

His mother's new vulnerability was a major concern. In addition to writing, he phoned every Sunday afternoon. The regular calls, letters and outings restored security and expectancy to her life. 'All they ever talk about is the weather,' she denigrated her fellow-residents. But one day, he found her discussing with her neighbours whether to play Delia Murphy or the Kilfenora Ceilidhe Band on the tape recorder which had once recorded Graham Hill. She had no such reservations about priests, and enjoyed well-advertised friendships with Canon Cahill and fellow-*Irish Press*-reader Father Quinlan. She was less charitable towards Miss O'Meara: 'That one would keep you gassing all day. I don't know why she can't find something better to do than buttonholing visitors. She's a menace.'

Her spirited neighbour was a match for his mother. Until his mother grew wise to her strategy, Miss O'Meara waited in ambush for him each fortnight. She told him how her father had introduced the wireless to the midlands and delivered batteries to the Portumna home of twenties cult-figure Henry Seagrave. 'He was the first to drive at two hundred miles per hour.' She gripped his arm: 'Two hundred miles an hour in 1929 – can you imagine it?

'You didn't know about poor Baron Hanley? He died a pauper over in Chicago, and his body wasn't claimed for six weeks. He blew all his money on the Irish tours. But wasn't he a bright spark just the same, like Prince Monolulo with the ostrich feathers and racing tips? Didn't he add a bit of colour to our lives? Will you ever forget the state car?'

Balancing on her wavering stick, Miss O'Meara related how her grandfather had heard Daniel O'Connell speak. 'There were bonfires everywhere. The streets and fields were full of horses, donkeys and carts, and the coaches of the grander people. The square was jammed. Men and women hung out of every window and balcony. He spoke for three hours and such was the cheering that every bird in the town was terrified and didn't return for days! My grandfather, Lord rest him, said that O'Connell was the first man who'd given self-respect to the ordinary people and the courage to get up and campaign for their rights. And he won freedom for the English Catholics too! But aren't we a gas race? Always spouting about freedom and the rest of it but that was something to be proud about and there's not even a plaque to show that it happened – or where.'

Mise Éire. Past Miss O'Meara's indignant head, he could see the sitting-room inmates nodding off. Mrs O'Brien, the retired teacher, stooped and widowed Mrs Ryan, Johnny Rourke the farmer and former nurse Miss Wrigley. Their individuality subsumed in the pallid anonymity of the institutionalised but each with his or her own little bit done for country and community. These were the people to whose grandparents Daniel O'Connell had spoken.

'Do you know, they may be all half-asleep in there now, but what a store of history they are? I said to Sister Luke the other day, if the schoolchildren came down here, they would learn more about real history in five minutes than all that bang-bang stuff in the books. Amn't I right? Next time, I must talk to you about Sacco and Vanzetti – and poor Harry Gleeson just down the road from here, also executed in 1941 for something he hadn't done. What do you think of the people of New Inn who kept their mouths shut while an innocent man was hanged for a murder committed by a local patriot?'

His mother enjoyed more outings than Miss O'Meara. 'Weren't those stone masons men of faith and artistry, ma'am?' An encounter with a scholarly priest complemented a visit to restored Duiske Abbey.

Birdsong enhanced the pastoral mood as they strolled along the lazing Barrow. Children freed from school waved distantly from the old bridge; trout jumped tentatively. He told his mother of his London art lessons and how soaring Gothic had freed up space previously confined by the Norman and Romanesque styles. 'A little learning's a dangerous thing.' She touched her head.

He succeeded in getting her to take a short annual break from the nursing home. Like a draped Henry Moore, she gathered her tweed coat in the car's front seat. 'There's nothing like a holiday.' Expectancy enlivened her posture. On the way to Clare, they made a surprise detour to one of her favourite places, Clomnacnoise.

Farmers conversed on hay-scented Shannon uplands. One could imagine the shock as the Norse stormed ashore from their intimidating longboats. His mother remembered a verse from 'The Dead at Clonmacnoise':

> In a quiet water'd land, a land of roses,
> Stands Saint Kieran's fair city:
> And the warriors of Erin in their famous generations
> Slumber there.

They motored under leafy arches into Bodyke, where she met a former pupil. 'What do you think of that Kylie Minogue one, whose father came from your place?'

'Don't talk to me.' His mother shooed an inquisitive mongrel. 'Sure in Tipperary, we've a fellow named Boy George who dresses up as a woman. And they're all making millions. Where did we go wrong at all?'

'Many's the time your father and I cycled here from Scarriff.' His mother surveyed the Boudinesque sands of Lahinch before returning to dine and gossip with fellow-guests at the Atlantic Hotel. Unexpected escorts accompanied them around Fanore Head into Galway Bay. 'Flying fish, have you ever seen anything like it?' She pointed to the splashing dolphins.

Outriders of surpliced rabbits preceded them along the lane to Corcamroe Abbey. They paced the green-set jewel whose ribs had weathered into harmony with the Burren ruggedness. His mother parted the lichen on King Conor O'Brien's tomb: 'Great days then in Clare. Our own kings and the choirs singing out across those hills each evening. And then the English came and destroyed everything.' He steered her across the new graves of those who basked in the reflected glory. 'We'd a fellow named Niall of the Nine Hostages who was raiding and kidnapping over there long before they ever bothered us.'

'God bless us; you'll never change!'

A long-mooted trip to Bundoran provided the only disenchantment. One-armed bandits had taken over the seaside town his mother had known for its teahouses. She reared from her seat in Old Testament rage: 'Away from this noisy dump. Such a lovely place destroyed by the greed of gombeen men. Cromwell couldn't have done worse.'

'Do you ever see the inside of a church these days?' Each time he left the nursing home, his mother sprinkled his car with holy water. He conspired in the blessing by delaying to speak to a nun or resident. He told Owen Walsh how she continued to worry about his temporal life. 'I don't know how you carry on, with neither insurance policy or pension. What will you do when you get older and can't work?'

'A buxom nun from your mother's nursing home would be insurance enough for me.' The artist picked his way through the flattened tubes and discarded brushes and pulled up two paint-splattered chairs to the variegated table.

Survivors of the fireplace purges flooded the turps-marinated studio with colour and animation. Mahler competed with Rubensque nudes and dancing street scenes. Shelves listed under the weight of symphonies and tomes on Picasso, Van Gogh and Matisse, the favourite. A photograph of Owen with Siobhán McKenna graced the piano, on which he had allegedly danced naked with another actress. Ensconced for half a century beside Lad Lane's arch, the artist was the last of Baggot Street's once teeming Bohemian population. His beard bristled at the reminder that his 'Owen Walsh, Knock Hard' brass knocker was now flanked by a row of plastic office bells.

'These fucking Celtic Tigers are tearing the arse out of the city. Instant cobblestones and rip-off pubs. Temple Bar's now Covent Garden with Guinness. You blink and a landmark's gone forever. Dolly Fawcetts a car park like most city churchyards, the bells plundered from Bloom's St George's Church, centuries of tombstones piling up in Mary Street as trendies turn O'Casey's baptismal church into a theme bar. And nobody gives a damn. 'Inishfallen Fare Thee Well!' Owen banged the table. The spoon danced a jig: 'Dublin Corporation's sold out to the building spivs. The Meath hospital's gone; the Adelaide's next, Dublin will soon be like Phnom Penh. Lovely shops, intimate streets turned into apartment fortresses with remote-controlled gates that would make Ceausescu blush. Congeniality to concrete at the thrust of a bulldozer. More business for the guards and the shrinks, you wait and see. Swinging their demolition balls is the only way those developers can orgasm. 'Twould be a pleasure to get rid of them and their bloody canopy of cranes, and see an unrestored building again. Bricks that have served their apprenticeship, flaking paint, rusting wrought iron, a few weeds between the steps and the voices of three-dimensional people. Real Dublin, not this shitty pastiche. The poverty of the tenements? Jasus, those people had character and craftiness and style. They didn't spend all day glued to a welfare television.'

The artist lunged at the window; paint flakes flew from the shutters: 'When I came here, there were cherry blossoms on those trees and and you'd meet Behan or O'Flaherty on their way for a jar. Now, it's all suits and advertising gasbags. Or kit boys and girls, the earphone generation, all from the same bottle and all wired up to Radio Gaga. They obliterated Georgian elegance and Lampshades pub for that Mammon's glasshouse, I've seen more inviting privies. Look at those all-terrain vehicles and not a jungle in sight, only more bloody cars – going nowhere. Progress, my royal Irish arse. But it's an ill wind. After burying it in one improvement, they uncovered a mural of mine in Larry Murphys latest manifestation. Let's toast the fucking thing before it gets covered again.'

Jimmy was equally discountenanced when he was short-taken in the toilet-less streets one Sunday afternoon. A Cockney bouncer pointed: 'Can't you read that notice, pal? Toilets for Customers' Use Only.' 'What the hell's this town coming to when you can't have a slash without some foreign illiterate telling you how to read a sign? Say "Boo" to a black queue-jumper and you're called a racist. Manners and respect are in free fall. You can't walk in the street without some mobile diner spilling a coffee over you. "Get a life,"a BMW virago berated me last week, after I remonstrated with her for nearly running me down.

'Security guards, cameras, speculators and foreigners: the city's been sold out without anyone noticing. It soon won't be Ireland any more. The shops are like clinics, we're all just ciphers, even drinking's an industry. The pubs are gone to the dogs with muzak and TV, a civilised discussion's now impossible. If it's not some pop rock-ape or apette spouting "shit" and "fuck", or a live camel race from Abu Dhabi, some idiot will whip out one of these new phones and depress you even further with intimate details of his drab existence. Soon they won't even be able to shite without bringing their phone soothers. Mobile morons.'

A provincial town when he had returned, Dublin now seemed an overcrowded building site. A pensioner he knew had just made the final rounds of the shops and friends in Bolton Street where he has spent all his life. A developer had taken over his house and forced him out to the wilds of the Navan Road, where he knew no one and where there were no shops.

Michael Carroll took a more positive view of the changes. The artist stopped his bicycle by Trinity's railings: 'You journos only write about negativity and destruction. What about the thriving art? What about the innovative architecture and design?

'Pastel-coloured buildings have replaced the quayside dereliction. The Gate Theatre, City Hall and Royal Hospital glow, the National Museum's straight from Monet's palette. Fanlights and renovated railings coruscate, fountains animate Talbot Street and Earlsfort Terrace. Art galleries are mushrooming, flower and sculpture displays enliven Merrion Square and other parks. Henry Moore's anchored Yeats in ethereal bronze in Stephen's Green. Isn't it bloody marvellous?'

'Here's Owen Walsh. You can tell him yourself.' He pointed across Nassau street. Michael regained his pedals; Baggotonia was still too small for more than one artist.

His mother took longer to get into the car. 'These ould belts are a nuisance.'

But he delighted her six months before her illness as they passed Roscrea's sleepy houses and homely hotels. 'I don't know how I stayed so long on the other side.'

'Mind that cyclist; tell me more.' She looked over at him.

'I heard a tin whistle under College Green's portico the other evening. It beat anything I'd heard in the Albert Hall. No poet laureate ever matched Brendan Kennelly's effervescence; you could never compare London to here.'

'The Lord be blessed. Saul's conversion!'

A juggernaut thundered past and shook their car. 'Where on earth are you going now?' She looked around, as he detoured off the main highway near Dunkerrin.

'Somewhere quieter. We'll try just a little of the old road.'

'Only for a few miles, then. Isn't the sunshine lovely on the hedges? And the woodbine. Lord bless us, I haven't smelt it for years. The bends remind me of all those little gatehouses. 'Twas a terrible shame they were destroyed. Will you ever forget your favourite, the Ink Bottle Lodge? You made us stop there every time we cycled to the Roscrea hurlings.'

As they traversed what remained of the original switch-backed thoroughfare, he lamented the passing of the distinctive round landmark. He was told it had been demolished thirty years earlier. But as they turned a bend on the now little-used road it suddenly reappeared, right in front of them! A few stones were missing and a startled pigeon flapped through a door-less frame. But the lodge's black slates and round chimney were intact and it looked more like the equally redundant inkbottle than ever. So amazed was he at the joyous discovery that at first he feared it must be a mirage.

His mother forgot her fear of the dark ways and her antipathy to Ascendancy houses. She stepped out of the car. 'God bless us and save us, but it's like tasting bog tay again.' After walking around the lodge, she caught his arm. 'Will you ever forget the '*Fir ag Obair*' signs when we were cycling to Scarriff?' They laughed at the memory of the wooden 'Men at Work' notices, which invariably preceded a gang of council workers leaning on their shovels.

'Thanks for reminding me of the Scottish Fiddle Orchestra concert and Dick Warner's Shannon film. Marvellous to see Scarriff docks and Holy Island again.' There was an unaccustomed softness to his mother's voice as they resumed driving. 'You're happy now, living in your own country?'

'It took some time but I'm getting used to it!'

'Last week was the anniversary of my first dance with Alfie Rogers.' She gazed out the windscreen.

'Alfie Rogers – the man who was shot in Killaloe?'

'Yes. Alfie was a great dancer. That night was one of the happiest of my life.' She saw a horizon farther than his. 'But then the Tans came to Clare and destroyed everything. They burned houses, sacked towns and shot at farmers working in the fields. While a lot of people talked about doing something, Alfie and his friends decided to fight. When he told me he was going up to Woodford,

I never thought I wouldn't see him again. The Tans roared into Scarriff looking for them. They ransacked our house but we didn't tell them anything. Somehow they found out where Alfie and the lads were. They captured them on the other side of Whitegate and brought them to Killaloe, where they tortured them.'

His mother started to sob. 'We got word that they'd been caught and that someone had seen the boat taking them down the lake. But before anything could be done to save them, the Tans shot them the next night. A man cycled from Killaloe and told us that their bodies were lying on the bridge.'

'That was terrible.' He changed gear gently. 'But it was a long time ago and we have to press on with our lives.'

'I will *never* forget.' She turned to him. 'You see, Alfie Rogers was my special friend. We were young and we laughed at how different we were in ways but we often spoke of a future together.'

So this was the big secret she had kept from her children for all those years. Hardly surprising that she abhorred the English. No wonder she had always feared the worst. 'God knows where we'd have gone together.' His mother dabbed her eyes. 'But I suppose it was His holy will and I accepted it. I cried for months because I never got the chance to say goodbye or comfort him. I will never forgive those who deprived him and his comrades of their young lives. But they are safe with God and nothing else can harm them now. When I met your father, I told him about Alfie. But he was the only one who knew how much he meant to me, until today.

'Now, maybe, you'll understand why I will never be reconciled to the English who made me and so many Irish people suffer. You're very lucky, not knowing the king's head on your stamps nor having to kow-tow to the coloniser. Nor waking up, wondering which of your friends will be killed today. We were ordinary simple people and all we wanted was to govern our own country. But so many good people had to die before they would allow us that.'

Alfie Rogers was much more than a name on a weatherbeaten monument. Hitherto, the Independence war had been something he had read about in books. But his mother had experienced its horror in real life. He would never argue with her over politics again. 'They were brave men, all right,' he said as he eased the car back on to the main road.

17

For three days his mother's condition remained unchanged. But on Friday morning, he was wakened by her agitated breathing. Though in adjacent rooms, he feared they were now farther apart than they had ever been. Nurse Ryan took his mother's pulse. 'That's liquid in her lungs; my injection will clear it completely.' His mother had deteriorated. Her elusive expression mirrored that of his father on his final day. More weary than he had ever before seen her, she had started to withdraw into herself. She would hardly ever see the Ink Bottle Lodge again.

Her breathing followed him down the corridor to the dining room. The Reverend Mother beamed a morning greeting, despite the responsibility of the burgeoning day with so many dependants. He suddenly remembered he had something to tell her: 'The mother's given me a great present.' The sister raised her eyebrows. 'Well, it's my birthday and to find her still alive despite all those gloomy prognoses was the best gift I could have hoped for!'

They shared a birthday toast of tea and brown bread. Through the broad window, he could see the early birds pecking their way through the flowers and vegetables which climbed to the hilltop Calvary. The sun was gilding the tip of the cross. 'Another grand day, thank God,' his father would have said. He heard the doctor's Renault 4. He excused himself and ran to meet the rural carer who lived remote from the expense-account world of communications acquaintances. The modem Peter Gilligan offered little comfort. 'She's fighting but her condition has definitely worsened.'

His mother was probably dying; he knew that now. But knowledge was one thing, acceptance another. He resumed his obstinate watch. He still hoped for a recovery of some sort. He held her hand. Tears trickled down his face as he willed her to continue that fight. He felt guilty for not appreciating earlier his mother's difficult life. He had sometimes reproached her for the negative influence of her worrying. 'Times were hard when I was bringing you all up. We never knew where the next penny was coming from. What else could we do only worry and pray?'

The stagnation which stifled thought in Ireland had also imprisoned her; the obsessive churchgoing and imagined maladies were likely fellow-children of a circumscribed and frustrated intelligence. Her books were her only means of escape. She had never realised her Irish Hospitals' Sweepstakes dreams: 'A fur coat, a Hoover and a trip to Lourdes!'

Sister Pauline glided in with fresh flowers: 'Your mother always appreciated nature. When she wakes up she'll be pleased to see these.'

The blooms' lively colours highlighted the increasing depersonalisation of the room. A tube led out of the plastic bag by the end of the metal bed; the bedclothes had been reduced to more clinical proportions. No longer casual ornaments, the religious objects projected a bolder, brassier presence.

How alive both the room and his mother has been only this day last week! She had been reading the *History of the Ely O'Carroll*, a rare work which Mary King of Parsons bookshop had unearthed. 'Will you come and look at this, a link between Mona Incha and Toomevara. It was Saint Domnan from Mona Incha who founded the church on Toomevara square in 650. Can you bate that?'

And how she had been looking forward to this weekend's break. She left in two new dresses to be altered and announced loudly enough for everyone to hear: 'I need them on Tuesday at the latest, I am going to Lahinch with my son.'

At least she hadn't aged as crankily as Jimmy, who increasingly fulminated against television advertisements, women with briefcases and loud music: 'I can't turn on the fucking tap, without being drowned in pop tripe.' Ten days earlier, he had persuaded his elder to share a Bloomsday horse-cab tour of Joycean Dublin. 'You're only trying to get me drunk so I'll pay.' Jimmy adjusted to the Edwardian upholstery, as they trotted northwards from their first Lincoln Inn port of call. By the time they descended to the Ormond Hotel, he was drunk and discomfited. 'Will you look at those myopic dandruffies. Your soulmates, all injected the wrong way, consulting their *Ulysses* like it was a bloody bible. Beards for the chinless. Their straw hats reveal a lot about their brains.'

'How's Molly?' He nudged a Bloom lookalike.

He loosened his tie. 'Soon it will be a national holiday. Joyceburgers, Joyce fellowships, Joyce jobs for the boys. James Augustine, patron saint of jarveys, innkeepers and every kind of academic and anaemic opportunist. And each holiday will begin with a reading. "Saint James, chapter six, verse four: And lo! there was muzak on Ormond Quay." What a load of Blooming bollocks. I'm going home.' Mistaking reality for art, an American student scribbled earnestly. 'Happiness is a bowel movement.' Jimmy brushed past him. As the inebriate one subsided into a motorised taxi, the Joycean enquired: 'Is he appearing later at Davy Byrnes?'

The window rattled as Danny approached with his wheelbarrow. *A Book of Hours* scene. 'My own mother went down with a stroke but she hung on for nine months. There's no telling with these things,' the gardener encouraged through the window.

'There's something special about people who work close to the earth. Yours is a more refined appreciation of nature and life,' his mother had once congratulated Danny.

'How are you, Mrs Lynch?' Nurse Ryan interrupted. 'A change of clothes and a new position and you'll be so comfortable you won't know yourself. A nice surprise for your son too: a letter from London. Maybe it's a love letter?'

It wasn't a love letter, but a florid note from his eldest daughter. 'Tell grandmam that I'm flying over to see her on Saturday. No red carpet, please; a cup of tea will do nicely when I arrive!'

'If anything ever happens to me, Laura is to get my engagement ring. She's a good girl.' Had his mother seen in Laura the free spirit she wished she had been? But the same girl had let him down more than once. She never delivered those photographs to David McClelland, nor the book he'd promised to Nevill Johnson. He would still have his London flat if she had continued to live there. 'I'll check out that library information for you next week, promise.' How they would get on when she arrived? At least he would see her, unlike her younger sister who had seldom communicated since the divorce.

The midday Angelus rang out. For his mother, alone with her history books, the sound would have spanned a millennium back to the time of Saint Domnan. It was wasted now on a pagan like him.

He brushed a stubborn fly from her hair.

The Reverend Mother bustled in the door. 'Siobhán, Sister Luke again. How are you now?' She addressed his mother as loudly as she had on Tuesday morning. But this time there was no response. This time his mother was not OK. 'Now, don't worry. She's comfortable and not suffering in the least.' Her words had the ring of the patient's shorthand. Three nuns from England escorted the Reverend Mother. One whispered: 'She won't last the day.' Was there no end to people's insensitivity? He remembered two visitors discussing a burial site beside his father's deathbed. He sat fearfully, wondering if his mother was still aware of his presence. He replaced the blankets any time she turned. She no longer mouthed prayers; her movements had become less agitated. He tried to encourage her: 'You're in safe hands; the rest will do you good.' But he felt a boldly growing certainty that they would never communicate again. Half of him fought to banish the gloomy thoughts. It was one o'clock on a summer afternoon, and his mother was still very much alive. That was the reality he should be celebrating. The door flew open. 'Racket Hall!' Sister Pauline shooed him out.

The vast countryside calmed him as he drove. It reminded him of pastures farther afield but his wandering ambitions were no longer imperative. It was his mother who was travelling. The progress of her decline was a shock. Her shrinking features were more set, her good and paralysed limbs equally immobile. Those once hyperactive hands had baked many a cake and given him many a wallop. Sad to see them now so still. She was surely breaking free, at last casting off the moorings of eight long decades. 'Your mother's a strong woman,' the doctor had informed him. He felt it was her stamina alone which was keeping her alive, those lungs and that heart which had first pulsated with life all those years ago in Clare. If only his mother could speak now, what things he could learn. She had told him about Alfie Rogers but how he wished that he had asked for more family history. Regrets for lost opportunities, were these to be death's biggest due?

Odd that it was only weeks since his mother had lamented with him at the demise of Parsons bookshop. 'Another bit of history gone, like Coole House. They were great to get that book for me and that was a nice thing you did, organising the little party for Miss

O'Flaherty and her companions.' Most of the books and bookcases had been sold during the previous days. An unaccustomed quiet reigned. Dust hovered where famous writers had once scintillated. But order was everything for May O'Flaherty. She fretted by the redundant cash register, under the bright wall patch from which her portrait by Owen Walsh had been removed.

'Miss Leahy, did you lock that back door? Miss O'Riordan, will you check that window again.' At six o'clock, they filed out the redbrick exit. For the final time, May bent down and padlocked the iron gate under the *Irish Times* sign. She was surprised when he invited her and the ladies across the road for a farewell drink. 'You know I only have a glass at noon with my lunch.' Her studious respectability reminded him of his mother.

'We can't see Parsons final chapter closed without a suitable rounding-off.' He took her arm at the traffic lights.

'Well, May O'Flaherty, I am shocked! Drinking in the evening as well as at lunchtime.' Mary Lavin emerged from a corner with her husband Michael Scott and daughter, Caroline. 'Beattie! What are you doing here?' Mary King suddenly saw Beatrice Behan and *Books Ireland* editor, Jeremy Addis. 'We were just passing by.' Michael Hartnett removed his cap. Owen Walsh held the door open for Garrett Fitzgerald. Artist Michael Carroll and journalist Michael O'Toole followed them in from the May sunshine. There were no speeches, only the murmur of reminiscing which gained strength with each round. Like flowers after a shower, the ladies of Parsons sprang to life. Despite the avant-garde wealth which had passed through the shop, May O'Flaherty confessed: 'The Catholic *Messenger* was always literature enough for me.' The proprietor smiled modestly when Mary Lavin reiterated: 'Parsons Bookshop, where there were often more writers on the floor than on the shelves!'

May remembered the first visit of the Oxford University Press representative. 'We still sold hardware and little nets for the children playing on the canal. When this pinstriped man walked in, his bowler banged against one of the hanging buckets. "Am I at the right address?" he enquired politely.' Mary Lavin laughed when May recalled how they would only know of Flann O'Brien's presence by a discreet cough from the dictionary section. After another medicinal glass, the proprietor revealed that her favourite had been Patrick Kavanagh. 'You would know Patrick was on the way, even before he arrived. He had great spiritual presence.' Patricia Ronan put her hand to her mouth and leaned over to Michael Carroll: 'God forgive me, but he was a rude ignorant bogman. He was always spitting – and you should see the way he searched the papers for racing tips, and then scattered the pages all around the place as he finished with them.'

Mary King confessed her fondness for John Broderick, who had rarely visited without his mother. She explained why Liam O'Flaherty stopped coming to Parsons. 'He grew jealous of Brendan, who'd taken a shine to his favourite girl in the shop. We missed Liam but not as much as Brendan, who'd reach through the railings and extract the papers every morning and then bounce back at lunchtime to pay. Frank O'Connor brightened many a dull day with his lovely white hair and Cork accent. But all our troubles fell away when Brendan crossed the door. He always lit up the place. We were the first to hear the column, before he trotted down to Burgh Quay. Brendan was a child who loved an audience. Patrick Kavanagh was always more sure of his talent. But despite his vulnerability, Brendan had great presence and Baggot Street was never the same after he died.'

The Mayo lady had read every book and knew who was behind each character. But she only smiled when Owen Walsh enquired: 'Was MacBride the ardent Mr Gentleman in that Edna O'Brien book?' She recalled Flann O'Brien's regard for Brendan Behan. 'Myles was so reserved, the opposite of the profligate Brendan. But he'd a soft spot for Brendan and always defended his work. Though they got on well, Brendan was a bit in awe of his elder, who dressed so conservatively compared to his own dishevelment. He made us laugh one day when he warned from the door: "Here comes Mr Magritte!"'

'Myles was the only one of the three of them to have a formal education. But he was generally so serious, you'd never associate him with that column. I felt he was disappointed, even bitter about his career, which makes it so ironic that everyone sees him as a comic. There wasn't much humour the rainy day I saw him tumble on Waterloo Road. His hat floated away in the gutter, as two students tried to help him. "Unhand me, your turnip-snaggers," he abused them. Instead of the journalism, I think Myles should have been writing something more substantial. The civil service job never allowed his ability full rein; what we saw was only a hint. Brendan summed him up well: "Myles is like the Titanic iceberg; most of him is under the surface. If he had a few rich ould ones like Joyce, God knows what he might have unleashed on us.'"

'Tell us, Mary, about the morning that Brendan and Patrick arrived together.' Turnstone Michael Hartnett watered his whiskey with poetic delicacy.

'We all held our breaths for the fireworks. But they greeted each other cordially and Patrick suggested they adjourn to Mooneys for a libation. "They b-barred me; we'll try Searsons," Brendan stammered.

'"I've a problem there," Patrick growled.'

'Between the two of them there was nowhere local they could go. They had to trudge off like a pair of delinquents to the wilds of Ballsbridge.'

At the last minute, he remembered to read out Lord Mayor Briscoe's salutations: 'We will miss you but Parsons will forever be part of Dublin's great literary heritage.'

'Never mind the literature; where now for the local news?' Michael Carroll fingered his bicycle key.

They all promised to meet again at Davy Byrnes, when Beatrice Behan would be retouching the murals by her father, Cecil Salkeld. 'Well done, Beattie,' the five ladies of Parsons chorused, when Beatrice revealed: 'That's me in the red dress running down the steps in the first picture. My father told me that if I was a good girl, he would paint me in and he did!'

Mary King tugged his arm as they left. 'I knew during the week that you were up to something. But we've a surprise for you too. The last volume of Patrick's poems to leave Parsons and we've all signed it. Give our regards to your mother. As she introduced you to literature, maybe she's the one we should be thanking for tonight.'

'A pity I had to leave her and all of Parsons real-life history to go to England – but at least I made the party.' He took the precious book.

The two nurses arrived together to make his mother's bed.

He remembered former Spanish girlfriend, Maria: 'Alcestis is just a story, altruism is fiction.' He told her how Grand Prix driver Mike Thackwell had spurned millions to teach handicapped children and showed her the St Paul's plaques which recorded Victorian acts of heroism, of lives sacrificed during rescues from fires, the Thames and the wheels of runaway coaches. 'Masochists.' She tossed her raven hair.

'Get up out of your seat and let the workers in.' Nurse Ryan unfolded a new pillowcase. The convent clock chimed six. Its rich tones were almost drowned by the crows' arrival. There was little soothing about their Stravinsky clamour, as they wheeled above the trees. For the first time, he saw them as symbols of fear, as the threatening harbingers of Van Gogh's last picture. Hope wrestled with despair once again. He opened the front door to a St Remy scene. Nuns and residents strolled past the flowerbeds. 'Sit down and enjoy the fresh air.' Miss Kenny moved up on her bench. But as the crows settled, he felt ashamed at such self-indulgence. How could he even consider enjoying the sunshine while his mother lay helpless and alone in there? He felt that he was making one of his regular visits. His waiting mother reading the *Irish Press*, the three short knocks to which she always responded: 'Is that you, Brendan? *Tar isteach.*' But the door advertised only sadness and foreboding.

The nurses had removed a bundle of medals from his mother's underclothes. Emblems of the Virgin Mary, the Sacred Heart, St Patrick, others from Fatima and Rome, the latter blessed by the pope himself. Wear had rounded them to sea pebble smoothness. Their inscriptions were indecipherable with ingrained dust but they had comforted his mother. He placed them on the bed beside her. The regular Rembrandt night party of nuns arrived. Silent around the sickbed, they seemed to bridge the widening chasm with meditation and compassion. 'She's safe in God hands.' A succession of neighbours called but now they didn't have much time for chat. 'She looks so peaceful,' said Miss O'Meara with unaccustomed brevity. Miss Kenny lingered by the door.

He thought of June days when, instead of being visited by strangers in a nursing home, his mother would have been greeting neighbours across the flowerbeds. 'You've a royal life on that rug of yours, Mrs Lynch. All you need are the corgis,' Dick Casey teased once, as he locked up the petrol pump. He regularly dabbed his mother's lips with water but it trickled down untasted, and each time he had to dry her chin. Though he desperately willed her to get better, he couldn't fool himself any longer. No one could reach her now. Altered and remote, she was drifting resolutely away. Her features spelt resignation but they also projected a quiet strength and control. She was navigating at her own pace towards some certainty beyond his earthbound comprehension. But he still as fiercely wanted her to live, to chat with her neighbours on scented evenings like this. In the street, a woman's voice called: 'Another scorcher tomorrow; water those roses.'

He was startled to find someone speaking beside him. 'Sleeping on the job, after only three days?' The Reverend Mother surveyed the patient. 'She's put up a great fight and it's wonderful consolation that she's not in pain.' He was proud of the struggle his mother had made for her life. He pondered over the phenomenon of existence and man's obsession with explanations and answers. The Bard had had no doubts: 'Shelley's not for dissection. Life and love are to be celebrated, not diminished by questions!' But man was weak and he was weak. He remembered his recent final Nesbitts meeting with fellow-journalist Declan. 'I'll buy, if you did your thousand words today.' The RTE man introduced a beautiful girlfriend. A fortnight later, he watched a hearse head off to Portlaoise with the body of his young friend.

It was sad to have no answer to his mother's decline and painful to see her so distant in those few hours since yesterday. This glorious evening could well be her last. How could others so casually destroy life? Only three hours north of Roscrea, men and women of accidental denominations were packing nails into bombs, and phoning taxi drivers to lonely murderous rendezvous. 'She's very peaceful.' Nurse O'Grady smoothed his mother's hair. His mother did not stir at all now. Her rosary beads lay motionless. He held her good hand. It was all he could do, as he hoped desperately that some of his fading optimism would transfer to her. If he could have prayed, he would have tried. Anything to help her who was so helpless. She was still breathing strongly, but with alarming pauses and sudden surges of inhalation. He wondered what, if anything, was going through her mind. But she didn't move or start as if troubled. She was finally free of the terrors which had darkened her healthier days.

He was ignorant of the church's latest version of eternity. But he was relieved that his mother accepted its security, as did the nurses and staff. She may have feared death, but she also believed in the certainty of another transcendent world, for which this life's travail was but a preparation. She was dying without debilitating doubts. Beside her pillow lay the cluster of medals.

Faith of our fathers, holy faith,
We will be true to thee till death.

Apart from odd sighs and sounds of creaking beds, the home was as silent as the dark outside. Midnight chimes rang out distantly. His mother had defied the prophets of doom again! She had survived another complete day to give him his finest birthday present. He was proud of her stamina and her will to live. Nurse O'Grady opened the door: 'It's tomorrow again.'

'Four-nil against the Jeremiahs. While there's life, there's hope!' He reassured his unanswering mother.

But for how long more?

18

The insistent knocking woke him up. Nurse O'Grady called: 'Brendan, you'd better get dressed and come in now.' Seven already? It wasn't. The clock had just turned three. It was unnaturally quiet. He could no longer hear his mother's loud breathing. He dressed quickly and combed his hair as he headed for the door. What vanity, but he remembered how important appearances were for his mother. At the foot of the bed there was someone he hadn't expected to see, the Reverend Mother. She was lighting the candles on the table from which the television had relayed its second-hand dramas.

'In the name of the Father, and of the Son, and of the Holy Ghost.'

Her presence and prayer told him all he needed to know. As he looked down at his mother, his worst fears were realised. How he wished her breathing were louder now. But it had subsided to mere gasps. Nurse O'Grady felt his mother's pulse: 'She's going.' He was silent, as was Martina, the nursing aide, standing opposite with the Reverend Mother. Spectators. His mother's head lay so deep in the white pillow that it seemed as if she was no longer there. She exhaled and, suddenly, she was silent. Her breathing ceased. Then, almost immediately, it restarted. Desperation triumphed. She's shown them again, he thought. He did not want her to die and while she breathed there was hope. But it was her final breath. Her heart had stopped. Her lungs rested for the first time in nine decades. That was how a life ended. The room filled with a disconcerting quiet.

'Dear Lord, into thy hands I commend my spirit,' the Reverend Mother read from *Prayers for the Dead*. She commenced a decade of the rosary. Her two colleagues made the responses; he heard his own voice answer with an unaccustomed Amen. Martina and Nurse O'Grady embraced him and, then, the Reverend Mother: 'There, now, she's gone to a better place, you need have no fear of that.' His tears mingled with theirs: 'I'm all right, don't worry. I'm only sad, I'll be OK in a few minutes.' He was overcome by grief and the raging frustration he had experienced at his father's death. How could the woman who last week so enjoyed Dromineer now be no more?

But what was the point of being angry now? She was gone. At least she could feel no more pain. How mercifully quick it all had been. A vast emptiness welled up inside him, like emigration and divorce all over again. No more letters nor chats after Sunday lunch. Never again would she wave a parting admonition from the nursing home door: '*Tóg go bog é*, drive carefully.'

He had returned to keep an eye on his mother; he had surely encouraged her with those outings and holidays? 'Thanks for showing me that Garda home,' she wrote, after she had once been restless in Roscrea. She in turn had provided some focus to his life. Without either planning or awareness, each had become dependent on the other. He sobbed for his loss, and the sorrow of someone for so long part of his life now lying there lifeless. He wept with the ineffable sadness of seeing another human being die. It was as if a part of him had died too, and of that he was certain indeed. He began to feel the weight of the years he had hitherto so blithely ignored. While the Reverend Mother and the nurse tidied the bedclothes, he looked despairingly at his mother's face. He watched for some tell-tale flicker which would show that she was still with them, that the events of the past few minutes had been an aberration. He would astound these professionals; they would be happy to acknowledge the triumph of his faith.

But will and hope as he did, the figure on the bed did not respond. His mother was dead. The rosary beads were entwined around her joined hands. The flickering candles behind the table cross highlighted the Caravaggio scene. The Reverend Mother gestured towards the door. 'You were very good to your mother, particularly over the past few days. We understand how hard it's been for you and it's sad for us too to lose someone. She was one of us, you know. But we all did our best. She had a peaceful death and one can't ask for more than that. Your mother is with God now. Let's all go down to the kitchen. Martina has gone ahead to make some tea.'

The Reverend Mother switched on all the lights and brought

down a tin of biscuits from the cupboard. Martina filled their cups. The intimate room, the early hour and company reminded him of his mother's Scarriff home. How rapidly her time had run from that kitchen to this. There had been awe, numbness and sadness in the presence of her death. But, guiltily, he began to feel relief. As if the arrival of what he had most feared had exorcised all the apprehension. A heavy weight was removed from his heart. He thought his three companions shared the same deliverance. 'Your mother was a gas character.' The Reverend Mother poured the milk. 'You may be sorry she missed the little holiday but she got almost as much pleasure from telling us about the new dresses and showing them off when they arrived! But while you may be disappointed, think of how terrible it would have been if she'd become ill while on the road. She was indeed fortunate in many ways. She enjoyed a long healthy life and, unlike so many poor people I've seen, she died without the least pain. We should all be thankful for that.'

Nurse O'Grady looked strange sitting down. She recalled how his mother had regularly kept her up to date on the state of other residents. 'You know I can't stand that so-and-so, God forgive me. But I saw her in Mass this morning and I didn't like the colour of her at all. Maybe you'd give her a knock, as if you were just passing by?' Martina refilled his cup. 'Do you remember taking your mother and two friends to vote in the Presidential election? After supporting the favourite, Brian Lenihan, they all laughed when you rushed back to Dublin to vote for Mary Robinson. "Three to one, it will be a wasted trip," your mother joked!' The Reverend Mother had recently lost her own Scarriff parents. 'There will be some great sessions when they all meet up and relive the old Clare days. They'll soon be discussing the Scarriff races, the regattas and the elections. "Dan Murphy's Door" will be sung; Biddy Earley will live again!'

Overcome by the weariness of grief and the wonder of death, they lapsed into silence. Disconcerted by the island of light, the eyes of nocturnal animals occasionally flashed through the French windows. 'You know, it's a lovely morning outside.' The Reverend Mother stood up. 'Wouldn't a little walk now do you the world of good? And afterwards, a well-deserved sleep.'

He gulped in the fresh air. How mild it was and brightening, even at five in the morning. The grass dampened his shoes as he picked his way through the narrow entry to the church grounds. His mother had regularly wheeled his father along this uneven trail. 'Nature and the river, even up to the week he died, it was your father's favourite walk.' The weeds rustled; a rat struck out for the opposite bank. The mouldering undergrowth smelled wholesome and earthy. The water swirled the long-tressed weeds and tumbled down the edge of a little dam. He started up the steep path to the crowded cemetery.

'Sure a town would be lost without a river.' From the mill below him, his mother had often traced the Moneen's course, as it circled Roscrea and headed for the monastery. He would never forget their last walk there. All those daffodils, all that gaiety and promise.

In the far distance, the plains rose up to meet the encircling rim of the wooded Slieve Blooms. The sky grew brighter, the light's progress palpable. The sun's first rays flashed over the top of the razor-etched hills and dispersed the wreaths of mist. He gasped, as it threw instant warmth on the high place where he stood above the still town. Still but no longer silent. The first tentative call of an awakening bird was taken up within seconds from every slope and branch. The Respighi chorus soared and dived in salute to the new morning. Wings glinted like a John Behan sculpture; the air pulsated with the birds' hymn to life.

'Honest to God, 'twould do your heart good to listen to the birds some mornings.' But his mother would not hear them ever again. He tried desperately to cling to the image of her alive. He flung his hands in the air as if to restrain time. But all the willing in the world could not retard its impartial progress. His mother was dead. There was no one now to relate to, no one who really cared. He sat down on the surround of a grave and sobbed uncontrollably. A curtain fluttered from a distant window, a sight which normally would have evoked erotic thoughts or suspenseful Hopper scenes. But the movement came from some irrelevant existence – the world in which people fussed and rushed. And spoke about religion but forgot how to care. The only religion was Life. The only reality was Life, the song of those birds, the drama of sunrises and sunsets. Today was the only day worth living for. But there would be no more todays for his mother; the tomorrow which had obsessed her every moment had finally arrived. How fleeting it all had been. Her rushed childhood into teaching, her confrontation with murder, her escape into marriage and children, her desolation at her husband's death and now the arrival of her own.

He wept for the absence of the love there had never been between them, a maternal soul she hadn't been. 'An encouraging word, an affectionate gesture? Our parents' generation was too busy trying to survive to have time for that horseshit,' Jimmy once admonished. But his inability to enjoy a stable relationship owed much to the fear of women instilled by his mother's neurotic ways. His obsessive search for freedom was surely a reaction to the repression, and the reason he could accept neither job nor marriage limitations. His intolerance and readiness to judge, rather than understand, were likely offspring of her dogmatism. He was the stage Irishman's mother's son after all.

Jimmy also reminded: 'Ireland's scholastic past, Parnell and O'Connell – wasn't it your mother's hard-earned encyclopaedia which first started you off on that tack? As well as on that travelling and art nonsense. Without her, where would you have been?' He felt ashamed for resenting his mother's inadvertent stifling of his travelling ambitions. It was time he celebrated her more positive legacy, time to constructively get on with the rest of his life.

An early-starting motorcycle signalled the town's awakening. He roused himself to descend. Heavenly perfume enveloped the bridge and soothed his senses with visions of carefree Clare holidays. Wild woodbine. He picked a ruby and orange bough, an appropriate bouquet for his mother's final journey. Her room had been transformed. The nuns had brought bunches of flowers which enlivened it with colour and fragrance. 'An occasion of sorrow but also a time to celebrate such a complete life.' Sister Pauline placed a vase on the window sill.

Dignified and composed, his mother looked youthful in her favourite cream blouse – as if going on a holiday after all. The years' erasure reminded him of his father's dead face, illuminated from within with the character and courage with which he had confronted life's disappointments The morning light played on her white bedspread. He placed the woodbine beside her joined hands and resumed his seat. 'Soon you'll be in Toomevara with the Sergeant.' He patted her rosary-entwined hands.

He was wakened by a knock on the door. A sturdy Clare traveller his mother had often befriended. 'Ah, me oul' segotia, I'm shocked entirely with the news. Me people knew your mother's up in Scarriff from eighty year back. Many's the long chat we had about the good days. It's like losing one of the family, I'll miss her.' His mother had enjoyed their chats; the woman would miss her regular donations. He parted with a precious fiver. Through the window, he watched her hasten to Hogan's corner pub and smiled for the first time in three days.

He dozed off again. A slim lady in summery white top and blue jeans was tugging at his shoulder. 'A fine way to greet a visitor, I must say.' His unreliable daughter. A rare day, he was with two of his own flesh.

'I'm very sorry about grandmam. But you should be happy that you took such good care of her. Doesn't she look like a teenager in her bright clothes?' He told her of his early rising and how he needed a siesta. 'Move over. I'll be happy to stay here until you wake. Coming over to Ireland won't be the same without her.' Laura sat down. 'Despite her funny ways, she was always lively and interesting, and you'd never know what she'd come out with next. "Tell that fella to mend his ways or there'll be skin and hair flying." I was amused to see her treating you as if you were still a child. I often thought of telling her, the cheek of it, speaking to my dad like that. She was very cross with you for ringing the dinner bell that day and bringing absent-minded residents out for second helpings. "Will your father ever grow up?" Do you remember the great night we had when we brought her for a meal in Killaloe? She really enjoyed it. It would be a fine thing if a father treated his daughter to a return visit there – and a great way to celebrate her life.'

'The modern generation doesn't beat about the bush.' He opened the door. He wondered how they would get on after such a long separation.

19

On the bright June Sunday, they brought his mother back to Toomevara. The nuns, residents and Shep watched from the shadow of the boundary wall. Miss Kenny cried quietly; Miss O'Meara gave him an encouraging wave. The hearse crossed over the stream, turned left on to the main road and accelerated. He thought of Sean O'Faoláin's mother's funeral: 'A walk or a trot, sir?' On roads once enlivened by ponies and traps, the dozen cars were left in the wake of juggernauts and faster vehicles. They travelled at a speed at which his mother wished he had always driven. She passed for the last time the road which led to Ink Bottle Lodge and the familiar landmarks of Moneygall's hurling field and tailor Dick Quinlan's house.

The enduring sturdiness of Knockane castle signalled their little village. They reached Gleesons and Ollatrim. At Shelley's Cross where his mother and he had waved to Dev, summer picnickers now blessed themselves for her. 'Grandmam's home again.' Laura pointed to their original house. At Looby's corner, the new sergeant stood to attention and saluted. An appropriately official welcome home for the former Sergeant's wife. 'Still some bloody dacency left in the world.' He startled his daughter. Only ten days since his mother and he were here on their way to Dromineer.

And now her dead Mass was being celebrated in the same church. Her bright pine coffin rested on a trolley outside the altar. The fresh-faced priest turned around. 'Let death not be a sorrow but a celebration. Particularly when we are marking the end of such a long and consistently religious life.' He spoke of the deceased's practical charity, her work with the Red Cross and the itinerants' movement. 'The influence of such good deeds multiplies like the ripples of a stone thrown in a pond. It reaches out to embrace, inspire and encourage many.'

'He's very eloquent.' His atheistic daughter inclined her head. Her grandmother's faith might yet redeem pagan London.

The undertaker beckoned him to join the bearer party. He picked his steps on the shadows cast by the noon sun. His mother had put on weight as she had grown older. But this day he would have carried her to Gurtagarry or further, to postpone the moment of her final departure. They approached his father's grave. His eyes misted as he recalled the solitary uniformed mourner riding high in the dust of the Gunner's funeral. The sergeant had lived the family motto – *Semper fideles*. And now both his parents were gone.

Only the mooing of riverside cows disturbed the silence. 'May the Lord have mercy on her and all the souls of the faithful departed.' The priest waved a farewell blessing. The holy water droplets slid down the varnished lid. The nameplate flared, as the coffin tilted. It touched the bottom of the grave with a scraping thud.

Laura dropped in the flowers she had brought from Roscrea. He followed them with the first handful of clay. The coffin gradually disappeared with each shovelful. It grew to a dark earth carpet which soon covered his mother completely. People came up and shook his hand. Billy and Tim Delaney, Dan Casey, Andy Harty, Mrs Coleman, Paddy Boland, his mother's favourite bank official Mr Holland and his old friends Chum and Chris Shanahan. Like a *This Is Your Life* cavalcade, he met Nicky Galvin and several of his former schoolmates. He tardily recognised Billy O'Brien who had relieved him of his belief in Santa Claus. 'Many a devotions hymnbook we shared,' Johnny Kennedy reminded him.

'A very lively woman and a great correspondent. She certainly knew how to keep us fellows on our toes.' Former government minister Michael O'Kennedy stood out in his suit. John Bourke and Jim Hickey patted the top of the earth mound with their shovels. An expectant robin alighted on Guard Coleman's nearby headstone. His mother was once more with all her former neighbours. Like a welcoming committee, they flanked the newly turned earth. Auntie Hannah and Auntie Maggie, Dick Casey, Mick French Shea, Ned O'Donoghue, Tom Tuohy, Dr Murphy, the Graces, the Ryan Barneys and Searsons. James Shanahan held his arm. 'The sergeant helped me with forms when I was going to England after the war. He and your mother were a mighty couple. We're glad to have them both back with us for good.'

Looking across Donovan's fields and the rise towards Blean and the Devil's Bit, he knew his parents could not be in a better place than this Laodicean village they had served so well. His mother was reunited with the husband she had loved. Finally at home, to rest forever under Toomevara's unassuming green slopes. She would never be lonely again.

A Madonna alien to his mother's favourite shrieked in the background, as Laura and he entered the funeral pub. 'I never thought your mother would be responsible for such sabbath excess – but didn't she and the *Irish Press* go at the right time.' Brother-in-law, Patrick, held his pint aloft. 'I'll tell you one thing. Lots of talk now about Celtic Tigers, but the real tigers were people like your mother and father, and the other Gardai. After centuries of slavery, they taught us that law and order was for everyone. They held the country together until we put down our roots, not indeed that they ever got much reward for it.'

'Our father often joked at how his pension was eventually bigger than his salary.' Colm emerged from the scrum. His brother spoke with an accent that was distinctly German after so many years in that country. He had put on weight and his red hair had darkened. 'My children now play Irish traditional as well as classical music. Our mother had much more influence than she ever realised! It seems as if it was only yesterday that I was opening the gate after the ride from Nenagh school. Will you ever forget our mother's pessimism – "There might be a drop of rain yet"? And the summer day she sent you down to collect *Figaro*?'

Jimmy had had a headstart. 'Jasus! But with a son like you, it's amazing that the woman lasted as long as she did. If anyone deserved heaven, she did. You went to England to get away from her, but you came back in the end. Don't think because she's died that you'll escape her now.'

His aunt Sarah surprised him. 'Did your father never tell you that it was he who took over our Clonmany barracks from the departing British? And, unarmed, he forced out Free State soldiers to establish the first Garda barracks in Castleisland? You did a good thing, returning for your mother. You prevented her from being institutionalised. She told us about all the outings – though she insisted you still drove far too fast! You say it's a pity that there was

216

never much love between you. But wasn't your practical help more important for her than fine words? You brightened up her last years and gave her someone to focus her attention on. You showed her that she wasn't alone. Now, wasn't that real love?'

'The last of the crusaders.' Jimmy raised his glass.

'An Irish loving which we'll celebrate this evening.' his daughter put her arm inside his.

'Perhaps you should go away for a break now.' Sarah suggested.

'Don't encourage him,' Laura interrupted. 'He's already talking of travelling to Asia – at his age! I'll talk him out of that nonsense tonight.'

'My daughter's beginning to sound like my mother!'

'Wasn't your mother a devil for the praying?' Uncle Joe brandished a fresh drink. 'If that woman doesn't get up there, the rest of us can jump into the Shannon and forget about it. I remember her visiting once and, bejasus, she was like the Scarlet Pimpernel. We sought her in the front and out the garden, before we eventually tracked her down. When a neighbour enquired if Mrs Lynch had arrived, we said: "Yes, but she's not staying with us at all. She's over beyond with Your Man in the chapel." She must have been shocked at the way things changed. Say what you like about the religion, but didn't it lift us out of ourselves? Didn't it give us some standards?'

From the corner behind Joe rose the high-pitched voices of two pensioners. 'Bad cess to that Blueshirt blackguard Mulcahy, he murdered the seventy-seven,' raged the unmistakable voice of Din Reidy.

'At least he was Irish, unlike that bloody Spaniard who killed Collins.' Jimmy Keogh!

'A good job our mother isn't here, she'd make short work of that anti-Dev man.' Colm produced his camera. 'Now, let's have a photograph before we all leave. A little smile, please!' They blinked in the sunshine outside the family home. The whirrings froze the scene for eternity. The camera was put away, the da Vinci tableau dissolved.

'I won't return now for a while.' Colm got into Sarah's car. 'But come to Germany and we'll go down to Prague or Budapest for a few days.'

The last of the cars accelerated away. There was no one but his daughter and himself on the afternoon street. Another show was over. Unpegged tents and reproachful white patches which would soon regain their greenness, as if no one had ever stopped there. Was that the murmur of a pitch-and-toss school? It was only the muted buzz of a television which, as they leaned over Mick Dalkey's bridge, was happily outrun by the caters and cinques of the constant stream: 'For men may come and men may go…'

'Killaloe, chauffeur!' Laura pointed to the car, where once Mrs Regan commanded, 'Grenanstown.' So long since he had spent an evening with his daughter. He studied her from the corner of his eye as they drove. They had some unfinished business to discuss. 'How life goes on.' Laura led the way to Peter's Restaurant through a Breughel throng of pint-laden anglers. Opening the door, he was suddenly proud of his blue-eyed daughter, so elegant in her slim black dress and matching stilettos. His appearance-conscious mother would be most impressed. The meal would surely be a success? Life's strange symmetry. A twenty-five-year old London lady coming to dine beside the distant birthplace of her grandmother, whose friend had been killed just yards away by fellow-English.

'What a view!' Laura pulled in her chair.

From the window table of the former railway station, they looked across the Shannon to the strip of houses which marked the Scarriff road. Nature and history combined in the swell of the slowly moving river as it skirted Brian Boru's Fort and slid past St Flannan's Oratory. The sun flooded the water with shades of orange and mauve, reflections rippled on the restaurant wall. Below them stretched the arched bridge on which Alfie Rogers had been shot. It seemed ancient history now, as daytrippers lazed on the riverbank and a boat tied up with a party of animated French. They could have been at Asnieres or Argenteuil. He poured the wine: 'Sunday afternoon on the island of La Grande Jette!'

'Seurat to you too.' His daughter raised her glass. 'Though I thought I'd never forgive you for all those bloody art lectures you dragged us to. Mozart and Chardonnay; you're more European here now than we are in England.' They faced the ribbon of road which had joined his mother's life to theirs and touched glasses. 'To you, grandmam!'

Their soup and bruschetta reminded Laura of restaurant visits with her grandmother. 'She'd always say: "Nothing for me, thanks, only a little something on a plate." Then she'd scoff everything in sight – particularly the cakes.' He surveyed his re-blonded offspring through the growing wine haze. A typical profligate child of the nineties, seduced by transitory fashions, a kaleidoscope of overpriced baubles and synthetic pop groups. She had known neither censorshop nor the blue-flamed demise of a final gas shilling. 'Why should I feel guilty for enjoying myself?' Guilt was alien to her, all right. She had never got around to visiting hospitalised Nevill Johnson. 'By the time I got home from work each evening, I was knackered. You can't run around London like you can in smaller Dublin. Colindale was even farther away. That's why I couldn't deliver those David McClelland photographs so quickly.'

The loss of that London flat still rankled. 'Why didn't you stay in Acton? If you had, I'd now have a base to return to?'

'You must be joking. That place was in the boonies, two bus rides away from all my friends in Fulham. You were over in Ireland doing what you wanted to do. I had to live as well. Believe me, I endured it as long as I could.'

He paused and carefully refilled their glasses. 'Well, if you tried, that's good enough, I suppose.'

'Perhaps we should keep more in touch from now on, then there might be less misunderstandings? And you might finally consider calling Marina. The divorce is history; time you both buried your differences.'

'As her elder, I suppose I'll have to make the first move. But she had better bite her tongue in the future!'

The setting sun fringed the hills with crimson. Laura put down her glass. 'A pity grandmam didn't enjoy nights like this. Dining, relaxing, and getting tipsy in pleasant surroundings. I thought it was really sad when she told me that, at my age, she'd to ask permission to go to a dance. And she also missed out on the modern Ireland she helped to build.'

He christened the second bottle. 'The luck of the generations.'

'Wild Irish salmon for a London Rose, chicken Cordon Bleu for the long in tooth.' The Belgian, Peter, flourished their dinner.

'What would you be saying now about life, after all your eventful years?' Laura picked up her knife and fork.

'"The happy man is the man who lives objectively. Bertrand Russell, *The Conquest of Happiness*, Chapter 17, verse 2!' he intoned. 'Life's like a marriage of convenience, a necessary compromise – and it's bloody wasted on the young. But read *Ulysses* or *The Ginger Man* and you'll never be sad or lonely.'

'You're off again. Patrick Kavanagh, Brendan Behan, Harry Kernoff. A litany to match grandmam's Blessed Virgin, St Anthony, St Jude, St Theresa of Lisieux. You should know there's now a new Irish litany. Chris de Burgh, Bob Geldof, Van Morrison, Sinéad O'Connor, The Corrs, U2, Hothouse Flowers, Westlife.'

'Mere noise and motion! You all see life through a lens, like holiday photographers. Get out there and experience it. If you don't, you won't have lived. And if it's rough going sometimes, always remember that while you're striving you're living. As Ernest Hemingway said, the world is still a great place to buy in...'

' – *Don't* mention him again. I'll never forget that time in Paris when you showed us all the writer's places. The Closerie des Lilas, "Hemingway drank there." The Rue Mouffetard, "Hemingway lived there." Marina said when you weren't listening: "And there's the bloody quayside – Hemingway pissed there." All we wanted in the heat was a nice cool ice cream, not a sermon.'

'No more sermons – but how sad that your grandmother didn't have your positive outlook.' He topped up her glass.

'A shame, all right, that she never enjoyed early-morning croissants. Or that she hadn't a perfect son!'

He looked out at the Shannon. 'I should have shown more understanding, not reacted so self-righteously to her attitudes. We had too many arguments.'

'Maybe. She enjoyed a good argument?'

His heart suddenly lightened as he acknowledged that the search for perfection was over. The broad river seemed to wash away all the trivia, all the irrelevant. The world would no longer be the black and white canvas of his dogmatic upbringing. He would learn to accept the imperfections of others and of himself. Past differences must yield to the same current. 'Life flows and renews itself like that river going to the ocean. We're all part of the wonderful symmetry of things.'

'The wonderful symmetry of Chardonnay.' His daughter held her glass to the light.

With such a reassurance of continuity, he experienced a resurgence of contentment and power. His species might be freshly fallen from the trees but it had achieved wondrous feats. Frightened he might remain in the dark and loneliness but he felt he knew who he was, where he had come from and where he was going. That which he could direct in his life, he would. For the rest, he would flow with the great tide which was bigger than all men. It was as if he was donning his togs for a bike race. His limbs tingled; he was in control once more. He had re-established a relationship with his mother; he could surely do the same with his daughters.

'I'll phone Marina.'

'Grandmam's first miracle!' Laura raised a congratulatory glass. 'You're off again.'

'I've been dreaming of replacing the camper. New towns, the brows of new hills. Pete Hogan's just returned from sailing around the world. I think I'll try Asia before I get any older:

For the temple-bells are callin', an' it's there that I
    would be –
By the old Moulmein Pagoda, looking lazy at the sea.'

Laura put down her knife and fork. 'Get a grip for heaven's sake. You're too ancient for that long-distance stuff. You're the wrong side of fifty, not a teenage backpacker.'

'Too old, my arse. Dervla Murphy cycled to India in her thirties. Yachtsman Tristan Jones has just re-circumnavigated the earth at the age of fifty. Being old is an accident. What matters in life is what one does, not a statistic.'

But not unaware of ageing's debilitating Plimsoll Line, was it fear of lapsing into his contemporaries' excuses which drove him now? Luckily, seniority had its compensations. Once inaccessible studies opened like long-awaited flowers in the light of wisdom and experience. Time, suddenly so precious, was finally appreciated.

Life began at fifty.

'With so little work, how are you going to pay your way?' his daughter raised a sceptical eyebrow.

'I now have a house to rent out!'

'My father a landlord, whatever next? As you well know, human life's particularly cheap in Asia. Many foreigners disappear there,' she persisted. 'And are you aware of malaria, hepatitis, dengue fever and all the other fatal illnesses you can contract?'

'I've fulfilled all my responsibilities and I'm off. Spectating is death. One lives only with movement and challenge. As Lorenzo de Medici said to Michelangelo: All of us are half-man and half-God, and if we use that which is half-God in us, we can perform the Twelve Labours every day.'

'That reminds me of the graffiti I saw in World's End last week: "Reality is a delusion induced by alcoholic deficiency."'

He refilled Laura's glass. She leaned across the table: 'I never told you that grandmam wrote to me, asking about your Pall Mall book award ceremony.'

Despite all her republicanism, his mother had been interested in hearing about royalty! He recalled the blazing gas flambeaus, Lord Strathcarron's presentation, the applauding Prince Michael and Lord Montagu. He felt like Airey Neave of Colditz, as he realised for the first time that he had conquered once impregnable St James's.

His daughter held her glass to his: 'To you again, grandmam, *our* royal!'

It moved him to see her sparkle, and how his mother most assuredly lived in her looks and mannerisms. And what indeed was death? A link might be broken but a person could hardly be dead if his or her influence extended beyond the grave. Children played Irish music in Germany because of his mother. Immortality after all!

Peter surprised them at the door:

> She stepped away from me and she moved through the fair,
> And fondly I watched her go here and go there.

'Your mother recited that for me as she was leaving the restaurant – the first time I'd heard anyone deliver an Irish poem!'

They emerged into night that was almost bright as day, each rooftop reflected the moon's embrace. Laura hummed 'You've got it'. Hand in hand, they crunched across their pebbled shadows to the Shannon's edge.

'St Brendan and Thor Heyerdahl navigated by those stars. Socrates and Christ observed what you are seeing now.'

'Words are superfluous,' Laura hinted.

There lies the port: the vessel puffs her sail.

The water gurgled and glinted. Old indeed, he would show them. He would have some stories for his daughter next time they returned here.

His heart jumped as he remembered that Filipino film. Night stars over the old Spanish church, dancing glow worms, smiling people, beautiful women. Now there was nothing to stop him from voyaging. Go he very soon would, on his big Conradian adventure. Like his mother, he would explore a long-awaited New World. Like his mother, he too was free at last!

Or was he?

Beckoning images of Christ and Kitchener; it might take some time. From birth to final breath, he knew that his mother would prove his most constant travelling companion. No divorce from her. He knew that he would remember her with every Angelus bell, every muezzin's call. A fish splashed unseen. Spangled riches rippled in their direction. Laura broke the silence: 'Isn't it lovely? A perfect summer's night in Ireland.' He surveyed the flawless star-laden sky. It pulsed with vitality and light. Not a cloud threatened its sublimity. He turned slowly to his daughter: 'There might be a drop of rain yet!'

Her laughter rang across the refulgent river, followed by his own. The echoes reverberated from the sleeping houses and played tag with them as they made their unsteady way across the bridge.